CRASHING THE TEA PARTY

Mass Media and the
Campaign to Remake American Politics

PAUL STREET AND ANTHONY DIMAGGIO

Paradigm Publishers
Boulder • London

Published in the United States by Paradigm Publishers, 2845 Wilderness Place, Boulder, CO 80301 USA.

Paradigm Publishers is the trade name of Birkenkamp & Company, LLC, Dean Birkenkamp, President and Publisher.

Library of Congress Cataloging-in-Publication Data

Street, Paul Louis.
    Crashing the Tea Party : mass media and the campaign to remake American politics / Paul Street and Anthony DiMaggio.
        p.   cm.
    Includes bibliographical references and index.
    ISBN 978-1-59451-944-4 (hardcover : alk. paper) —
    ISBN 978-1-59451-945-1 (pbk. : alk. paper)
    1. Tea Party movement. 2. Mass media—Political aspects—United States. I. Dimaggio, Anthony R., 1980– II. Title.
    JK2391.T43S77 2011
    320.520973—dc22   2011009209

Printed and bound in the United States of America on acid-free paper that meets the standards of the American National Standard for Permanence of Paper for Printed Library Materials.

Editorial production by the Book Factory.

Designed and Typeset by Patricia Wilkinson.

14   13   12   11   1   2   3   4   5

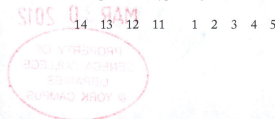

Contents

The Tea Party mythology—that it is a grassroots, "insurgent" movement bent on overthrowing the "establishment"—has taken root in the corporate and even independent liberal media . . . which [advanced] this conservative manufactured myth, that the Tea Party is separate from the Washington establishment, that it is "fighting" the beltway . . . that Tea Party candidates are outside of the political establishment. In simply reporting the Tea Party as a separate entity from the Republican Party, many media sources have helped perpetuate the false notion that its leaders represent a new political movement. In even using the brand "Tea Party" we perpetuate the idea that it is not the same old Republican Party.
 —Adam Bessie, September 20, 2010[1]

Push Republican principles; just don't ever actually concede to anyone you talk to that this is all about returning Republicans to office.
 —Chicago Tea Party organizer to a handful
  of local chapter members, April 2010

The other party's candidate is not simply depicted as unworthy of public office, but is connected to alien forces within the society that threaten to overwhelm decent folk—libertine sexual behavior, communists, criminals, people of color demanding more than they deserve. The Republican Party, thoroughly modern itself, poses as the bulwark against unsettling modernity.
 —William Greider, 1992[2]

The timidity of a Democratic Party mesmerized by centrist precepts points to the crucial fact that, for the poor, minorities, the working-class, anticorporatists, pro-environmentalists, and anti-imperialists, there is no opposition party working actively on their behalf. And this despite the fact that these elements are recognized as the loyal base of the party. By ignoring dissent and assuming the dissenters have no alternative, the party . . . marginalizes any possible threat to the corporate allies of the Republicans. Unlike the Democrats, however, the Republicans, with their combination of reactionary and innovative elements, are a cohesive, if not a coherent, opposition force. . . . The character of the Republican Party reflects a profound change: radicalism has shifted its location and meaning. Formerly it was associated with the Left and the use of political power to lift the standard of living and life prospects of the lower classes, of those who were disadvantaged under current distributive principles. Radicalism is now the property of those who, quaintly, call themselves "conservatives" and are called such by media commentators.
 —Sheldon Wolin, 2008[3]

With economic pain at the highest level ever seen by most Americans, and with minorities especially hard hit, we're seeing a revolt not by people of color, nor the unemployed, nor the foreclosed upon. Instead, we're seeing a revolt by the white middle class. It's a revolt against the very notion of a positive role for government in helping people. It's a revolt against Latin American immigrants. It's a revolt against Muslim Americans. And it's a revolt against our black president. . . . Opportunistic and rightwing Republican politicians, business front groups, and media outlets like Fox have ginned up the hatred.

 —Matthew Rothschild, October 2010[4]

---

1. Adam Bessie, "Media Spreads Tea Party Leaders as 'Anti-Establishment' Myth," Media-Ocracy.
2. William Greider, *Who Will Tell the People? The Betrayal of American Democracy* (New York: Simon and Schuster, 1992), 274–275.
3. Sheldon Wolin, *Democracy Incorporated: Managed Democracy and the Specter of Inverted Totalitarianism* (Princeton, NJ: Princeton University Press, 2008), 206.
4. Matthew Rothschild, "Rampant Xenophobia," *The Progressive,* October 16, 2010, 8.

Prologue

Making Tea from the Top Down

As during the Boston Massacre and the mass protests that followed it in the late winter of 1770, "the laboring classes . . . formed the bulk of actors . . . at the [Boston] Tea Party" of December 16, 1773.[1] The working, or "laboring," class aspect of the historic event was evident not just in the social composition of the cadres who moved from "Old South" (the Boston meetinghouse where the patriots approved and planned their soon-to-be-famous assault on British tea) to British cargo ships that fateful evening. It was clear also in how the action—remembered in official public memory as "the destruction of the tea" (not "the tea party") until the early 1830s—sent up the refined tea-making rituals of the British elite and its colonial representatives. What came later to be called the Tea Party was, historian Alfred F. Young notes, "a mock enactment of the making of tea. The cry in Old South, 'Boston harbor a teapot tonight,' set the tone. The spirit of the day and night, after two weeks of suspense, was one of festive euphoria." Furthermore,

> to "make tea" in Boston harbor mocked the genteel tea ritual. Tea, as Mercy Otis Warren wrote, was "an article used by all ranks in America," but among the better sort the conduct of brewing, pouring, and serving tea was an elaborate, mannered class ritual managed by women. Among the well-to-do, it required the elegant silver teapots, creamers, and sugar bowls crafted by silversmiths like [Boston's Paul] Revere, the tea caddies, serving trays, and tea tables made by skilled woodworkers, and the porcelain cups, saucers, and

serving dishes imported from abroad. For the boarding parties—all but a minority of them able to wield block and tackle and lift and break open 350-pound chests—to "make tea" in Boston harbor was a parody of class and gender [and] . . . another way to channel class resentment.[2]

Young's reflection on the real Boston Tea Party provides an interesting backdrop for the analysis of the elite 2009–2010 Tea Party phenomenon presented in this volume. The latest and most important right-wing effort to date to appropriate the legacy of the American Revolution and Tea Party for Republican electoral purposes, the current cardboard cutout incarnation depicted in the chapters that follow is a fake-populist aristocratic operation. It can make no legitimate claim to the egalitarian historical mantle handed down by the rugged, predominantly artisan- and laborer-based movement that conducted a genuinely popular and radical, quasi-revolutionary action in Boston Harbor in December of 1773. It is, as liberal *New York Times* columnist Paul Krugman wrote early on, in April 2009, "AstroTurf (fake grass roots)," largely "manufactured by the usual suspects"—by right-wing Republican operatives (for example, Richard Armey, director of the reactionary advocacy group FreedomWorks). It is "supported," Krugman noted, "by the usual group of right-wing billionaires" (e.g., the superopulent, archreactionary capitalists and polluters Charles and David Koch).[3] Ironically enough given its insistent claim of liberal media bias against it, the contemporary Tea Party owes its existence and relevance largely to the corporate media, a critical economic and ideological asset of the business elite. Thanks to the dominant media's distorting hall-of-mirrors effect and to related factors of U.S. political culture, the party's significance has been magnified far beyond its actual numbers, and its real character has been grossly misrepresented to the American public.[4]

In painting this unflattering picture of the current Tea Party, we hardly mean to suggest that the Democratic Party and its affiliated activist and policy infrastructure do not also betray the popular legacy of the American Revolution in service and connection to "the better sort." Right-wing Tea Party "movement"* leader John O'Hara is not wrong when he notes that "'Astroturf'—a term for fake activism playing off the 'grassroots,'" can be legitimately applied to "many protests on [what passes for] the left, funded by [leading global financier] George Soros and the like."[5] The liberal organization MoveOn.org and the White House–affiliated group Organization for America (a direct outgrowth of Barack Obama's election campaign) are excellent cases in point: They are top-down, staff-driven agents of the Democratic Party beneath and beyond their claims to represent progressive citizens and voters from the bottom up. We share Krugman's sense that the Tea Party deserves considerable criticism from liberals and progressives, but we remain painfully aware that the "leftmost" side of the narrow American "one-and-a-half-party system" (Sheldon Wolin) is deeply subordinated to the moneyed and imperial elite.[6] The Democrats and the not-so-liberal and not-so-activist progressive movement are no small part of what has allowed the contemporary Tea Party (and the right-wing Republican agenda that the Tea Party rebrands in the false rebel's clothing of grassroots insurgency) to become a relevant factor in American political life. Like the richly media-magnified and media-approved 2004–2008 Obama phenomenon and the 2007–2008 Obama presidential campaign,[7] the Democratic Party itself is a great example of false populism and fake grassroots. Democratic Party corporatism and liberal and progressive timidity in regard to that corporatism help create a popular activism vacuum that "the Tea Party" and its elite sponsors, managers, and publicists exploit, with critical support from the corporate media (and not just from that media's rightmost organs like FOX News) and at no small peril to fading democratic prospects. The Democrats' corporate centrism is a critical part of the Tea Party story, we feel. We are highly critical of, and *chilled by,*

---

*In this volume we will consistently put the word "movement" in quotation marks in connection with the Tea Party. The 2009–2010 Tea Party's claim to be an independent and insurgent social and political movement—a claim that is strongly reflected and reinforced in the mass media coverage it has received—should, we think, be viewed with a heavy dose of skepticism. The reasons for our skepticism will be discussed in an explicit fashion in Chapter 6.

the Tea Party phenomenon—a development we view with deadly seriousness—but we hardly mean to encourage readers to simply cower under the umbrella of the Democratic Party or its current standard-bearer, Barack Obama, the supposedly socialist nemesis of "the New American Tea Party movement."

1

The Tea Party Does Not Exist

Reflections on a Not-So-New "Movement" and the Deeply Conservative Essence of U.S. Political Culture

Almost Overnight: "The New American Tea Party"

It didn't take long for President Barack Obama to become the new King George—provocatively and preposterously aligned with Marx, Hitler, and Lenin—in the shrill rhetoric of a supposedly vast new American social and political "movement." In the late winter and early spring of 2009, just months after the first black president's inauguration, consumers of American news and politics were presented with a purportedly great and novel protest phenomenon—a supposedly new "third force," in the words of the *Wall Street Journal*, in the nation's political life—"the Tea Party."[1] Wrapped in the potent historical symbolism of the American Revolution, this swiftly emergent "movement" seemingly out of nowhere spoke the traditional national language of "freedom" and "liberty" against the supposedly "left," "big government," and even the "socialist" and "Marxist" agenda of the president and his fellow "radical" Democrats. Its participants and conductors had been curiously silent about the significant expansion of the federal deficit under the big government presidency of the messianic-militarist Republican war president George W. Bush, who transferred massive billions of taxpayer dollars to defense contractors and Wall Street investment firms and significantly advanced government assaults on cherished civil liberties. But here they were in the streets because of the "out-of-control spending" and statist agenda of a black Democrat in the White House.

This revealing inconsistency notwithstanding, the American people beheld "the New American Tea Party," said to be a great, bottom-up, citizens' "backlash" against the "radical left" Democratic totalitarians in Washington. By early 2010, as leading Tea Party co-ordinator and propagandist John O'Hara claimed, "Few Americans haven't heard of the Tea Parties." This was an exaggeration: An April 2010 poll by the Pew Research Center showed that 31 percent of Americans had never heard of "the Tea Party and 30 percent had no opinion of it." Nevertheless, 69 percent awareness of something called "the Tea Party" was not irrelevant, and the rest of O'Hara's assertion was unassailable. "Love them or hate them," O'Hara continued, "they are in the news, they are growing, and they are making a difference in the political arena."[2] With notable rapidity, supporting "the Tea Party" became something like popular shorthand for anger about the state of life and politics in the United States—a lightning rod for a sense of being "pissed off" about how things were going in America under the greatest economic crisis since the Great Depression.

It wasn't the first time that people on the American right had tried to use the legacy of the Boston Tea Party against "big government" Democrats (see Chapter 2 for details) But in early 2009 and through 2010, the term "Tea Party" caught real fire for the first time in America's heavily mediated political culture. A Google Web search in late 2010 found that attention to the Tea Party was extensive, as mentions of the group were competitive with mentions of other political institutions such as the Democratic and Republican parties and discussion of President Barack Obama.

In the spring and summer of 2009, after a summer in which "Tea Party" activists received extensive media coverage of their efforts to disrupt congressional town hall meetings on Democratic Party "health reform," "the Tea Party" became a leading target of fear, loathing, disgust, and mockery on "liberal," Obama-friendly media outlets like MSNBC's Rachel Maddow and Keith Olbermann shows and the widely read liberal Web site Huffington Post. The term "tea-bagger" became standard liberal opprobrium for right-wing "Obama-haters" (and even, in our experience, sometimes for Obama's left critics). Nonetheless, an April 2009 Rasmussen Reports survey found that "fifty-one percent of Americans have a favorable view of the 'tea parties' [Tax Day protests held across the country by 'Tea Party' activists on April 15, 2009] held nationwide last week, including 32 percent who say their view of the events is very favorable."[3] A WorldPublic Opinion.org poll in August 2010 found that fully 52 percent of Americans felt "sympathy" for what the survey designers called "the Tea Party movement."[4] A December 2009 NBC/*Wall Street Journal* poll found that "the Tea Party activists—those angry opponents of health care reform and government spending who flooded last summer's town hall meetings—are *now more popular than Democrats or Republicans*" (emphasis added). The survey showed that 41 percent of likely voters had a favorable opinion of "the Tea Party," compared to 35 percent for the Democrats and 28 percent for the Republicans, leading the *Los Angeles Times* to conclude that "*if the Tea Party really were a party* it would be at the top of the food chain" (emphasis added).[5]

The designers of a Pew Research Center survey of U.S. voters in April 2010 almost seemed to think that the Tea Party was in fact an independent political party. It gave respondents the following possible choices as answers to the question, "Which of the following groups best represents your views right now?" "(a) Democratic Party, (b) Republican Party, (c) Tea Party, (d) Some other group, (e) None of these, (f) Don't know." "Tea Party" got the nod from 28 percent of Republicans and 30 percent of Republican-leaning Independents.[6]

"In the space of one year," leading right-wing pollsters Scott Rasmussen and Douglass Schoen proclaimed in the late summer of 2010, "*the Tea Party movement became the most potent political force in American politics*, with the potential to change America" (emphasis added).[7] This assertion was far too strong, as (we shall see) are numerous other Tea Party claims made by Rasmussen and Schoen. Nevertheless, the "Tea Party movement" already boasted a number of victories in the electoral arena by the time Rasmussen and Schoen wrote. It was reported to have played key roles in a number of races, including the election of Republican Scott Brown to the U.S. Senate in the special election to fill the late Edward Kennedy's seat in January 2010 and in the later U.S. Senate Republican primary victories of Joe Miller (Alaska), Mike Lee (Utah) and Marco Rubio (Florida) and the U.S. House primary victory of Charles Perry (Texas). Self-described "Tea Party candidates" won 2010 Republican primaries in Kentucky (Rand Paul for a U.S. Senate seat), Illinois (Robert Dold for the Tenth Congressional District), Arizona (Sharron Angle for a U.S. Senate seat and Jesse Kelly for the Eighth Congressional District, a House seat), Colorado (Ken Buck for a U.S. Senate seat), Wisconsin (Ron Johnson for the U.S. Senate), Florida (Allan West for the Twenty-second Congressional District), and Delaware (Christine O'Donnell for the U.S. Senate). According to *New York Times* reporter Kate Zernike in September 2010, in an article looking forward to the November midterm congressional elections, "Of the 18 Senate races that [the paper] considers competitive, there are 11 where the Tea Party stands to be a significant factor. While it is harder to predict the Tea Party's influence in the House races, given the diffuse nature of thousands of local groups across the country, there are at least 48 out of 104 competitive seats where it could have a major impact."[8] The next month, Zernike reported in a front-page *Times* story that "enough Tea Party–supported candidates are running strongly that the movement stands a good chance of establishing a sizeable caucus to push its agenda in the House and Senate" (emphasis added).[9] Bloomberg News reported breathlessly, "*Thirty-One Percent of Likely Voters Say They Support the Tea Party.*"[10]

By mid-September 2010, the Tea Party phenomenon was the subject of—or played a central role in—no less than thirteen books available through Amazon.com.[11] Consistent with the notion that "the Tea Party" had become a major factor in U.S. political life, Newt Gingrich, a likely presidential contender in 2012 and the former Speaker of the House of Representatives, dedicated much of his 2010 book, *To Save America*, to channeling core "Tea Party" themes. He explicitly linked his fate to the "the Tea Party movement" by claiming that the United States was oppressed by a deadly conspiracy of "secular socialists" that included Democrats, big business, most of academia, and nearly all of the media. "The secular-socialist machine represents as great a threat to America as Nazi Germany or the Soviet Union once did," Gingrich intoned, using language tuned to the hyperbolic and paranoid spirit and style of "the Tea Party."

The Myth of a Great, Authentic, Nonpartisan, Antiestablishment, and Grassroots Social Movement

Though much of the discussion of "the Tea Party"* strikes us as excessively dramatic and exaggerated (Rasmussen and Schoen's book is an egregious example), we think there should be little doubt that the Tea Party is of considerable significance in contemporary American political history. The large quantity of high-decibel coverage and commentary it has received in the mass media since the spring of 2009 has—along with sponsorship, funding, and direction provided by top Republicans and corporations and political investors (e.g., the Koch brothers)—granted it a relevant place in America's political life. But what is the Tea Party phenomenon exactly, and where might it lead? Even though there has been a considerable amount of discussion of the Tea Party in mass media news and commentary, there has been too little systematic and comprehensive investigation of it as a social, political, and—as shall receive particular emphasis in this study—media phenomenon. We seek to overcome this gap by providing a thorough investigation based upon our in-depth and on-the-ground analysis undertaken during late 2009 and 2010.

In its own public relations and according to its own supporters, the Tea Party represents a great independent, nonpartisan, "grassroots," "insurgent," and "anti-establishment" uprising of "the people" against concentrated power and wealth. (The word "grassroots" appears at least forty times in O'Hara's 2010 book, *The New American Tea Party*.) By O'Hara's account in his widely read book, the Tea Party is "a powerful grassroots movement" that "has involved millions of Americans in the political process like never before and has permanently changed the political landscape of our time."[12] It is "genuinely a grassroots movement—something quite rare on the left or right." It is, O'Hara claims, "[an] organic grassroots uprising"

---

*We will dispense from this point with the use of quotation marks around "the Tea Party." They are intended to express our skepticism about the actual existence of a distinct and coherent 2009–2010 Tea Party anything like its standard self- and media description.

without "any sort of command and control infrastructure." It is motivated by a "nonpartisan" determination to create "a chance for the people to speak to the politicians for a change." It reflects "the power of an informed, driven citizenry" and enlists "participants and organizers who run the gamut of the political and socioeconomic spectrum."[13] Dick Armey argued in September 2010 on the Public Broadcasting System's *NewsHour* that the Tea Party was an "outside-the-body, bottom-up group" seeking to reform the nation's political system by and for the American people.[14] Gingrich claimed that "the rise of the Tea Party movement is a great example of the American people's courageous tradition of rejecting elitism."[15] Right-wing activist Joseph Farah chimed in with the grandiose claim that "the Tea Party Movement is the most dynamic and powerful *grassroots* political movement witnessed by modern-day America. It arose spontaneously—and in the nick of time—to save this country from an advancing, fatal drift away from self-government, liberty and the promise of greater prosperity for future generations."[16]

Such flattering self-description is to be expected from Tea Party "movement" leaders like O'Hara and Armey* and from a Tea Party opportunist and/or ally like Gingrich. More startling perhaps is how ready allegedly disinterested and "neutral" observers and commentators have been to describe the Tea Party in remarkably similar, "movement"-friendly terms. In early September 2010, the *New York Times* Web site defined "the Tea Party movement" as "a diffuse American grass-roots group that taps into antigovernment sentiments."[17] In a February 2010 portrait of what he called "the Movement," writer Ben McGrath at the elite liberal weekly magazine the *New Yorker* referred to the Tea Party as "*the social movement* that helped take Ted Kennedy's Senate seat away from the Democrats" (emphasis added). McGrath mused that "the Tea Party movement,

---

*Armey was, in his role as director of the far-right Washington-based advocacy group FreedomWorks, a major player in the making of the 2009–2010 Tea Party. FreedomWorks, as the *New York Times* reported in August 2010, "has done more than any other organization to build the Tea Party movement." O'Hara is "external relations manager" at the far-right Heartland Institute, a national "free market think tank." He is a long-standing Republican campaign activist and a leading figure in the development of the 2009–2010 Tea Party movement.

identified by some commentators as the *first right–wing street protest movement of our time*, may be a reflection of the how *far populist sentiment* has drifted away from the political left in the decades since the New Deal" (emphasis added). McGrath noted without disapproval the Tea Party's claim to represent "the needs and worries of ordinary Americans" against both leading parties and "the political class in Washington" and Tea Party activists' claim to carry the historical mantle of the civil rights movement of the 1950s and 1960s.[18]

According to Zernike in her widely read *Boiling Mad*, the Tea Party may have been "fortified by well-connected Washington groups like *FreedomWorks* . . . and also by [Fox News right-wing superstar] Glenn Beck." But "even aside from these well-connected supporters," Zernike continued, articulating a reigning media refrain, "the Tea Party [is] *an authentic popular movement*, brought on by anger over the economy and distrust of government in both parties."[19]

On the widely consulted, supposedly authoritative Wikipedia Web site, the entry for "Tea Party Movement" in August 2010 listed politicians who had garnered "grassroots support" from "the modern-day Tea Party movement." The publishers of Rasmussen and Schoen's book described the phenomenon on Amazon.com as "*a classic populist uprising*" and "an *authentic grassroots movement* of concerned American citizens demanding to be heard by an out-of-touch political establishment"—an impressive nonpartisan rank-and-file citizens' revolt against both of the nation's big business and big government parties (emphasis added). According to Rasmussen and Schoen, the Tea Party is "*a genuine grassroots phenomenon* [that] has *unprecedented broad-based support* [and reflects] *a spontaneous outpouring of [mass] anger*" (emphasis added).[20]

In September 2010, David Paul Kuhn, the chief political correspondent of the widely read Web site RealClearPolitics, announced that the Tea Party was an expression of the fact that "politics has moved from top-down to bottom-up." By Kuhn's account in an essay bearing the ominous title "R.I.P. Political Establishment," it was a great new leaderless and popular phenomenon akin to a raw elemental force of nature:

The orchestras have overtaken the conductors. . . . Politics is increasingly de-centralized and influence more democratized. The tail easily wags the dog. . . . "The Tea Party is part of something. Something is not part of the Tea Party," said Republican strategist Alex Castellanos. "The phenomenon we are talking about is, yes, *not a left-right phenomenon as much as it is a bottom up phenomenon."* . . .

No single factor . . . sparked this movement. Tea Party activists want it to remain decentralized and independent of party leaders. One popular book within the Tea Party movement is the business text, "The Starfish and the Spider: The Unstoppable Power of Leaderless Organizations." The starfish does not depend on a head to survive or even operate. If you cut off the arm of a starfish, it can regenerate.[21] (emphasis added)

A cover story in *Time* magazine the same month informed readers that "the political movement . . . that calls itself the Tea Party" was a programless and "diffuse collection of [popular] furies and frustrations" that had "upended the elite of the Republican Party" from "Nevada's high desert to Kentucky's rolling coal hills." *Time's* political correspondent Michael Scheurer called the Tea Party a "rebel movement" and "popular movement" that reflected and channeled "populist revolt" against "elites," "establishment candidates," and "the two major parties." Reflecting on the Tea Party's political accomplishments to date, Scherer concluded, "'We the People' are making their voices heard."[22]

By the summer of 2010, leading media outlets sometimes discussed the Tea Party as if it were an independent third party, separate from the Republicans. *USA Today* reported in September 2010 that a North Carolina resident *"would like to vote for a Tea Party candidate, but if one isn't on the ballot, he is prepared to vote for the Republican instead"* (emphasis added).[23] According to one common media trope in the summer and early fall of 2010, on the eve of pivotal midterm elections, Republican leadership had just recently sensed the pro-GOP electoral significance of the great popular Tea Party movement and was trying to harness it to party purposes.[24] But it might be too late for the Republicans, presumably the enemies (along with the Democrats) of the Tea Party. So mused *Wall Street Journal* columnist Daniel Henninger, who wrote the following after Tea Party candidate Christine O'Donnell won the GOP primary in Delaware for a

U.S. Senate seat in mid-September 20010: "As the Tea Party gained attention and its candidates won primary elections, the political establishment began to understand that the movement . . . wasn't just about picking off this or that incumbent. The movement is massing to *hand the establishment a decisive defeat.* Six months ago, this would have been laughable. No longer" (emphasis added).[25]

The Rancid Manipulation of Populism by Elitism

The conventional, quickly entrenched, and mainstreamed "movement"-friendly description and imagery of the Tea Party are highly misleading, in our opinion. The claims that the party represents a refreshing, independent-nonpartisan, antiestablishment, insurgent, grassroots, populist, and democratic force and constitutes a leaderless and decentralized popular social and political protest movement are, we show, deeply inaccurate—every bit as false as Tea Partiers' fallacious claim that Barack Obama, the Democratic Party, and the nation's dominant corporate media are part of the "radical socialist Left." *Crashing the Tea Party* exposes an ugly, authoritarian, and fake-populist pseudomovement directed from above and *early on* by and for elite Republican and business interests. Its active membership and leadership are far from "grassroots" and "popular," far more affluent and reactionary than the U.S. citizenry as a whole and even than the segment of the populace that purports (at the prompting of some pollsters) to feel "sympathy" for the Tea Party. The real Tea Party phenomenon discovered here is relatively well off and Middle American (not particularly disadvantaged), very predominantly white, significantly racist, militaristic, narcissistically selfish, vicious in its hostility to the poor, deeply undemocratic, profoundly ignorant and deluded, heavily paranoid, wooden-headed, and overly reliant on propagandistic right-wing news and commentary for basic political information. Many of its leaders and members exhibit profound philosophic contempt for collective action; a disturbing and revealing uniformity of rhetoric across groups, cities, and regions; a stunning absence of real and deeply rooted local organizing; and a predominant prioritization of Republican electioneering over grassroots protest of any kind.

The Tea Party portrayed in this book is *not a social movement*, but rather a loose conglomeration of partisan interest groups set on returning the Republican Party to power. Despite protestations to the contrary,[26] the Tea Party is Astroturf and partisan Republican to the core. We find little to no evidence that it is a manifestation of local populism. It is not an "uprising" against a corrupt political system or against the established social order. Rather, it is a reactionary, top-down manifestation of that system, dressed up and sold as an outsider rebellion set on changing the rules in Washington. Far from being antiestablishment, the Tea Party is, we feel, a classic, right-wing, and fundamentally Republican epitome of what the formerly left political commentator Christopher Hitchens once called "the essence of American politics": "*the manipulation of populism by elitism*" (emphasis added). "That elite is most successful," Hitchens wrote in a 1999 study of the Bill Clinton presidency,

> which can claim the heartiest allegiance of the fickle crowd; can present itself as most "in touch" with popular concerns; can anticipate the tides and pulses of public opinion; can, in short, be the least apparently "elitist." It's no great distance from Huey Long's robust cry of "Every man a king" to the insipid "inclusiveness" of [Bill Clinton's slogan] "Putting People First," but the smarter elite managers have learned in the interlude that solid, measurable pledges have to be distinguished by a "reserve" tag that earmarks them for the bankrollers and backers.[27]

In the American party system, the Democrats are perhaps best equipped and most experienced when it comes to playing the deceptive, co-optive, and system-sustaining role that Hitchens (writing about a Democratic president) observed. It has long been the Democrats' job to police and define the leftmost parameters of acceptable political debate. For the last century, it has been the party's assignment to play "the role of shock absorber, trying to head off and co-opt restive [and potentially left] segments of the electorate" by posing as "the party of the people." The Democrats performed

this critical system-preserving, change-containing function in relation to the agrarian populist insurgency of the 1890s, the working-
class rebellion of the 1930s and 1940s, and the antiwar, civil rights,
antipoverty, ecology, and feminist movements during and since the
1960s and early 1970s (including the gay rights movement today).[28]
The Democratic Party, not the GOP, has been most adept at ruling
in accord with what David Rothkopf, a former Clinton administration official, in November 2008 called (commenting on president-
elect Obama's corporatist and militarist transition team and cabinet
appointments) "the violin model." Under the violin model, Rothkopf said, "you hold power with the left hand and you play the music with the right." In other words, "you" gain and hold office with
populace-pleasing, progressive-sounding rhetoric even as you actually govern in standard service to existing dominant corporate and
military institutions and class hierarchies.[29]

Nevertheless, the Republican Party is hardly immune from the
desire to wrap corporate and plutocratic policy in the fake rebel's
clothing of populist connection to the needs of aspirations of the "the
little guy." The campaigns and presidencies of Richard Nixon,
Ronald Reagan, and George W. Bush were highly adept at claiming
to represent hard-working ordinary Americans in a struggle with
concentrated wealth and power. The GOP's more transparently aristocratic and corporate essence has hardly prevented it from working
to create popular, grassroots illusions about its regressive agenda.
The Republicans require votes from tens of millions of middle- and
working-class people to gain elected office, and therefore they also
and quite logically seek to manipulate populism—to create the sense
that they are of and for "the people" in opposition to the privileged
and powerful.

The result is highly unattractive. As the left-liberal journalist and
author William Greider noted in his classic volume *Who Will Tell the
People?* the Republican Party is plagued with a critical dilemma when
it comes to winning elections. "After all," Greider wrote, "it is the
party of business enterprise . . . the party that most faithfully represents the minority, namely wealth holders." It "overcomes this hand-
icap," Greider observed, with no small help from the Democratic
Party, which has "retreat[ed] from its own [onetime] position as the

party of labor and the 'little guy.'" The GOP also succeeds, however, by blurring partisan differences in "sexy advertising [candidate] images," by pushing patriotic themes, and "mainly by *posing as the party of the disaffected*. From its polling and other research data," Greider noted—in a passage full of rich meaning for our understanding of the 2009–2010 Tea Party phenomenon—the Republican Party "concocts a *rancid populism* that is perfectly attuned to the age of political alienation—a message of antipower" and "us against them" (emphasis added). In the Republican version of us against them, the "us" is God-fearing, white, and patriotic Americans and their traditional values and institutions. The "them" is "drawn from enduring social aggravations—wounds of race, class, and religion, even sex." Conveying a political mood of "resentment against established power and 'elitist liberals,'" distrust of major institutions, and a sense of powerlessness even as this sense is "concocted" by right-wing elites, this "rancid populism"* gets very, very ugly: "The other party's candidate is not simply depicted as unworthy of public office, but is connected to alien forces within the society that threaten to overwhelm decent folk—libertine sexual behavior, communists, criminals, people of color demanding more than they deserve. The Republican Party, thoroughly modern itself, poses as the bulwark against unsettling modernity" (emphasis added).[30]

The Tea Party and U.S. Political Culture

We find the 2009–2010 Tea Party phenomenon to be the leading contemporary example—indeed, an epitome—of Greider's rancid populism. Along the way, we see it also as an unappealing, deeply authoritarian embodiment of numerous other and interrelated, overlapping, and core characteristics of U.S. political culture:

---

*"The term 'populism,' so abused in modern usage," Greider noted in an important observation, "is now applied to almost any idea or slogan that might actually appeal to ordinary people." Greider's point is especially well taken with regard to the Tea Party, which numerous commentators insist on describing as populist despite its predominantly elite and plutocratic agenda, character, and backing.

- The disproportionate influence of concentrated wealth in America's dollar democracy, where "politics," in Progressive Age philosopher John Dewey's haunting words, becomes "the shadow cast on society by big business" and "representative democracy" comes to mean representation for giant corporations and the illusion of popular governance by the majority.[31]
- The relentless capture of popular political energies in the painfully narrow and business-friendly spectrum of acceptable debate imposed by the reigning American winner-take-all "two-party system."[32]
- The general ("all other factors being equal") preference of the powerful business elite for Republicans (instead of Democrats) in top offices. This preference reflects the fact that the Democrats possess more urban, minority, and labor-based constituencies than do the Republicans. Also, they tend to do slightly but significantly more than the GOP for working-class people and the poor when in power. This preference is reflected in a curious double standard. Corporate interests and their front groups (we include core Tea Party institutions in the latter category) restrict their relentless attack on "big government," "deficits," and "ideology" to Democratic officeholders, who are constantly lectured by business and the right on the need to "steer to the center" and reduce government spending. Corporate interests ignore the epic, ideologically driven, and indeed extremist contributions of Republican administrations and officeholders to the expansion of government.[33]
- A disingenuous, largely business-crafted war on deficits, "entitlements," and "big government" that seeks to "starve" only what French sociologist Pierre Bourdieu called the left hand of the state: the parts that reflect past popular victories in the struggle for social justice and democracy. The right hand of the state—the parts of government that serve, protect, and provide welfare for the opulent minority and dole out punishment for the poor—are not targeted for dismantlement.[34]
- The triumph of emotion-heavy advertising and branding over rational deliberation and serious policy consideration when it comes to popular political choices.[35]

- The triumph of electioneering over serious social and popular movement-building in a political culture that reduces most of the citizenry to a managed electorate. This political culture teaches ordinary people to see meaningful democratic politics as being about little more than occasional participation in periodic elite-crafted, candidate-centered "electoral extravaganzas" (Noam Chomsky) or electoral "symbolic" "spectacles" (Murray Edelman).[36]
- Deadly mass ignorance and no small amount of sheer stupidity regarding history, politics, policy, and more.[37]
- The powerful hold of dramatic Manichean and nationalistic symbols of good and evil. "Thus, on one hand," wrote the leading propaganda critic Alex Carey, "an extravagant idealization of the Spirit of America, the Purpose of America, the Meaning of America, the American Way of Life. On the other hand, the extravagant negative idealization of Evil secularized in communism/socialism as, sui generis, in all places and at all times, malevolent, evil, oppressive, deceitful, and destructive of all civilized and humane values."[38]
- A strong fundamentalist attachment on the part of deeply conservative Americans to religious and political *archaism*— a "fondness for singling out privileged moments in the past when a transcendent truth was revealed, typically through an inspired leader, a Jesus, a Moses, or a Founding Father." As the veteran political scientist Sheldon Wolin notes, the well-known American-capitalist "zest for change" curiously "coexists with fervent political and religious convictions that bind the identity of the believers to two 'fundamentals,' the texts of Constitution and the Bible and their status as unchanging and universal truths." The deeply inflexible reactionary mind-set reflected in archaism's hold is reinforced by the chaotic pace and nature of the change imposed on daily life and culture by the relatively unbridled corporate capitalism that reigns in the United States.[39]
- A culture of national militarism wherein the U.S. military holds a privileged, highly popular place in American political culture and efforts to call attention to the adverse consequences

of becoming smitten with military power—for example, extravagant taxpayer expense—are deemed beyond the parameters of acceptable debate.[40]

- A neoliberal culture of narcissistic self-interest wherein the key policy question is *"what's in it for me?" and* "public issues can only be seen as private concerns." This culture sees "human misery [as] largely defined as a function of personal choices," consistent with what the distinguished left social critic Henry A. Giroux calls "the central neoliberal tenet that all problems are private rather than social in nature."[41]

- The stupendous reactionary power of giant transnational communications conglomerates like Time Warner, Disney, and News Corp to shape and often distort reality in an age when less than ten global corporations control more than half of all print and electronic media in the United States.[42]

- The strong hold of an ostensibly color-blind racism that denies the continuing role of numerous objectively racist institutional practices, structures, and policies in the sustaining of harsh racial inequality in the United States.[43]

Off Center: The Rightward Drift, the Far-Right Echo Chamber, and the Paranoid Style

The Tea Party phenomenon epitomizes three additional factors in American politics, which deserve a more extended discussion. The first factor is the rightward drift of the nation's political and policy environment over the last generation. The American public looks at the contemporary bipartisan system as increasingly polarized along a left-right continuum, with Democrats moving dramatically to the left and Republicans moving somewhat less dramatically to the right. But the deeper truth is that Republican politicians have become far more reactionary far more dramatically and quickly than Democrats have become "liberal." In fact, the rightward shift of the Republican Party is the main cause of polarization. Democratic activists and officials became somewhat more liberal throughout the

1960s and 1970s, but that shift subsided by the 1980s. By the 1990s and in the post-2000 period, these activists were moving further toward the center. Throughout this entire period, however, Republican activists became nearly twice as conservative, never moving back to the center. The limited move to the left by the Democratic Party, moreover, is due not to its increased willingness to challenge conservative public policies, but to the defeat and subsequent exodus of center-right southern Democrats from the party beginning in the 1960s. From the Carter administration onward, Democrats have grown increasingly conservative in their embrace of neoliberalism and in their declining support for worker protections and entitlement programs. The political system has become more polarized in the last few decades, as the Republican Party has moved to the right at a far greater pace than the Democratic Party has embraced any sort of progressive politics.[44]

The second factor is the rise of what communication scholars call a "right wing echo chamber."[45] Over the last two decades, the American right has constructed an imposing media empire. The right-wing media machine's outlets include newspapers like the *New York Post* and the *Washington Times*, Fox News, Fox radio, a range of "public affairs" broadcasts on cable television, and a vast talk radio network that leans far to the right and promotes a nearly constant assault on the supposedly socialist Democratic Party, on the allegedly "liberal" mainstream media, and on purportedly dangerous left activists, groups, and causes. The audience for these far-right media outlets is considerable, with a significant number of Americans now describing talk radio (predominantly right wing) as a regular component of their daily news consumption.

It's not just any kind of news, however, that right-wing media purvey. The real message of these outlets is heavily ideological and propagandistic. "Those who get their news about politics from conservative media outlets may be hearing a great deal about politics," political scientists Jacob Hacker and Paul Pierson note, "but what they are told is heavily slanted towards Republican interpretations, even on issues—such as the size of the deficit or whether Weapons of Mass Destruction have been found in Iraq—on which there are correct (but politically inconvenient) answers." In addition, the "conservative media empire [is] closely coordinated with conservative [Republican] political elites." Right-wing media outlets confer regularly with leading Republican operatives to produce an intensely right-partisan form of news coverage and commentary that contrasts sharply and favorably (for many right-wing news consumers) with the narrow, bland, and officially neutral style of the mainstream media. The political reach and relevance of this harshly propagandistic "news" and commentary are enhanced by the fact there is little on the "other" (left and liberal) side that can compete with right-wing talk radio and Fox, where "a former high-level Republican political operative and practiced practitioner of political spin, Roger Ailes, has served from the outset as CEO."[46]

One of the many ugly consequences of this new, right-wing media empire is the emergence of a viciously circular self-reinforcing balkanization or polarization among conservative news and talk radio readers, listeners, and viewers. The same reactionary messages are promulgated throughout right-wing radio, television, and print and among Republican officials. These views have grown more and more impervious to counterclaims and challenge. Those who get their news primarily from Fox News, for example, are now remarkably unwilling to follow any other television media sources. The closed-off mental, moral, and political provincialism that has resulted is fraught with authoritarian peril.

The third factor is what esteemed American historian Richard Hofstadter called "the paranoid style in American politics." By Hofstadter's account in 1964, reflecting on the far-right "Goldwater movement," this "style" was an "old and recurrent phenomenon in our public life which has been frequently linked with movements of suspicious discontent." Notable for extreme and often badly misdirected anger, the paranoid style is characterized by "heated exaggeration, suspiciousness, and conspiratorial fantasy"—a sense that mysterious and nefarious forces have infiltrated and subverted the land, including the highest reaches of government and politics, threatening to enslave the republic. Paranoid-style groups and individuals tend to speak, think, and write in chiliastic and melodramatic terms, claiming to have discovered—and urging militant opposition to—powerful elitist forces of darkness. Examples past and present include mid-nineteenth-century nativist claims that "the Monarchs of Europe and the Pope of Rome are at this very moment plotting our destruction and threatening the extinction of our political, civil, and religious institutions"; late-nineteenth-century Populist warnings about "the secret cabals of the international gold ring"; 1950s McCarthyism's crusade against communists "high in this government"; and the 9/11 "Truth movement" (which insists that the al Qaeda jetliner attacks of September 2001 were an "inside job" conducted by the Bush administration to justify U.S. occupations in the Middle East and South Asia). These and other examples of paranoia in American history are a fairly predictable outcome of (a) the contradiction between the nation's ubiquitous claim to be a model democracy and the harsh authoritarian political and policy realities imposed by the deeply entrenched, structurally empowered supercitizenship of concentrated wealth and empire and (b) the relative absence from American political and intellectual discourse of commonsense class-based structural analyses of the aforementioned underlying conflict between capitalism and democracy. As Hofstadter noted:

> Perhaps the central situation conducive to the diffusion of the paranoid tendency is a confrontation of opposed interests which are (or are felt to be) totally irreconcilable, and thus by nature not susceptible to the normal political processes of bargain and compromise. The situation becomes worse when the representatives of a particular social interest—perhaps because of the very unrealistic and unrealizable nature of its demands—are shut out of the political process. Having no access to political bargaining or the making of decisions, they find their original conception that the world of power is sinister and malicious fully confirmed. *They see only the consequences of power—and this through distorting lenses—and have no chance to observe its actual machinery.*

As Hofstadter knew, powerful political actors who are not and do not feel "shut out of the political process" have not uncommonly exploited and fanned the paranoid style to win support from those who are and/or do feel powerless in the face of existing social and political forces. The paranoid style draws heavily on mass ignorance about the actual machinery of power, which is quite unmysterious in the commonsense class analysis that is so sadly taboo in the United States, where left thought is largely shunned by dominant educational and media institutions.[47] As we see in Chapter 5, Hofstadter's paranoid style is currently experiencing an elite-sponsored, big money-, and big-media-enabled return to the center of American politics—a return that that is intimately bound up with the rise of the Tea Party.

The Tea Party Did Not Happen

The Tea Party has taken on a political relevance beyond its limited and archconservative, "super-Republican" core, we feel, thanks above all to the "hall-of-mirrors" effect of modern American mass media.[48] The Tea Party has had an outsized impact because its supposedly new message—little different in core fundamentals from the basic probusiness, antipoor messages of an evermore right-wing and unpopular Republican Party (the real political party that the Tea Party has been rolled out to rebrand)—appeals to a mass corporate media that favors reactionary false-populist protest over genuinely grassroots and progressive social movements. This preference has inflated the Tea Party's meaning and brand far beyond what it would enjoy without media hype. One of the great ironies of the contemporary Tea Party, we show, is that it owes much, even most of its significance to the very mainstream media it insistently (and absurdly) accuses of liberal and left bias.

One draft title of this book was purposely ironic and paradoxical: "The Tea Party Does Not Exist." The title was discarded for commercial reasons, but it accurately and significantly reflects the content of this study. In saying that the Tea Party does not exist, we do not mean to deny the reality of Tea Party institutions, leaders, activists, members, backers, and supporters. Neither do we deny a coherent historical Tea Party phenomenon that emerged in early 2009 and continued through 2010 and (we expect) beyond. All of these things exist, of course, and together they hold real political and policy significance. We are not among those liberals and progressives who can be rightly accused of "not taking the Tea Party movement seriously."[49] We observe, however, that

- the real 2009–2010 Tea Party is very unlike the advertised version in terms of structure, membership, purpose, popular participation, partisan identification, and ideology/worldview.
- there is a significant disconnect between (a) the political beliefs and ideological orientation of those who tell pollsters they "approve of" and/or "feel sympathy for" the Tea Party and (b) the real Tea Party phenomenon discovered here.
- the 2009–2010 Tea Party is a top-down caricature of the real, actually popular, and (in its time) radical Boston Tea Party of 1773.
- the 2009–2010 Tea Party is a significantly *mediated phenomenon*. Literally, it is a largely a creation of the corporate media, which have given it revealingly outsized and favorable coverage and magnification. And here we mean the entire mass media, not just the right-wing communications empire (of "conservative" talk radio, Fox News, the *Wall Street Journal*'s editorial page, and the like) that serves as a leading Tea Party organizer and as Tea Partiers' main "news" source.

Our draft title was inspired in part by French philosopher Jean Baudrillard's provocatively titled book *The Persian Gulf War Did Not Happen* (1991). Of course, Baudrillard knew the 1990–1991 U.S. war on Iraq occurred. Bombs were dropped, depleted uranium poisoned the air and water of Mesopotamia, soldiers and civilians died or were maimed, and buildings, roads, and other infrastructure were destroyed. Nothing in Baudrillard's book questioned the experiences and suffering of the people involved. But the Gulf War differed markedly from previous wars. It was primarily a scripted media event—a "virtual war" that was useful in different ways to both sides of the conflict. It was a mediated and, of course, highly one-sided war. It took place on Iraqi soil and inflicted most of its damage on the Iraqi people even as the dominant media called the United States "a nation at war" and identified the enemy as Saddam

Hussein, whose regime was allowed to survive the savage, one-sided imperial assault. The Gulf War did not "take place" the way previous wars had, Baudrillard felt, because the suffering and even a uniform understanding did not penetrate the people at home who watched the events on CNN.[50]

We do not accept all of Baudrillard's analysis of the Persian Gulf war. We think his book is written in an unnecessarily difficult and bloated style that is all too sadly characteristic of much postmodern writing and theory. We are not postmodernists. Nevertheless, we are struck by how well Baudrillard's take on the original U.S. Iraq war fits our sense of the corporate-mediated Tea Party phenomenon. And beyond this parallel with Baudrillard, another deserves mention: the notion of "both sides of the conflict" having a vested interest in the mediated/media-created history. Liberal, Democratic-affiliated institutions and media (MSNBC's talk show roster, for example) have demonstrated their own commercial and ideological investment in the inflation of the Tea Party phenomenon and threat, in addition to the ways that this inflation limits the spectrum of debate to voices representing an increasingly centrist Democratic Party and a Republican Party that has moved radically to the right over the last few decades.

Popular Resentment and "Anything That Looks Like Alternative Politics"

The real Tea Party phenomenon examined in this book is different not only from the one depicted by the "movement" itself and the mass media but also from the version suggested by those progressives who have bought into the illusion that the Tea Party is "an authentic grassroots movement" and even a "populist uprising" that we on the left should be treating with respect (not ridicule).[51] We certainly see little point in mocking or jeering at the Tea Party and agree that it should be taken with deadly seriousness. However, we do not believe that the Tea Party has meaningfully mobilized and connected with the working-class and disadvantaged people that "the Left" should be organizing in common opposition to concentrated wealth and corporate-state power.[52] This belief about the Tea

Party simply does not jibe with what we have learned over months of in-depth, on-the-ground investigation.

Our research does not offer much support for left progressives pursuing a "left-right" alliance with the Tea Party. It does not elicit from us much, if any, desire to reach out across the ideological spectrum to find hidden compatriots on the right. We find ourselves responding to left and liberal calls for progressives to connect with the Tea Party in much the same way that the radical political scientist Adolph Reed Jr. replied to left calls for common cause with the angry, "antistatist," right-wing militia movement in the 1990s. Reed argued that

> in desperate times we strain to find something to celebrate . . . to grasp at anything that looks like alternative politics.
>
> . . . The substance of . . . ostensibly progressive defense of the militia movement goes something like this: the militia supporters are by and large working class; they often are recruited from especially depressed local economies; their membership expresses their alienation from politics-as-usual; therefore, we shouldn't dismiss their populist frustrations.
>
> . . . But defending them on these grounds is naive and short-sighted, and reflects a broader, perhaps more insidious tendency—including a kind of accentuate-the-positive bias toward *whatever looks like autonomous, populist action*. . . . I haven't seen anything to suggest that I shouldn't judge the militiamen by the company they keep politically. Nor have I seen any signs among them of a substantive vision for political and economic reorganization that would allay my fears.
>
> . . . Yes, government is ultimately a means of coercion . . . [but] . . . the state is the only vehicle that can protect ordinary citizens against the machinations of concentrated private power. Even though it does function as an executive committee of the ruling class, the national state is the guarantor of whatever victories working people, minorities, gays, women, the elderly, and other constituencies we embrace have been able to win—often enough against the state itself. . . . I don't get a sense of anything compatible with this perspective from the militia movement.

. . . There's not much reason to think that the militia movement's politics are anything other than paranoid proto-fascist. To say that they're not all racist, sexist, or xenophobic is both bizarre and beside the point. Organizationally and ideologically they're plugged into the most vicious, lunatic, and dangerous elements of the right.[53]

We do not wish to overdo the analogy here. The real Tea Party described in this book is much less working and lower class than the 1990s militias were. It is much less of an actual grassroots movement and far less paranoid and less proto-fascist (we find the Tea Party predominantly neoliberal-authoritarian, not particularly fascist or proto-fascist in orientation) than the 1990s militia phenomenon. Nevertheless, Reed's Clinton-era formulation remains useful, we think, for contemporary progressives, who have little to gain—and much to lose—from trying to find and make meaningful common cause with false-populist and racially exclusive right-wing organizations that claim to oppose "big government," that describe the Democratic Party as socialist and Marxist, and that call for the restoration of an unfettered authoritarian "free-market" system. (Such a system would amount to a world without vital citizen protections against private power or viable public avenues for the promotion and defense of social equity.) We see the interest of some contemporary progressives in "working with" the Tea Party as a sign of leftist desperation in a difficult time. Bill Clinton and Barack Obama—both young, new, charismatic, eloquent, and false-progressive corporate-Democratic presidents[54]—have played a key role in silencing relevant left protest. Today, as in the 1990s, some of our fellow progressives seem overly willing "to grasp at anything that looks like alternative politics" and to overlook the deep and dark downsides of rightist false populism.

We do see the Tea Party as a real challenge to the progressive forces with which we identify. We view it as a reason for serious, determined, real grassroots, and, yes, angry movement-building—the creation of an independent, oppositional, and working-class politics on the left. Popular resentment abhors a progressive vacuum. In the deadly absence of serious left organizations and politics on the scale required today, the Tea Party and the broader, hard Republican right it represents and rebrands threaten to become evermore successful in capturing and misdirecting ordinary middle- and working-class people's justifiable populist outrage. Thanks to its enmeshment in and captivity to the (not-so-)leftmost side (the Democrats) of the business- and empire-dominated American "two-party" (or "one-and-a-half party") system (the Tea Party portrayed here is equally enmeshed with and captive to the other, rightmost dominant U.S. business party), "the left" today is simply not up to the job of expressing and acting on popular and working-class interests, consciousness, and anger from the bottom up. This leaves the field of harnessing and channeling popular passions and consciousness all too dangerously open for the top-down, Tea-Partying, false-populist politics of the hard right. The last thing we wish to do in this book is follow in the footsteps of the tepid, liberal, "professional left" by holding up the Tea Party menace (quite real, to be sure) to encourage citizens and activists to cower under the umbrella of the Democratic Party and its current figurehead, Barack Obama. Justice and democracy require the sorts of rank-and-file people's organizing and independent movement-building and protest the Tea Party purports to exemplify. This can be provided only by a relevant left, something that barely exists in the United States today. "Where are the progressives?" E. J. Dionne rightly asked in a September 2010 column on the Tea Party's media-created success in magnifying its impact beyond its small numbers. "Sulking is not an alternative. . . . The tea party may be pulling a fast one the country. . . . But if it has more audacity than everyone else, it will, I am sorry to say, get away with it."[55]

Distinctiveness of the Book

This is not the first book published on the 2009–2010 Tea Party phenomenon, but it is the most rigorous and scholarly study yet to appear on the subject matter. There is much of anecdotal value and historical and journalistic substance in some of the Tea Party books that have appeared so far.[56] We are struck, however, by the relative absence of serious, painstaking research and intellectual rigor (both empirically and theoretically) in all of these volumes,[57] most of which appear to have been constructed hastily to appear on the eve of the

2010 midterm elections (widely taken to be a critical moment in the history of "the modern-day Tea Party"). *Crashing the Tea Party* is the first systematic, investigative, and scholarly analysis of the 2009–2010 Tea Party phenomenon. Our research included attending Tea Party rallies, meetings, and other events during the spring, summer, and fall of 2010 throughout the Chicago metropolitan area, following electronic correspondences with Tea Party groups, and conducting discussions with Tea Party members. At the same time, we provide a larger macroanalysis of interest groups and their relationship to the political system, the private economy, public opinion, and the mass media. We also incorporated insights from historians, consistent with our interest in bridging divides between subdisciplines that are overly separated in U.S. scholarship.

Book Structure

The argument of this book beyond this introductory chapter is developed across seven chapters. Chapter 2 revisits the original/actual/real (Boston) Tea Party (December 16, 1773), suggesting fundamental social-historical, political, and class differences between the original Boston Tea Party and the contemporary "movement" that claims the mantle of that iconic event in American and revolutionary history. Chapter 2 also notes the original Tea Party's shifting and contested treatment (including the right's recurrent reactionary, top-down appropriation of a popular, plebian and radical, significantly bottom-up episode in the American Revolution) in the American public memory and provides a brief historical sketch of the Tea Party caricature that arose in 2009.

Chapter 3 provides an in-depth examination of contemporary Tea Party demographics, composition, belief, and ideology. Looking beneath survey data showing widespread popular sympathy for the Tea Party, our findings on the "movement's" core makeup and leadership and its regressive, authoritarian, and reactionary beliefs and partisan history and goals diverge sharply from those who claim that the Tea Party has mobilized a broad, diverse, and "grassroots" spectrum of the U.S. populace in an independent, antiestablishment people's protest against the nation's dominant institutions and power structures.

Chapter 4 builds on Chapter 3's discussion of Tea Partier identity, values, and worldview to demonstrate the significant degree to which the phenomenon in question is in fact—despite the insistent contrary protestations of its participants—*deeply racist*.

Chapter 5 paints a disquieting portrait of the Tea Party as an archauthoritarian and extremist phenomenon.

Chapter 6 shows how the Tea Party fails to match its common description as a social movement. This final chapter also reflects on the critical fake-populist "dissent-manufacturing" role that the nation's dominant corporate mass media have played in creating the Tea Party phenomenon and its current political relevance.

Written immediately after the midterm congressional elections (widely taken to be the main gauge of "the new American Tea Party's" relevance), Chapter 7 revisits our key findings in light of the results (a great Republican and Tea Party triumph), reflects on the future (or lack thereof) of the Tea Party phenomenon in U.S. politics and offers some modest suggestions for reasonable and effective political responses on the part of U.S. political progressives.

Chapter 8 is an unexpected and pleasant surprise. It relates our argument and findings to the remarkable, progressive public worker uprising that broke out in Madison, Wisconsin, in response to the extreme anti-labor policies of Wisconsin's right-wing, Tea Party–approved Scott Walker in February of 2011. It assesses the Midwestern labor rebellion within and beyond Madison as a sign of progressive revival and response to the Tea Party threat to justice and democracy.

2

"Turning the World Upside Down"
From the Original Tea Party
to the Current Masquerade

Hegel remarks somewhere that all facts and personages of great importance in world history occur, as it were, twice. He forgot to add: the first
time as tragedy, the second time as farce.

—*Karl Marx, 1852*[1]

The "Whole Body of the People"
on the Road to Independence

The Boston Tea Party of December 16, 1773, sparked the third and
last great crisis of Britain's rule over its North American colonies.[2]
The first Tea Party was sparked by an attempted government
bailout of a giant English corporation, the British East India Company, in the form of the British Parliament's passage of the Tea Act,
an early example of what today might be called "corporate welfare."
For reasons that had nothing to do with the Americas, the East India Company—a colossal merchant-capitalist trading firm—was
failing to turn a profit for its well-heeled English investors. It was
also failing to provide the hoped-for tax revenue that the British
Empire needed to consolidate control over recently acquired possessions on the Indian subcontinent. Facing severe financial diffi-
culties, the company was deemed too big and important to be
allowed to fail.

Parliament hoped to find the East India Company's salvation in North America. Tea, once a preserve of the rich, was now consumed by all social classes in England and its colonies. To stimulate sales and save the company, the British government, now headed by Frederick Lord North, offered it a series of rebates and tax breaks permitting it to dump low-priced tea on the American market, undercutting smugglers and established merchants alike. Beyond the goal of rescuing the corporation, the expected money raised through taxing the imported tea would help defray the costs of colonial government and undermine colonial assemblies' significant control over public finances in North America.

A British tax on imported tea was not new in the colonies. In an effort to extract more revenue from its North American possessions, England in 1767 passed the Townshend Act, a bill to tax tea, paint, paper, lead, and glass as they arrived in colonial ports. The tea tax survived the repeal of the other Townshend Duties in the wake of large-scale street protests after the Boston Massacre (March 5, 1770—when British troops fired into an angry crowd of poor Bostonians, killing a handful), which followed a two-year colonial boycott of imported British goods. The effects of the tea tax were minimal, however, because American merchants had long "honestly smuggled" (as John Adams put it) tea from Holland.

In the British view, the 1773 Tea Act was beneficial for all concerned. Parliament would increase its revenue from the colonies, the company's politically powerful investors would profit, and the colonies would enjoy cheap tea. But the colonists were already obtaining low-priced tea under the existing arrangements, and the legislation undercut established North American merchants. By providing a source of revenue for colonial governments independent of the colonial assemblies, the bill threatened the independent power of the colonists' proud and relatively autonomous representative bodies. And many colonists believed that to pay consumption excises on what promised to be a large new subsidized volume of English imports would be to surrender the core principle over which the colonists had been fighting London since the Stamp Act crisis of 1765—no taxation without representation.

Steeled by years of dedicated "nonimportation" struggle, northern colonial leaders determined to reject the empire's "tea bribe." Colonial port authorities in Philadelphia and New York refused permission for ships carrying East India Company tea to anchor in their harbors. In November 1773, however, a British tea ship did succeed in docking in the harbor of Boston, the hotbed of the colonial nonimportation cause since the mid-1760s (with Boston in the lead, the colonists had waged a successful nonimportation struggle in response to the British Stamp Act of 1765). Boston was also the site of a symbolically powerful confrontation with British imperial power in March 1770—the Boston Massacre and its aftermath. Massachusetts's widely unpopular colonial governor, Thomas Hutchinson (whose Boston mansion had been ransacked by an angry crowd of colonists in the wake of the Stamp Act), decreed that the ship could not leave the harbor until it had unloaded its tea and paid the tax on it.[3] The colonists recognized that Hutchinson's sons were poised to profit as the East India Company's two new Boston agents. Hutchinson agreed to negotiate with colonial leaders chosen by "the Whole Body of the People." The negotiations failed, and more tea ships arrived in Boston Harbor.

On December 16, 1773, after a large town hall meeting in Boston's Old South Meeting House, approximately 150 colonists outfitted as Mohawk Indians boarded three British vessels from Griffin's Wharf and tossed more than 300 chests of tea—valued at nearly £10,000 (more than $4 million today)—into the water. The action took three hours. A crowd of 1,000 to 2,000 watched. It was a well-planned, highly coordinated military action. An armed detachment was placed on Griffin's Wharf to prevent any tea from landing. Many of the participants carried muskets or pistols on the advice of leading Boston revolutionary Sam Adams. As distinguished social and political historian Alfred F. Young recounts, "The boarding parties risked arrest and prosecution. . . . All participants risked life and limb. Several British naval vessels, marines aboard, rode in the harbor, and more troops were stationed at Castle William on one of the harbor islands. . . . The crowd on the wharf thus served as insurance against military intervention."[4]

It was a pivotal moment in pushing the colonists and Britain on the road to war and American independence. Faced with the perceived necessity of showing "whether we have, or have not, any authority in that country" (Lord North), Parliament passed what the

Americans called the Coercive and Intolerable Acts. The English shut down the Boston port until the East India Company was compensated in full. The second Coercive Act tore up the 1691 Massachusetts colonial charter, vastly curtailing town meetings and authorizing the colonial governor to appoint members of the Massachusetts Council, thereby ending the colony's unique right to elect the members of its own governing body. The third Coercive Act let British officials accused of wrongdoing be tried in another colony or province or in England itself, far from popular juries in Boston. The final Coercive Act permitted British officials to billet redcoats (imperial soldiers) in colonists' private homes. General Thomas Gage, the top British commander in America, replaced Hutchinson as governor of Massachusetts, putting the most proudly independent and rebellious colony in North America under direct British military control.

In response to the tea action, the empire struck back like never before. It was determined that there would be no humiliating British retreat as there had been in response to colonial resistance to the Stamp Act (1765) and the Townshend Duties (1767). The British government's reaction to the original Boston Tea Party united colonists and the colonies in common opposition to what they widely saw as an intolerable threat to their already considerable political freedoms. The die was cast. The Coercive Acts "were the last straw. They convinced Americans once and for all that Parliament had no more right to make laws for them than to tax them."[5] The colonists were well on the road to the open military conflict that broke out in the battles of Lexington and Concord on April 19, 1775, and ultimately to the independence declared in July 1776.

Reversing the Traditional Order

More than being a critical episode on the path to national independence, the great tea action also helped establish the American Revolution as a social movement.[6] The Tea Party was "unique," Young notes, "in many ways that later generations have not always been willing to recognize."[7] Unlike some other early American revolutionary events (the raiding of Hutchinson's mansion in 1765, the recurrent tarring and feathering of British colonial tax authorities, and the Boston Massacre and its aftermath, for example), the tea action remained from start to finish in the hands and under the direction of the Boston merchant class and its independent Whig leadership, organized as the Sons of Liberty.[8] Nevertheless, "the destruction of the tea" (as the event was generally described in early American public memory through the early 1830s) was the single largest popular action of the decade leading to the onset of war between England and its North American colonies. At the two mass meetings held in late November and at two climactic December gatherings at Boston's Old South (the leading site also of meetings and speeches against the Boston Massacre), attendance reached 5,000. The last Old South event was the largest meeting ever to have occurred in Boston. The crowd flooded into the streets, fed by attendees from surrounding towns. Traditional legal property qualifications for town meeting participation were abandoned, and "the laboring classes" formed the bulk of the participants.[9]

Besides being a quasi-military action (the "most revolutionary act of the decade"),[10] the Tea Party upended the traditional social and political order. Previous colonial protests had mocked the traditional order, but, Young notes, "the action against the tea ships—destroying 9,659 British Pounds['worth] of private property belonging to the powerful East India Company, defying Parliament, defying the whole array of British officials and military might in the colony—*this was truly turning the world upside down*" (emphasis added). The event was characterized by "festive euphoria" as muscular male colonists (who could lift and break open 350-pound tea chests) poked fun at the genteel British and aristocratic teatime ritual by "making tea" in Boston Harbor, turning the "harbor [into] a teapot," and "making so large a cup of tea for the fishies." Class distinctions among the original Tea Partiers were leveled or at least suspended and cloaked by the participants' common American Indian disguises and personas. As Young notes, "It was a masquerade that released [participants] from the usual norms." The tea protest was "an exhilarating reversal—aggressive, quasi-military, destructive and carnivalesque."[11]

"To Masquerade as Commoners":
The Official Rediscovery of the Tea Party

The Boston Tea Party was seared in the personal and private memories of those who participated and witnessed the dramatic event, but it was played down in the early American republic's publicly sanctioned collective memory. It did not figure prominently in the official history crafted by the upper-class keepers of the young nation's public memory. For those historical gatekeepers, the Boston Massacre (1770) and the Battles of Lexington and Concord (1775) were far more appealing as commemorative events. As an "unmistakably willful and provocative, a true act of revolution,"[12] the tea action did not fit the reigning elite national narrative, which cast the British as aggressors and the colonists as defenders of their own liberties. Cultural authorities in the early republic were less than eager to promote an event that highlighted the Revolution's plebian heritage—its reliance on the anger, solidarity, strength, and agency of the urban laboring and popular classes.[13]

The Tea Party gained a central, even iconic place in the nation's public memory—in the North at least—six decades after it actually occurred, in response to an upsurge of radical labor activism and social contestation in the mid-1830s. Both sides of the labor-capital conflict of the Jackson era sought to appropriate the Revolution's heritage to their own purposes. For early New England trade unionists like Seth Luther, the Tea Party (as the event was now commonly called) was a useful example of legitimate collective action against propertied interests by ordinary citizens.[14] With northern labor and antislavery activists seizing upon the radical traditions of the Revolution in struggles against northern and southern concentrations of wealth and power, the history-conscious northern elite moved to provide its own spin on the American Revolution. The Tea Party emerged as an officially sanctioned iconic event as elite politicians and their parties—the Democrats and the Whigs (the latter seeking by its name to wrap its elite mercantilist agenda in the democratic legacy of the Revolution)—scrambled to "masquerade as commoners" in a supposedly new "age of Democracy and the common man."[15] Against the backdrop of rising popular activism and radicalism and related upper-class fear of "mob violence" in the 1830s, the relatively orderly tea action struck some northern elites and collective memory-keepers as "safe" in comparison to "other [revolutionary] events (the Stamp Act riots, the mobbish Massacre, the grim tarrings and featherings." The term "tea party," common in popular parlance, now emerged in book titles and newspaper stories in part because it was "a frivolous name for a serious event—undermining its radical potential."[16] From the mid-1830s on, the Boston Tea Party took a central, honored place in the official history and public memory of the American Revolution. It has been claimed by left and right ever since.[17]

In 1970, radical historian Howard Zinn cited "the great tradition of the Boston Tea Party" while defending his and other anti–Vietnam War activists' civil disobedience in federal court. Zinn hit on the same theme when speaking at an antiwar rally of 50,000 on the Boston Commons in 1971. Two years later, during celebrations marking the two hundredth anniversary of the Tea Party, a large crowd at Boston's Faneuil Hall cheered speeches calling for the impeachment of Republican president Richard Nixon and for government action against oil companies said to be profiteering in the emergent energy crisis. Before the last speaker had finished, the People's Bicentennial Commission, the Boston Indian Council, and environmental and antiwar activists led a march that concluded with a reenactment of the Tea Party near the former site of Griffin's Wharf. Protesters dressed in colonial garb boarded a tea ship replica, hanged an effigy of Nixon, and dumped three empty oil drums into Boston Harbor. A crowd of 40,000 looked on and cheered.[18]

The Rise of the "Tea Party 2.0"

Not to be outdone by the New Left when it comes to appropriating the iconic legacy and symbol of the "Boston patriots," the late-twentieth-century and early-twenty-first-century American right has identified itself with the 1773 action again and again. According to the standard media narrative, the latest, most spectacular, and most successful right-wing effort to claim the legacy of the Boston Tea Party began on February 19, 2009. That's when CNBC business news editor Rick Santelli, in a broadcast from the floor of the Chicago Mercantile Exchange, criticized the Obama administration's plan to refinance mortgages, announced the day before. Santelli denounced the plan for "promoting bad behavior" by "subsidizing losers' mortgages," and he called for "a Chicago Tea Party" in which traders would gather and dump bad derivative securities in Lake Michigan. A large number of traders around Santelli cheered his proposal, much to the amusement of the CNBC anchors. Video of Santelli's instantly famous Tea Party "rant" went viral on YouTube and across cable news after it received a "red siren" headline on the right-wing news aggregator Web site Drudge Report.[19]

According to the *New Yorker*'s Ben McGrath and *New York Times* reporter Kate Zernike, this is when "the movement" against Obama was first inspired to join together under the shared Tea Party banner. Web sites sprang up within hours of Santelli's broadcast. John Shilling, an eighteen-year-old student in Hilton Head, South Carolina, launched a site (called 92percentgroup.org) dedicated to opposing the administration's Homeowner Affordability and Stability Plan. Another young web activist, Zack Christensen, quickly renamed his site chicagoteaparty.com, calling it "the official home of the Chicago Tea Party." The same day, reteaparty.com went live to coordinate "Tea Parties." The founders reported that by the next morning they had received 40,000 e-mails, and by March they were reportedly receiving 11,000 visitors a day.

A Facebook page was created a day after "Santelli's rant" by arch-Republican, business-sponsored propaganda and advocacy group FreedomWorks, which called for "simultaneous Tea Party protests" across the country. Quickly, FreedomWorks coordinated a "Nationwide Chicago Tea Party" protest across more than forty different cities for February 27, 2009, creating the first national modern Tea Party protest.[20]

Santelli's outburst and the rapid "grassroots" response—financed and coordinated by the right wing of the Republican Party[21]—was hardly the first time that the American right had tried to use the legacy of the Boston Tea Party against "big government" Democrats. During the 1980 presidential campaign, the Libertarian candidate Ed Clark—sponsored by brothers David and Ed Koch, two leading capitalists who would play important financial roles in seeding the early Tea Party of 2009—told *The Nation* that libertarians were going to hold "a very big tea party" because citizens were "sick to death" of taxes.[22] In 1994, under the encouragement of the leading Republican representative and House Speaker Newt Gingrich, Sharon Cooper (currently a state representative in Georgia) published a book titled *Taxpayers' Tea Party*.[23] Four years later, on April 15, Dick Armey, the ultraconservative Republican House majority leader from Texas—and future head of leading Tea Party funder and coordinator FreedomWorks joined a fellow right-wing representative from Louisiana for a curious ritual in Boston. They "boarded *Beaver II*, the tea ship replica, put a copy of the federal tax code in a chest marked 'tea,' and dumped it in the harbor."[24] Throughout the 1990s and earlier, the Boston Tea Party theme was used by antitax protesters on Tax Day. FreedomWorks (formed in 1984) held protests outside post offices across the country every April 15. As Zernike observes, it "even proposed the idea of a modern-day Boston Tea Party. In 2002 it launched a website for the U.S. Tea Party. 'Do you think our taxes are too high and the tax code too complicated? We do!,' the site proclaimed as 'The Star Spangled Banner' piped in the background." In 2007, Armey and FreedomWorks president Matt Kibbe wrote an op-ed article "proposing the Boston Tea Party as a model of grassroots pressure on an overbearing central government." They couldn't get it published. Armey's own spokesman "thought the historical comparison was boring. But all that changed in the first months of 2009."[25]

Ron Paul Versus "Tea Party 2.0"

The contemporary Tea Party was launched by Texas representative Ron Paul, an actual opponent of the political establishment. An authentic libertarian who seriously opposes imperial wars and advocates drug decriminalization, Paul gave the name "Tea Party" to the rallies for his 2008 presidential run. During a Boston fund-raising event for his campaign on December 16, 2007 (the 230th anniversary of the Boston Tea Party), Paul evoked the "Tea Party" to emphasize his fiscal conservatism and strict "small government" stance in a fundraiser that garnered $6.01 million, reported to be the largest single-day campaign finance take in history.[26] As iconoclastic journalist Matt Taibbi noted in September 2010, Paul's genuine libertarianism meant that he could never be taken seriously by the Republican establishment, but the curious success of his insurgent campaign and brand name was not lost on GOP elites, which "s[aw] the utility of borrowing his insurgent rhetoric and parts of his platform for Tea Party 2.0—this second-generation Tea Party" that "came into being a month after Barack Obama moved into the White House."[27]

Seattle's Keli Carender Versus Binghamton's Trevor Leach

In an effort to demonstrate what she considers the authentically grassroots composition and origins of the Tea Party movement, Zernike claims that the real progenitor of "the movement" was not Santelli but a hip young Seattle-based conservative blogger and activist named Keli Carender. According to many of the Tea Party leaders with whom Zernike spoke, including top Republican player Dick Armey, Carender organized the "the first Tea Party" protest in Seattle without any outside assistance on President's Day, February 16, 2009, the day before President Obama signed his economic stimulus bill into law.[28] The Carender narrative strikes us as disingenuous. The Republican right has a much longer history of working with the Tea Party brand (shown to be quite profitable by Ron Paul). Establishment Republican institutions and media seized on Santelli's rant to create a handful of national Tea Party organizations almost overnight. And Carender did not actually use the term "Tea Party" (she called her action a "Porkopolus Protest"). We suspect that the story line of Carender as the sparkplug is part of the Tea Party establishment's effort to make the distinctly aged, privileged, and top-down "movement" look younger, hipper, more insurgent, and more antiestablishment than it really is.

A better candidate for the mantle of youthful progenitor of the post-Obama Tea Party, we think, is Trevor Leach. Just four days after Obama's inauguration, Leach, chairman of a local chapter of

Young Americans for Liberty, and about two dozen others poured a few gallons of carbonated pop into the Susquehanna River in Binghamton, New York, to protest Governor David Paterson's obesity tax on soda. Besides staging its action earlier than Carender did, Leach's group explicitly borrowed from the language and iconography of the original Tea Party, wearing Indian disguises and pouring a beverage into a natural body of water.[29] This action dovetailed nicely with a concerted beverage industry's lobbying and pressure campaign claiming that soda taxes (designed to fill gaping state revenue holes and to improve citizen health) were elitist and statist assaults on working people and democracy. Corporate lobbying succeeded in defeating efforts to impose soda taxes in New York and across the country over the next seventeen months. The American Beverage Association spent $9.4 million in the first four months of 2010 to fight New York's proposed tax (a model for similar levies across the country)[30] that Trevor Leach and his early band of post-Obama Tea Partiers protested over the waters of the Susquehanna. We have no direct evidence that young Americans for Liberty received money from the beverage industry prior to or after its Binghamton action (but the likelihood seems high). Nevertheless, the chief beneficiaries of the Binghamton Tea Party—like the nationwide Tea Party phenomenon that would arise in subsequent months—was the corporate sector, not "we the people."

"To Masquerade as Commoners" II and as Victims

The contemporary Tea Party is profoundly different in its own time from the original protest whose name and legacy it has appropriated. Even without counting the many elite political and economic players (e.g., Dick Armey, the Koch brothers, Glenn Beck, Fox News owner Rupert Murdoch) that have provided its most important base, its -local participants and activists are considerably more privileged and less popular than the Boston Tea Party participants were in their time. The ideology and beliefs of the modern Tea Party are, as we shall see, deeply reactionary, narrow, regressive, ossified, selfish-narcissistic, proestablishment, and authoritarian—quite different from the egalitarian, giddy, and "upside-down" spirit of the 1773 Tea Party. Whereas the original/real Tea Party dramatically advanced a profound political and structural break—the separation of the colonies from England—the current Tea Party is militantly dedicated to the preservation of the existing social and political status quo. It is a corporate-mediated monument to the business and political elite's long-standing effort to "masquerade as commoners"—to Christopher Hitchens's "manipulation of populism by elitism." The Boston Tea Party owes its central place in the nation's collective consciousness to real accomplishments and actions supported by most of the engaged American citizenry. The current farcical version owes its place in the popular imagination largely to the modern corporate mass media, which creates dangerous illusions about the nature and even the existence of a "popular movement" called the Tea Party.[31]

The modern Tea Partiers we observed in the Chicago area claimed that their "tax rebellion" was continuous with the American revolutionaries' struggle against "taxation without representation." But the contemporary Tea Party's ability to mobilize right-wing voters to remove the Democratic majority in the U.S. House of Representatives during the 2010 midterm elections speaks to significant differences in political power between current Tea Partiers and the colonists, who lacked the ability to significantly influence elections and win stronger representation within the British government of their time. Moreover, regardless of what one thinks of the Obama administration and its policies, analogies between tyrannical British colonialism (strangely mixed up with socialism and Marxism in the Tea Party worldview) and the Obama administration suggest that the modern Tea Party grossly misconstrues centrist, procorporate policies (accompanied by some concessions for the poor) as dictatorially left and unduly oppressive of business interests.[32] Little legitimately links the complaints and agenda of the original revolutionary Tea Partiers with those of contemporary Tea Party adherents.

The Past as Prop

Last August, one of us (Street) visited the historically preserved Old South Meeting House in downtown Boston. Old South is most well known for its role in the original/real Tea Party protest. Street asked the Old South volunteers if their historical site (preserved as a museum in the 1870s) had seen more foot traffic than usual with the rise of the modern Tea Party movement. A volunteer quickly answered, "No, not at all: Those guys couldn't care less about the real history of the Tea Party. . . . We don't see them, even when they have one of their rallies downtown." Apparently, the Tea Party label or brand—the iconic image of a popular-revolutionary event that right-wing "patriots" do not care to deeply understand or remotely investigate—is sufficient for contemporary imitators, for whom the past is little more than a superficial propaganda field to be mined in service to contemporary political agendas.[33]

3

Tea Party "Super Republicans"
Who They Are, What They Believe

Popular Resentment, Left Vacuum

The real Tea Party phenomenon portrayed in this volume is different not only from the version presented by the "movement" itself and the mass media. It is also different from the character some progressives have given it, which coincides to no small degree with the media narrative and that of the Tea Party itself. According to a number of prominent progressive left thinkers and activists, the left* ought to reach out to the Tea Party and connect with its members as potential allies in promoting left-wing causes. Many, perhaps most of the Tea Partiers, this hopeful (some might say desperate) line runs, are working-class people "we on the left should be organizing." For example, in the summer of 2010 Washington-based antiwar activist Kevin Zeese called for progressives to recruit "traditional conservative" Tea Party activists—described as "confused" by Zeese—to join a "left-right antiwar coalition" to demand "the

---

*Like "the Tea Party," the term "the left" is an overly broad and often vaguely defined term that is thrown around rather loosely and often as a term of derision in the reigning political and media culture. Perhaps someone should consider penning a book or at least an essay titled "The Left Does Not Exist."

end" of "the American empire" and form "a broad-based anti-war movement not limited to the 'left.'"[1]

The most prominent Tea Party commentary on the left has come from radical intellectual Noam Chomsky, who has argued that the Tea Party represents legitimate popular anger that "the left" would do well not to ignore or mock. Chomsky framed the Tea Party's success as "sign of the failure of the left" because Tea Party supporters have "real grievances" rooted in the stagnation of American wages, the growth in unemployment, and bipartisan attempts to dismantle the social welfare state.[2] Chomsky warned that growing public anger, expressed by Middle America and the poor, carried with it the specter of radical right-wing violence.[3] Chomsky advanced more elaborate and grave reflections, evoking the memory of early German Nazism:

> Right now . . . there is a right-wing populist uprising. It's very common, even on the left, to just ridicule them, but that's not the right reaction. If you look at those people and listen to them on talk radio, these are people with real grievances. . . . And in fact they are getting shafted. For 30 years their wages have stagnated or declined, the social conditions have worsened . . . so somebody must be doing something to them, and they want to know who it is. Well Rush Limbaugh has answered—"it's the rich liberals who own the banks and run the government, and of course run the media, and they don't care about you." Either they just want to give everything away to illegal immigrants and gays and communists and so on. . . . The reaction we should be having to them is not ridicule, but rather self-criticism. Why aren't we organizing them? I mean, we are the ones that ought to be organizing them, not Rush Limbaugh. There are historical analogs, which are not exact, of course, but are close enough to be worrisome. This is a whiff of early Nazi Germany. Hitler was appealing to groups with similar grievances, and giving them crazy answers, but at least they were answers; these groups weren't getting them anywhere else.
>
>   . . . The liberal Democrats aren't going to tell the average American, "Yeah, you're being shafted because of the policies that we've established over the years that we're maintaining now." That's not going to be an answer. And they're not getting answers from the left.

So, there's an internal coherence and logic to what they get from Limbaugh, Glenn Beck, and the rest of these guys. And they sound very convincing, they're very self-confident, and they have an answer to everything. It's a crazy answer, but it's an answer. And it's our fault if that goes on. So . . . don't ridicule these people, join them, and talk about their real grievances and give them a sensible answer, like, "Take over your factories."[4]

The potential for mass violence is reflected in the story of Joe Stack, to which Chomsky drew attention in his 2010 address to the Left Forum in New York City. Stack, who committed suicide by flying his plane into an IRS office building in Austin, Texas, symbolized the rage of society—many members of which felt they were being left behind in light of growing economic desperation and increased official talk about cutting social welfare, balancing budgets, and framing "big government" as the overarching societal problem. Stack himself lamented corporate corruption in light of a tax system he saw as blatantly favoring the rich. His attack on corporate America highlighted the industrial decline and outsourcing felt in Harrisburg, Pennsylvania—once the heart of steel production in America—where he had attended school. Stack's anger as a "tax protester" was most specifically directed at the IRS, amid an audit being conducted against him following the 2000 dot.com bust, in which he claimed he earned no income and was forced to raid his retirement savings in order to make ends meet. Chomsky highlighted the Stack anecdote as merely one example of "those who have been cast aside as the state-corporate programs of financialization and deindustrialization have closed plants and destroyed families and communities." Stack was not simply antigovernment. He was enraged by the federal government's disproportionate service to the rich and powerful.[5]

The bipartisan assault on popular social welfare programs, accompanied by the worsening economy and an official commitment to bailing out corporations deemed "too big to fail," has played an important role in creating a political environment in which widespread distrust of officialdom provides fertile ground for Tea Party messages. The Tea Party's major appeal to the general public is that it is selling popular rebellion at a time when the public is understandably enraged about an economic crisis that neither party has been willing or able to pull the country out of.

The Tea Party's specific policy proposals tend to be strongly opposed by the American public. However, the group's general anxiety over the worsening state of the American economy *is* shared by the mass public. In a CBS/*New York Times* poll conducted in April 2010, both Tea Partiers and the general public agreed that "the most important problem[s] facing the country today" were the economy more generally and the lack of jobs more specifically.[6] This rational, understandable concern with the dire state of the U.S. economy and the implications of the economic crisis for American workers and the growing number of unemployed (throughout 2008 onward) have brought Tea Party supporters and the general public together to some degree.

Much commentary on the left emphasizes the increasing failure (or unwillingness) of the Democratic Party to make social welfare for the poor and unemployed a significant priority during the great economic crisis. The party has pursued some policies that benefit the disadvantaged to some extent—such as an expansion of Medicaid, a legal prohibition on denying health care due to "preexisting conditions," an extension of unemployment benefits, and federally funded stimulus and public works hiring. These changes, however, are seen (with reason) by much of the left (and the larger public) as terribly inadequate in light of the larger commitment of the Obama administration to bailing out elite financial and corporate interests at massive taxpayer expense.[7]

"The Little Guy": How Grassroots?

Legitimate popular anger *is* widespread across the nation—anger that could be channeled in egalitarian ways by progressive and democratic forces. But "Tea Party populism" is largely the result of top-down manufactured rage, created and disseminated by a combination of official, corporate, and media-based voices at the expense of genuine grassroots empowerment. It is being used to pursue probusiness policies that will only accelerate the dramatic growth of inequality and the stagnation of working- and middle-class incomes that have occurred over the last four decades.

The context of increasing public desperation seems well fit for the application of noted liberal historian and journalist Tom Frank's "Kansas thesis"—a downtrodden white working class picked off by the manipulative, fake-populist right wing after being abandoned by elitist corporate Democrats. Resentment, the argument runs, abhors a vacuum. If a genuinely popular working-class political party and reasonably angry social-democratic progressives do not exist to give forthright and actionable answers to irate and aggrieved working people, it is left, the thesis holds, to reactionary forces to capture and channel popular wrath in authoritarian, regressive ways by a right wing that falsely represents itself as antiestablishment.[8]

In fact, however, the real Tea Party phenomenon beneath the "populist" branding and media imagery does not appear to rest on an especially working-class base. How grassroots and popular is the Tea Party? Leading Republican and Tea Party media icon and organizer Glenn Beck asked in March 2009, "What happened to the country that loved the underdog and stood up for the little guy?"[9] That's who the "insurgent" and "antiestablishment" Tea Party movement was speaking for, according to Beck: "the little guy." "Talk about grassroots," a small-town Kentucky Tea Party activist—a middle-aged working-class woman—told *New Yorker* writer Ben McGrath in the fall of 2009. "This is as grassroots as it gets."[10]

Not really. National data suggest that the Tea Party's core support is not particularly made up of working-class "underdogs" ground up by deindustrialization and corporate globalization. To be sure, such people were no doubt present (in large numbers perhaps) among the 52 percent of Americans who "feel sympathy for the tea party movement."[11] But feeling sympathy for a vaguely defined, deceptively marketed and poorly understood, media-scripted "movement" is not the same as being an active supporter or a direct participant in that "movement."

A poll conducted by the Program on International Policy Attitudes (PIPA) in August 2010 suggested real differences between the values of the survey respondents who felt sympathy for the Tea Party movement and actual Tea Party institutions and ideology. The Tea Party complains insistently about "big government," but just 31 percent of "Tea Party sympathizers" reported that their main concern was that government is becoming too big. Over half (55 percent) said that their biggest worry was that government "is not following the will of the people." Even among a "hard core" that told PIPA they were "very sympathetic to the Tea Party"—one in five overall— only 46 percent cited major distress over "big government." More of this group—47 percent—expressed greater concern with Joe Stack's main issue: government's lack of democratic responsiveness.[12] This finding is consistent with long-standing majority popular American opinion, which—well to the left of both major U.S. political parties and dominant media and the business class on economic issues—has long been primarily concerned not with government power or size per se but with the disproportionate influence exercised over politics and policy by concentrated wealth and power.[13]

Social movements consist of (1) an "activist core," full-time members who make it their first priority to promote the movement;[14] (2) voluntary part-time participants (sometimes referred to as a "conscience constituency"), who contribute to the movement out of ideological attachment; and (3) the sympathetic public on the outskirts, which indicates ideological support for the movement but has yet to participate directly in any substantive way.[15] The Tea Party appears to contain all three components required of a social movement, but support appears to be strongest at the margins (among the general public) rather than within the core. The size of the core and the size of the conscience constituency groups in the Tea Party are vastly exaggerated in public discussion. Their numbers are so small that they resemble the structure of an interest group rather than a social movement. Like other privileged and affluent interest groups, the Tea Party employs its significant resources to expand the size of the sympathetic public surrounding the group, but the core and conscience constituency remain quite small. The outermost layer of the Tea Party (its sympathetic public) *does* resemble the size of the sympathetic public surrounding effective social movements, something that reinforces the tendency of pundits and much of public to think of the Tea Party as a popular "movement."

How big are the Tea Party's core and conscience constituency? The signature Tea Party narrative of freedom and liberty versus big government (equated with evil "socialism" in the "movement's" standard rhetoric) is certainly more common, probably close to uniform among the much smaller group of Americans who can be properly identified as core Tea Party participants and activists. But this group does not appear to be very large. Defining "Tea Party activists" as those who attended a rally or donated money to "the movement," an early April 2010 CBS/*New York Times* survey found that this category comprised 20 percent of Tea Party supporters and 4 percent of Americans overall.[16] In a similar vein, a mid-February 2010 national survey by the Opinion Research Corporation found that just 2 percent of respondents had given money to any organization associated with the Tea Party movement. Five percent reported attending a movement rally or meeting and 7 percent reported other active steps to support the Tea Party, either in person or through e-mail or on the Internet."[17]*

The closer one gets to the core of the Tea Party's base, the more elite the "movement's" "grassroots" support looks. Organizations such as FreedomWorks, Americans for Prosperity, the Tea Party Express, and Our Country Deserves Better produce the bulk of Tea Party events and actions. They have an interest-group structure and a relatively small number of members, and they rely heavily on corporate funding and organizing from the Republican Party.[18] Little is left of the Tea Party phenomenon apart from these groups. Local chapter organizing is sparse, and attempts to bring the meager resources and organizing of these chapters together at the national level have largely been a blatant failure.

Angry though they may be, the right-wing "populists" at the "grassroots" of the Tea Party phenomenon are not particularly disadvantaged or working class. Neither are they particularly well off. We see them as relatively affluent within the heart of Middle America. A March 2010 Pew Research Center poll found that 24 percent of

---

*Even these numbers are far too high for the activist contingent, for they find little support in the observational data on "movement" participation and activism we will present in Chapter 6.

Americans "agree with the Tea Party movement." ("Agree with" is certainly a stronger level of support than "feel sympathy for.") Besides being significantly older, and disproportionately more male and white (non-Hispanic) than most Americans, Pew's "Tea Party backers" were considerably more college educated and more likely to enjoy higher family incomes than the general public. Pew determined that the "backers" were considerably more nationalistic ("patriotic" and flag-displaying), more religious, more likely to be registered to vote, and more likely to possess a gun (see Table 3.1).[19] *

In April 2010, a CBS/*New York Times* poll asked respondents if they considered themselves to be "supporter[s] of the Tea Party movement?"—a stronger question than whether they agreed with the Tea Party. The *Times* reported that "Tea Party supporters" were wealthier and better educated than the general public. The survey found that 75 percent of supporters had a college education; 76 percent enjoyed household incomes above $50,000 (including 20 percent receiving more than $100,000); 78 percent described their financial situations as "good" or "fairly good"; 65 percent identified as either middle or middle upper class; 59 percent were men; 75 percent were 45 or older; and 89 percent were white.[20] A National Association for the Advancement of Colored People (NAACP) study found that the poor and unemployed were underrepresented in the Tea Party. The study examined membership in various Tea Party groups, including Resistnet, FreedomWorks, 1776 Tea Party Patriots, Tea Party Nation, and Tea Party Patriots, finding a very weak relationship between unemployment and Tea Party membership.[21]

A CNN poll in February 2010 poll found that Tea Party activists (including those who had given money to Tea Party groups and/or participated in Tea Party rallies) had considerably higher incomes, were more highly educated, and were more likely to be male, Caucasian, rural, conservative, and Republican than the general population.

National survey data suggest that Tea Partiers, although largely hailing from Middle America, are not generally representative of

---

*The general public was more likely to be employed than was the Tea Party cohort in Pew's research, but this simply reflects the fact that the "Tea Party backers" demographic is older, with more retired people.

TABLE 3.1

Demographics of Tea Party Supporters		
Demographic Group	*Agree with Tea Party*	*General Public*
Male	56%	49%
Age 18–29	8%	21%
30–49	33%	34%
50–64	33%	26%
65 and over	23%	17%
Education		
High School or Less	38%	47%
College Graduate	35%	28%
Income		
Less than $30K	18%	31%
$30–75K	31%	31%
$75 and Over	36%	25%
Registered to Vote	87%	76%
"More Patriotic than Most"	51%	33%
Display the Flag	75%	58%
Religious Attendance		
Weekly or More	49%	38%
Seldom or Never	18%	25%
"Have a Gun"	47%	33%

SOURCE: Pew Research Center for the People and the Press, "Distrust, Discontent, Anger, and Partisan Rancor: The People and Their Government" (April 18, 2010), at http://people-press.org/report/606/trust-in-government.

the larger public—and this is true of its most dedicated followers as well. Those deeming themselves "strong supporters" were disproportionately middle-aged or older and white, as well as overwhelmingly Republican and conservative, when compared to the general public (see Table 3.2).[22]

Our observation of local Tea Partiers throughout the Chicago metropolitan area found generally the same demographics described in national polling data. We were able to find very few active Tea Party organizers, nothing close to the numbers that would constitute an expansive national "movement." The overwhelming majority of those we spoke with and observed at meetings and at rallies, however, were articulate and well dressed and appeared to hail from middle- and upper-middle-class backgrounds. The vast majority appeared to be over forty years of age, and there was a significantly larger presence of men, although a substantial number of women also participated. All participants were openly conservative, and the vast majority indicated that they were Republican either in their partisan identification or their voting patterns. Most suggested that they saw voting as the most important form of political participation in politics today. Most also attempted to distinguish themselves as patriotic, freedom-loving Americans and considered themselves far more patriotic than moderate Republicans, centrists, and those on the left. Finally, many represented themselves as God-fearing Americans, at times framing private property rights as "God given." Participants attributed a sort of godlike wisdom to the Founding Fathers and their alleged support for "constitutionally mandated" "limited government." In those we observed, "free-market," laissez-faire capitalism was almost a religion in and of itself.

Elite Tea Partiers are far outside the ideological mainstream. At the national level, the CBS/*New York Times* poll's Tea Party activist cohort was almost identical in socioeconomic terms to the poll's broader Tea Party "supporter" group. But the activists were considerably angrier at Washington, more disapproving of Obama, more favorable toward Glenn Beck and Sarah Palin, more likely to think the economy was getting worse and that quality jobs are a thing of the past, more likely to say that violent acts against government were justified and that the income taxes they paid were unfair, and more likely to think that Palin could be an effective president.[23]

TABLE 3.2

Strong Tea Party Supporters		
Demographic Group	*Tea Party Activists*	*General Public*
Male	60%	50%
White	80%	71%
College educated	40%	28%
Rural	50%	38%
Urban	9%	21%
Conservative	77%	40%
Vote Republican	87%	46%
Income: Under $30K	8%	28%
$30–50K	18%	19%
$50–75K	32%	17%
More than $75K	34%	25%

Within Tea Party Differences: Strong Versus Weak Supporters		
Demographic Group	*Strong Supporters*	*Weak Supporters*
Republican/lean Rep.	82%	64%
Conservative	78%	58%
White	91%	83%
Male	61%	49%
Age: 18–29	6%	19%
30–39	6%	11%
40–50	16%	20%
51–65	39%	27%
Over 65	33%	24%

SOURCE: http://i2.cdn.turner.com/cnn/2010/images/02/17/rel4b.pdf.

"All You Capitalists"

Tea Party leader John O'Hara underscores the elitist nature of the Tea Party's base. In *The New American Tea Party*, O'Hara claimed that "Tea Party participants and organizers *run the gamut of the political and socioeconomic spectrum*" (emphasis added).[24] At the beginning of Chapter 1, O'Hara related the incident that is so commonly mentioned as the spark that set off the Tea Party fire—Rick Santelli's February 19, 2009, CNBC rant against President Barack Obama's alleged call for responsible homeowners and taxpayers to "pay for your neighbor's [bad] mortgage." By O'Hara's account,

> following this line, the Chicago trading floor on which Santelli had been standing erupted in yelling and screaming. This typically happens because each stock is rallying or declining. Santelli's rant was interrupted by a nearby trader who quipped, "Maybe we should all stop paying our mortgages; it's a moral hazard."
>
> Stock traders cheering at the political statements of an on-air business reporter? Talking about pointlessness of paying a mortgage as a kind of moral hazard? It was like a scene from *Atlas Shrugged,* except, thankfully, the monologues were shorter.
>
> These traders . . . were not ideologues or talking heads, nor were they activists or lobbyists. They were *simply working people who wanted the freedom to continue working and enjoy the fruits of their labor in a fair way* (emphasis added). Santelli's complaint about the unfairness of rewarding the irresponsible behavior of those who didn't play fair resonated.
>
> If one small rant could get a trading floor on its feet, was it possible that others felt the same? . . . That people could get their hackles up over the minutiae of mortgages is pretty damning. . . . That's where we [the Tea Party] came in.[25]

Chicago floor traders have an average annual salary of $86,000.[26] To refer to them as some sort of rank-and-file people's entity undermines the official Tea Party "grassroots" and "populist" narrative. So does the fact that Santelli, the "Paul Revere" of the Tea Party's "Second American Revolution," is a former futures trader and former vice president of Drexel Burnham Lambert, once a leading Wall Street investment banking firm. O'Hara omitted Santelli's call (in his outburst) for "*all you capitalists*" to join him in forming a "Chicago Tea Party" that would "dump . . . some derivative securities" in Lake Michigan. "It was a delicate pose," writes Ben McGrath—"financial professionals more or less laughing at debtors while disavowing the lending techniques that had occasioned the [financial] crisis."[27] It was also a hypocritical and ironic pose given the financial sector's well-documented role in the offshoring of livable wage employment for millions of American workers over the last four decades.

The irony of it all is captured by essayist Adam Bessie, who observes that the supposedly populist and antiestablishment "Tea Party grew from outrage—outrage at the prospect of 'subsidizing the loser's mortgages,' with a call to 'capitalists' to come protest."[28] Tellingly enough and contrary to the dominant narrative of the contemporary Tea Party as a populist, antiestablishment uprising that targeted elite financial interests, Santelli's famous eruption did not attack the billions of taxpayer dollars being used to prop up the bad real estate debts and unsecured derivative losses produced by financial giants like AIG and Goldman Sachs—gargantuan public bailouts backed by subsequent Tea Party champions like Sarah Palin and many other leading Republicans.[29] Santelli directed his rage at the White House's Homeowner Affordability and Stability Plan, a $75 billion program that cost less than one-hundredth the cost of the bank bailouts of 2008–2009. This was "one of the few bailout programs designed to directly benefit individuals, many of whom were minorities, and who were close to foreclosure."[30]

"While the big bank bailouts may have been incomprehensible to ordinary voters," *Rolling Stone* writer Matt Taibbi noted in September 2010, "here was something that Middle America had no problem grasping: The financial crisis was caused by those lazy minorities next door who bought houses they couldn't afford—and now the government was going to bail them out." Taibbi noted the elite-directed, business- and Republican-structured nature of the supposedly grassroots uprising that followed Santelli's corporate-mediated meltdown:

Suddenly, tens of thousands of Republicans who had been conspicuously silent during George Bush's gargantuan spending on behalf of defense contractors and hedge-fund gazillionaires showed up at Tea Party rallies across the nation, declaring themselves fed up with wasteful government spending. From the outset, the events were organized and financed by the conservative wing of the Republican Party, which was quietly working to co-opt the new movement and deploy it to the GOP's advantage.[31]

What They Believe

If the real Tea Party "grassroots" is distinct from the general citizenry in terms of its comparatively elevated socioeconomic status, its difference from the broader populace is more and sharply pronounced in terms of its values, ideology, worldview, and partisan identification. Tea Partiers stand well to the proestablishment right of a U.S. majority that stands well to the left of both major parties on a large number of key societal values and policy issues.

Pollsters Scott Rasmussen and Douglas Schoen argue that "fringe element[s]" make up only a small minority of the Tea Party's "mainstream" supporters.[32] Data from the CBS/*New York Times* poll, however, suggest that Tea Partiers are extreme in their opinions, demonstrating a significant chasm between the Tea Party and the rank and file citizenry it claims to represent (see Table 3.3).[33]

The Silent Progressive Majority

Rasmussen and Schoen think that the public is closely aligned ideologically with the Tea Party. They see both as conservative in their opposition to "big government," their support for "free markets," and their opposition to health care reform.[34] This image of the public is generally rejected in scholarly studies of public opinion, which show strong public support for specific liberal social welfare programs.[35] A vast amount of polling data contradicts the widespread assumption and dominant media trope that the United States is a "center-right

TABLE 3.3

Political Opinions of Tea Party Activists, Supporters, and the General Public			
Policy Opinion	*Tea Party Activists*	*Tea Party Supporters*	*General Public*
Disapproval of Obama	96%	88%	40%
Taxes Are Unfair	55%	42%	30%
Feel Anger Toward Washington	72%	53%	19%
Palin Will Make a Good President	75%	66%	26%
The Best Economic Years Are Behind Americans	64%	58%	45%
Violence Against Government Is Acceptable	32%	24%	16%

nation"—even a conservative country. National opinion polls suggest that Tea Partiers are clearly projecting their values upon a largely reluctant public, which views the lack of government support for progressive policies, rather than "big government" itself, as the major problem plaguing the political system. Public opinion is quite progressive in terms of majority support for the liberal state:[36]

- Sixty-nine percent of U.S. voters agree that "government should care for those who cannot care for themselves" (Pew Research, 2007).
- Fifty-four percent of voters agree that "government should help the needy even if it means greater debt" (Pew Research, 2007).
- Fifty-eight percent believe the U.S. government should be doing more for its citizens, not less (National Elections Survey, 2004).

- Twice as many Americans back more government services and spending (even if this means a tax increase) as do those who support fewer services and reduced spending (National Elections Survey, 2004).
- Sixty-four percent of Americans would pay higher taxes to guarantee health care for all U.S. citizens (CNN/Opinion Research Corporation Poll, May 2007).
- Sixty-nine percent think it is the responsibility of the federal government to provide health coverage to all U.S. citizens (Gallup Poll, 2006).
- Eighty percent support a government-mandated increase in the minimum wage (Associated Press/AOL Poll, December 2006).
- Eighty-six percent want Congress to pass legislation to raise the federal minimum wage (CNN, August 2006).
- Seventy-one percent think that taxes on corporations are too low (Gallup Poll, April 2007).
- Sixty-six percent think that taxes on upper-income people are too low (Gallup Poll, April 2007).
- Fifty-nine percent are favorable toward unions, with just 29 percent unfavorable (Gallup Poll, 2006).
- Fifty-two percent generally side with unions in labor disputes, whereas just 34 percent side with management (Gallup Poll, 2006).
- Fifty-nine percent of Americans support programs that "give special preference to qualified women and minorities in hiring" (Pew Poll, 2003).
- A strong majority of American voters think that the nation's "most urgent moral question" is either "greed and materialism" (33 percent) or "poverty and economic injustice" (31 percent). Just 16 percent identify abortion and 12 percent pick gay marriage as the nation's "most urgent moral question" (Zogby, 2004). Thus, 64 percent of the population think that injustice and inequality are the nation's leading "moral issues."
- Just 29 percent of Americans support the expansion of government spending on "defense." By contrast, 79 percent support increased spending on health care, 69 percent support increased spending on education, and 69 percent support increased spend-

ing on Social Security (Chicago Council on Foreign Relations, "Global Views," 2004).

- Seventy-eight percent of Americans support using "tax dollars . . . to help pay for" "food stamps and other assistance to the poor," while 80 percent support appropriating tax funding for "retraining programs for people whose jobs have been eliminated" (National Inequality Survey, 2007).

The CBS/*New York Times* Poll on Tea Party Supporters

An April 2010 CBS/*New York Times* poll's extensive survey of the beliefs of Tea Party supporters (TPS in this section) indicates that the supposedly popular base of the "populist" Tea Party "insurgency" stands well to the proestablishment right of majority opinion in the United States. Contrary both to O'Hara's claim that the Tea Party's base reflects "the gamut of the political spectrum" and to Tea Partiers' claim that their "movement" is "not a left-right phenomenon as much as a bottom-up phenomenon" (Republican strategist Alex Castellanos),[37] the poll found that 73 percent of TPS identified themselves as "Conservatives," compared to just 4 percent who were "Liberals" and 20 percent who called themselves "Moderates."[38] With the Tea Party cohort, we are clearly dealing with the far-right end of the American politico-ideological spectrum.

Furthermore, the CBS/*New York Times* survey found the following (see also Table 3.4 for an abbreviated representation):

- Just 20 percent of TPS surveyed were willing to place primary blame for the 2008–2009 financial and economic crisis on Wall Street and the Bush administration (Wall Street being the primary crisis instigator), compared to 54 percent of Americans who blamed Wall Street and Bush.
- Fully 92 percent of TPS preferred a "smaller government providing fewer services" to citizens (50 percent of the overall survey sample shared that opinion).
- Unlike 50 percent of the entire survey sample, only 13 percent of TPS believed that the federal government should spend

federal money to create jobs even if this meant increasing the budget deficit.

- Seventy-six percent of TPS thought the government should privilege deficit reduction over job creation—an opinion shared by just 17 percent of Americans according to the survey.
- Eighty-nine percent of TPS believed that President Obama had "expanded the role of government too much"—an opinion shared by just 37percent of Americans.
- Ninety-two percent believed that "Barack Obama's policies were moving the country more toward socialism." Support for this position was 40 percentage points lower among the general public, with 52 percent thinking Obama was promoting socialism.
- Eighty-four percent of TPS reported having an "unfavorable" opinion of Barack Obama (this view was shared by 43 percent of all Americans)—an opinion informed by the fact that 77 percent of TPS identified him as "very liberal" (only 31 percent of the overall sample agreed with that) and that 56 percent of TPS saw his policies as "favoring the poor" (just 27 percent of the overall population shared that opinion).
- Eighty-two percent of TPS believed that "illegal immigration is a very serious problem for the country right now"—an opinion shared by 60 percent of the overall population.
- Fifty-one percent of TPS believed that "global warming won't have a serious impact on the environment at all"—a belief shared by only 24 percent of Americans overall. Fifteen percent of TPS thought that global warming "doesn't exist"—an opinion shared by just 5 percent of Americans.
- Just 16 percent of TPS (compared to 39 percent of Americans overall) believed that gay and lesbian couples should be allowed to legally marry.
- Fifty-three percent of TPS, compared to 34 percent of Americans overall, felt that "Supreme Court's decision in *Roe v. Wade* (the decision that established a constitutional right for women to obtain legal abortions) was "a bad thing."
- Seventy-three percent of TPS thought that "white people and black people have about an equal chance of getting ahead" in

American society—an opinion shared by 60 percent of Americans overall and by 55 percent of "Non–Tea Party Whites."

- Fifty-two percent thought that "in recent years too much has been made of the problems facing black people"—an opinion shared by 28 percent of Americans overall and by less than 25 percent of Non–Tea Party Whites.
- 80 percent TPS felt it was "a bad idea to raise incomes taxes on households that make more than $250,000 in order to provide health insurance to people who do not have it"—an opinion shared by 39 percent of Americans overall.

TABLE 3.4

Differences Between Tea Party Positions and Those of the General Public		
Positions	*Percentage of Tea Party Supporters Who Agreed*	*Percentage of General Public Who Agreed*
Wall Street and Bush are to blame for the financial crisis.	20%	54%
It is better to have a smaller government with fewer services.	92	50
The federal government should spend money to create jobs even if this increases the deficit.	13	50
Deficit reduction is more important than job creation.	76	17
Obama has expanded the role of government too much.	89	37
Obama is moving the country toward socialism.	92	52
Unfavorable opinion of Obama	84	43
Obama is very liberal.	77	31

(continues)

TABLE 3.4 *(continued)*

Differences Between Tea Party Positions and Those of the General Public		
Positions	*Percentage of Tea Party Supporters Who Agreed*	*Percentage of General Public Who Agreed*
Obama's policies favor the poor.	56%	27%
Illegal immigration is a very serious problem.	82	60
Global warming won't have a serious impact on the environment.	51	24
Global warming doesn't exist.	15	5
Gays and lesbians should be allowed to marry.	16	39
Roe v. Wade was a bad decision.	53	34
Whites and blacks have an equal chance of getting ahead.	73	60
Too much has been made of the problems facing black people.	52	28
It's a bad idea to raise taxes on incomes over $250,000 to provide health insurance for those who don't have it.	80	39
Government benefits for the poor only help them remain poor.	75	38

SOURCE: CBS/*New York Times*, "Polling the Tea Party: Who They Are and What They Believe," *New York Times*, April 14, 2010, at www.nytimes.com/interactive/2010/04/14/us/politics/20100414-tea-party-poll-graphic.html#tab=4.

- More then 75 percent of TPS believed that "providing government benefits to poor people encourages them to remain poor"
  instead of "help[ing] them to stand on their own"—an opinion
  shared by just 38 percent of Americans overall.[39]

Consistent with the CBS/*Times* survey's finding that Tea Partiers
believed that Obama was too far to the left, three-quarters of Tea
Party supporters surveyed by Selzer and Co. in early October 2010
agreed that "Obama is too anti-business." Just one-third of all likely
voters shared that opinion.[40]

Our on-the-ground investigation of the Tea Party throughout the
Chicago area largely confirmed the polling numbers just cited. The
Tea Partiers we met and observed rarely attacked Wall Street at rallies and meetings. They focused their anger instead at the specter of
"big government" and "Obama socialism," epitomized in their view
by the federal stimulus program and the health reform bill. One important distinction we drew from attending local meetings when
comparing local observation to national polling data, was the con-
scious downplaying of social, religious, and moral issues by Tea Party
organizers. Those activists clearly saw the state of the American
economy and the Democrats' supposedly liberty-smashing and socialist response to the economic crisis as their priority issues. The
Tea Party events spent relatively little time on the social-moral issues
that the right has been so adept at exploiting in recent decades.[41] The
right-wing Republicans depicted in Tom Frank's classic study *What's
the Matter With Kansas?* moved working-class Middle Americans
away from the Democratic Party with "cultural issues" like guns, religion, gay rights, and abortion (Frank had remarkably little to say
about race and militarism), but the Tea Party we observed in and
around Chicago consciously elevated economic issues (jobs, taxes,
trade deficits, and more) over cultural matters to advance their cause.

The Tea Partiers as "Super Republicans"

The existing polling data do not fit the dominant "movement" and
media image of the Tea Party as a nonpartisan, independent, and

antiestablishment political force—or the idea that the Tea Party represents a potential third party apart from the Democrats and Republicans.[42] The survey data reveal that the Tea Party is a distinctly right-Republican group with little interest in bucking the reigning two-party system.

Contrary to John O'Hara's claim that the Tea Partiers run "the gamut of the political spectrum," the CBS/*New York Times* poll found that two-thirds of Tea Party supporters (compared to just more than one-quarter of all survey respondents) usually or always voted Republican in national and statewide elections. Fifty-four percent of TPS held a favorable opinion of the Republican Party, and, consistent with their pronounced reluctance to embrace third-party alternatives, a massive 92 percent reported a "not favorable" view of the Democratic Party. Fifty-four percent of TPS identified themselves as Republican, compared to just 5 percent who were Democrats. Just 4 percent of the cohort described themselves as "Liberal," compared to just 20 percent who were "Moderates" and an overwhelming 73 percent who identified as "Conservative." Eighty-four percent of TPS reported a "not favorable" opinion of the sitting Democratic president, Barack Obama—a view shared by just 33 percent of Americans overall. And when asked to list the living American political figure they admired most, TPS placed Republicans in each of their top eight positions, ranked as follows: Newt Gingrich, Sarah Palin, George W. Bush, Mitt Romney, John McCain, Ron Paul, Mike Huckabee, and George H. W. Bush.[43]

More telling, perhaps, in terms of what it says about the limits of their alienation from the GOP, 57 percent of the Tea Party cohort held a favorable opinion of George W. Bush. By sharp contrast, 58 percent of Americans viewed him unfavorably. Related to their comparatively high approval of the second President Bush, just 5 percent Tea Party supporters—compared to 32 percent of all Americans—thought the Bush administration was "most to blame for the current state of the nation's economy." The far-right, Republican Fox News media star and Tea Party icon Glenn Beck was viewed with favor by 59 percent of TPS—an opinion shared by 18 percent of Americans. Fully two-thirds of the Tea Party cohort held a favorable opinion of Sarah Palin. By contrast, Ron Paul—often cited by progressive advocates of a left-right coalition as an example of libertarian spirit that progressives can find common cause with in the Tea Party—was viewed favorably by just 28 percent of TPS.[44] The libertarian war critic Paul is more popular among Tea Party backers than he is among the Republican establishment, but his status among these supposedly antiestablishment "insurgents" is much lower than that of establishment pro-war Republicans such as Bush, Palin, and Beck.

Fewer than 1 in 5 TPS thought there was "a lot of difference between the Republican Party and the Tea Party movement." When asked whether "the country needs a third political party—a new party to compete with the Democratic and Republican Parties," 52 percent of TPS *disagreed*. The predominantly Republican Tea Party cohort was *less third party oriented than the American population as a whole*, according to the CBS/*Times* survey.[45]

The survey found that the "Tea Party activist" cadre had a stronger feeling of independence from the Republican Party than did Tea Partiers overall. Half of the activists viewed the GOP unfavorably. Most of those identified as "Tea Party activists" by a February 2010 CNN/Opinion Research Corporation poll described themselves (somewhat deceptively) as "Independents." Nevertheless, given (among other things) their own Republican views and history and their intense dislike of the supposedly socialist Barack Obama and the Democrats, the Tea Party activists showed little proclivity to bolt the Grand Old Party or the American winner-take-all two-party system. As CNN political writer Paul Steinhauser noted in February 2010, those activists seemed to see themselves every bit as caught within that system as left progressives who complain about the corporate and military direction of the Democratic Party, but who then line up in support of that party's candidates at election time.[46]

By the findings of an important Bloomberg News poll conducted between October 7 and October 10, 2010, 4 of every 5 Tea Party supporters who said they would vote on November 2 planned to cast their ballots for Republicans even though one-third described themselves as "Independents." Fully 85 percent of Bloomberg's Tea Party sample believed that "the economy will improve with Republicans in control of Congress." Eight of 10 Tea Party voters backed the "Pledge to America," the Republican Party's "road map for governing" in the wake of gaining control of Congress. As Lisa Lerer, a Bloomberg reporter, observed, "Tea Party activists, once on the fringe of the Republican mainstream, are fueling the party's momentum in the midterm elections." Lerer described Tea Party voters not as independents or anything like a third and autonomous force in American politics but rather as "*Super Republicans*" who were "more energized than other likely voters and more apt to view this election as exceptionally important" (emphasis added). The Tea Party cohort held no specific ideological or policy position that placed it outside the Republican Party. Tea Partiers were distinguished from other voters mainly by the fact that 56 percent of likely Tea Party voters viewed the November elections as "exceptionally important" (compared with 43 percent of all likely voters) and in that they were "more intense than other voters in seeking a rollback of the changes passed by the Democratic-controlled Congress." Bloomberg noted that Tea Party backers who planned to vote put a higher priority than other voters on lowering taxes. They also favored making people wait longer to receive full Social Security benefits and slashing money for research of Alzheimer's and other diseases as a way to narrow the deficit—exactly what one would expect from "super Republicans."[47]

There was no rank-and-file citizen's protest on the part of "Independent" Tea Partiers when the Tea Party protested Tax Day two blocks from the White House on April 15, 2010. The protest featured former Republican House representative Dick Armey, a former Republican House majority leader; Senator Saxby Chambliss, Republican of Georgia; Republican representatives Ron Paul of Texas and Steve King of Iowa; and longtime leading Republican strategist Grover Norquist, chairman of Americans for Tax Reform.[48]

"The Tea Party today," Matt Taibbi observed in September 2010, "is being pitched in the media as this great threat to the Republican Party; in reality, the Tea Party is the GOP."[49]

"The Tea Party movement may be a bit frisky and unpredictable," conservative writer Michael Brendan Dougherty noted in the *American Conservative* in April 2010, "but it will always have a warm cup to serve the GOP. In Nashville [during a national Tea Party Convention in the spring of 2010] the chanting went up tentatively at first, then gained force: 'Run, Sarah, Run!' Palin graciously accepted their adoration—then left in the company of the Republican professionals who make up her entourage."

"Even the most militant [Tea Party] rebels aren't upending the establishment," Dougherty added. "They're still playing safely within the confines of Republican orthodoxy." Dougherty concluded that "the Tea Party is nothing more than a Republican-managed tantrum."[50]

It is telling, of course, that the group's members "only took to the streets [to protest big government and deficits] when a Democratic president launched an emergency stimulus program."[51] They stayed home during the Bush years, when a Republican president combined massive war spending with large tax cuts for the wealthy.

Our observation of Tea Party chapters in the Chicago area reinforces the national data. The Tea Partiers we observed denounced the dwindling number of moderate Republicans as RINOS—Republicans in Name Only. They conceded that they saw themselves as Republicans and that the primary goal of their activism was to return Republicans to Congress in the 2010 midterms. The Tea Party activists we met and observed functioned as adjuncts to the Republican Party, although they represented the party's most extreme elements.

The same basic point extends to the politicians running in the 2010 congressional midterms as what Kate Zernike called "Tea Party candidates." By her calculation and the calculation of the *Times* in mid-October of 2010, "all" of the 138 Tea Party candidates contending for U.S. House and Senate positions in the 2010 midterms ran as Republicans. Not a single one ran as an Independent. Beyond extreme calls on the part of some Tea Party candidates for the abolition of the Internal Revenue Service and other key federal agencies and their common embrace of a harshly restricted interpretation of the U.S. Constitution, the Tea Party candidates' supposedly distinctive ideology identified them as little more than hardcore right-wing Republicans:

> While there is no official Tea Party platform, candidates share a determination to repeal the health care legislation passed in March [2010]. They vow not only to permanently extend the tax cuts passed under President George W. Bush and to eliminate the estate tax, but also to replace the progressive income tax with a flat tax or

a national sales tax. Several candidates advocate abolishing the Internal Revenue Service entirely.

. . . Many have called for a balanced budget amendment. They opposed newly passed financial regulation, and oppose cap-and-trade of carbon emissions.

. . . The candidates also promise to carry into office the Tea Party's strict interpretation of the Constitution.[52]

Although extreme, these ideas are hardly beyond the pale of an increasingly and evermore right-wing Republican Party. They are right-wing "super-Republican" prescriptions.

Tea Party Militarism

What about the foreign policy views of the Tea Party? How much basis is there for the hope—mentioned at the beginning of this chapter—entertained by some left progressives to find antiwar allies among Tea Party supporters? There is not much information on Tea Partiers' foreign policy attitudes. The existing survey data focus almost completely on their opinions on domestic issues. But the high approval that most Tea Partiers give to the openly messianic-militaristic George W. Bush presidency and to the militaristic and nationalistic Sarah Palin and Glenn Beck (founder of a "9/12 movement" that seeks to "return America to the sense of unity it felt on the day after 9/11") certainly suggests that the Tea Party is far more prowar than antiwar. So does the comparatively weak support that Tea Partiers give to the openly antiwar Tea Party inspirer Ron Paul. Palin, Beck and other leading prowar Republicans have been repeatedly featured at Tea Party rallies.

Antiwar libertarian voices were pushed to the margins as leading Republicans quickly asserted control of the originally more eclectic and genuinely popular phenomenon. In March 2010, antiwar conservative activist Allison Gibbs told journalist Kelley Vlahos that Tea Party "people boo when you bring up the fiscal irresponsibility of the two-front war overseas." Tom Mullen, author of *A Return to Common Sense*, told Vlahos that he was invited to speak in 2009 at a Tea Party rally in Montgomery, Alabama, and "took note of the overriding pro-war theme." Mullen "attempted to apply the common argument that taxpayers should not be forced to pay for everyone else's health care to overseas wars of choice. . . . I said, why is it right for the government to force you to fight for freedom in some other country?" Vlahos asked Mullen what reaction he had received: "He said, 'They were very polite.'"

Vlahos's concerns about the Tea Party, presented on Antiwar .com, seem to have been validated. "The current liberty/Tea Party movement—which started off, if not as a third-party libertarian endeavor, but as an alternative to the prevailing political status quo—is being co-opted," Vlahos worried, "by Republicans and right-wing conservatives who in the end cannot and will not accept libertarian positions against the war, the military-industrial complex, the war on drugs, and the growing police state."

Despite the Tea Party's declared top concern with reducing the deficit and shrinking the size of government, speakers at rallies we attended ignored the massive deficit-expanding military budget—more than $1 trillion each year, paying for half the world's military spending and maintaining more than 800 military bases across more than 100 nations worldwide—or the expensive U.S. wars abroad as drains on the American taxpayer and American society. Tellingly enough, in the spring of 2010, there were three Tea Party challengers of Ron Paul in the Republican primary. Among their criticisms of Paul was that he opposed the wars in Iraq and Afghanistan.[53] Prospects for renewing the antiwar movement through a left alliance with the Tea Party are dim indeed.*

Tea Party Religious Fundamentalism

Approximately half of Tea Party supporters consider themselves part of the "religious right," while more than half support the "Christian conservative movement."[54] An estimated 61 percent of

---

*To be sure, we understand the appeal of forming tactical issue alliances across ideological lines and have both met and worked with genuinely antiwar and anti-imperialist "Tea Party" libertarians of the Ron Paul variety in the past (DiMaggio at Illinois State University and Street at the University of Iowa).

Tea Partiers claim to be Protestant, consistent with the fact that Protestants are statistically more likely to identify as conservative and Tea Party supporters.[55] Forty-four percent of Tea Partiers claim to be "Evangelical" Christian, and Evangelicals are more likely to call themselves conservatives and to support the Tea Party.[56] More than half of white Evangelicals describe themselves as part of the Tea Party.[57]

Tea Partiers' values are heavily influenced by the religious right. Approximately one-half of Tea Partiers believe that the Bible is the "literal word of God," and Tea Partiers are statistically more likely than the general public to believe that the United States is a Christian nation, that abortion is wrong, and that gay marriage should remain illegal.

The faith-based background of the contemporary Tea Party may go far in terms of explaining group members' high levels of extremism and authoritarianism—topics to be explored in greater depth in Chapter 5. The same demographic groups that make up the religious right—including regular church attendees and Evangelical Protestants—are statistically likely to be supporters of the Tea Party itself. These groups are also consistently more likely to be authoritarian in their political leanings, scoring higher on questions measuring authoritarianism when compared to Catholics, mainline Protestants, Jews, and those attending church less frequently. Evangelical and regular church attendees are more likely to be part of an authoritarian strain of American politics that has "little tolerance for ambiguity" and expresses "antipathy toward intellectual[s]."[58]

"A Grassroots Citizen's Movement Brought to You by . . . Oil Billionaires"

In the Tea Party groups, as in other political organizations and indeed across the institutional landscape of the United States, participants are far from equal with each other in terms of power and influence. Both the CBS/*Times* poll and the CNN survey cited previously included among their definition of "Tea Party activist" any person who gave money to the cause. But we cannot realistically think that the title "activist" does justice to the participatory super–

Tea Party citizenship granted to the single contributor who gave a $1 million donation to the Atlanta-based Tea Patriots in mid-September of 2010. The *Washington Post* announced that the gift was anonymous but it is difficult not to believe that the giver communicated his or her interest in how the group decided to use the money: pouring it into "local tea party groups and get[ting] out the vote efforts on some of the most competitive congressional races."[59]

What sort of superactivist status should we give to the hyper-opulent, hard-right capitalist brothers and epic environmental polluters David and Charles Koch? As journalist Jane Mayer showed in an important *New Yorker* article on "the billionaires behind the hate" in August 2010, Koch Industries, the second wealthiest private company in the United States, has provided large-scale funding to seed and grow the Tea Party's "grassroots." Koch Industries deals in plastics, chemicals, and petroleum as well as commodities trading and financial services. The Koch brothers' companies have been fined frequently by the government, so they have a strong interest in deregulation. The Koch brothers, Mayer showed, had for many years poured millions of dollars (a comparatively small part of their $35 billion fortune) into the construction and maintenance of a far-right *propaganda infrastructure*, including probusiness think tanks and a public relations machinery to craft and disseminate persuasive plutocratic and capitalist messages. One of the Koch brother's projects is the Americans for Prosperity foundation (AFP), which funded a July 4, 2010, summit titled "Texas Defending the American Dream." This gathering, Mayer explained, was designed to work as a tool for promoting the "grassroots" Tea Party movement:

> Five hundred people attended the summit, which served, in part, as a training session for Tea Party activists in Texas. *An advertisement cast the event as a populist uprising against vested corporate power.* "Today, the voices of average Americans are being drowned out by lobbyists and special interests," it said. "But you can do something about it." The pitch made no mention of its corporate funders. The White House has expressed frustration that such sponsors have largely eluded public notice. David Axelrod, Obama's senior adviser, said, "What they don't say is that, *in part, this is a grassroots citizens' movement brought to you by a bunch of oil billionaires.*"[60]

AFP is for all intents and purposes a fake-popular "white hat" arm of the wealthy business interests. Its core function is to create the illusion of mass citizen support on behalf of lower taxes for the rich and the deregulation of industry and high finance. It has worked closely with the Tea Party since "the movement's inception." Just weeks prior to the initial Tea Party tax protests of April 2009, AFP ran a Web site that gave supporters "Tea Party Talking Points." By donating funds to inform and mobilize Tea Party protesters and spread "anti-government fervor," the Koch brothers helped "turn their private agenda" into what Mayer (mistakenly) calls "a mass movement." A Republican campaign consultant who has done research on behalf of the Koch brothers went further. "The Koch brothers," he told Mayer, "gave the money that founded [the Tea Party]. It's like they put the seeds in the ground. Then the rainstorm comes, and the frogs come out of the mud—and they're our candidates!"[61]

In October of 2010, the progressive blog ThinkProgress obtained a memo that outlined a June gathering held by the Koch brothers. Glenn Beck attended the meetings along with national business leaders, who strategized on how to win future elections for the Republicans and how to give fake-progressive cover for business propaganda against real and potential progressive reform. As liberal researcher Lee Fang noted

> The memo, along with an attendee list of about 210 people, shows the titans of industry—from health insurance companies, oil executives, Wall Street investors, and real estate tycoons—working together with conservative journalists and Republican operatives to plan the 2010 election, as well as ongoing conservative efforts through 2012. . . . Corporate "investors" at the Koch meeting included businesses with a strong profit motive in rolling back President Obama's enacted reforms[, including] several companies impacted by health reform . . . [and] the financial industry impacted by health reform . . . [and] several executives at the meeting have an incentive to stop Democrats and President Obama from addressing climate change and enacting clean energy reform. . . . Participants collaborated with infamous consultants who specialize in generating fake grassroots movements.

The leading business and right-wing participants in the June planning meeting "committed to an unprecedented level of support."[62]

The Kochs are hardly the only elite interest behind the early growth of the Tea Party, of course. As Adam Bessie observes:

The April 2009 Tea Party protests were heavily subsidized by the elite Republican foundation and advocacy group *FreedomWorks*, chaired by former leading congressional Republican Dick Armey. . . . "*FreedomWorks* had the resources to break the Tea Parties big," writes Michael Brendan Dougherty of *The American Conservative*. "The group commands a budget in the $8 million range and claims 902,000 members."

And to get big, Armey's organization has received financial support from big business. *FreedomWorks* received nearly $3,000,000 from the Sarah Scaife Foundation, which according to *Media Matters* "is financed by the Mellon industrial, oil, and banking fortune," and which donates major money to many conservative causes and think tanks. Further, Steve Forbes—of the "nation's leading business magazine" *Forbes*, famous for their list of the richest companies and people in the world—is on the board of directors.[63]

Bruce Bartlett, a conservative researcher who once worked at a think tank funded by the Kochs said that "the problem with the whole libertarian movement is that it's been *all chiefs and no Indians*. There haven't been any actual people, like voters, who give a crap about it. So the problem for the Kochs has been trying to create a movement." With the emergence of the Tea Party, he said, "everyone suddenly sees that for the first time *there are Indians out there—* people who can provide real ideological power." The Kochs, he said, are "trying to shape and control and channel *the populist uprising* into their own policies."[64]

But the Tea Party isn't particularly libertarian, as we have seen, and it would probably be at least as accurate to conclude that elite interests like the Kochs created the Tea Party from the beginning, compared to claims that such groups have sought to capture and channel the supposed populist uprising at the heart of the "movement."[65] To be sure, it does seem that the early days of the Tea

Party's first real flowering across the nation involved something of a genuine fluid, eclectic, and grassroots feel. As Ben McGrath notes:

> As spring passed into summer [in 2009], the scores at local Tea Party gatherings turned to hundreds, and then thousands, collecting along the way footloose Ron Paul supporters, goldbugs, evangelicals, Atlas Shruggers, militiamen, strict Constitutionalists, swine-flu skeptics, scattered 9/11 "truthers," neo-"Birchers," and, of course, "birthers"—those who remained convinced that the President was a Muslim double agent born in Kenya. "We'll meet back here in six months," Beck had said in March, and when September 12th arrived even the truest of believers were surprised by the apparent strength of the new movement, as measured by the throngs who made the pilgrimage to the Capitol for a Taxpayer March on Washington, swarming the Mall with signs reading "'1984' Is Not an Instruction Manual" and "The Zoo Has an African Lion and the White House Has a Lyin' African!"[66]

By the late summer of 2010, however, Tea Party Nation founder Judson Phillips told the *Washington Post* that the original grassroots feel of 2009 had given way to the development of something he called "Big Tea." "Many of the grassroots activists who started this movement 18 months ago," Phillips reflected, "look and ask the question 'Dude, where's my movement?' There is no question the movement has changed. The evolution of 'Big Tea,'" he felt, "is the logical result of where this movement must go."[67] It is clear, however, that big business and the related Big Republican Party were centrally involved in the creation of a "Big Tea" "movement" from the beginning.

There's nothing new, of course, in the right-wing manipulation of fake-grassroots pseudo-populism by and for the corporate plutocracy. As Fang noted in October 2010, "The fusion between the 'intellectual' conservative movement and big businesses opposed to regulations and accountability has a history in America dating back to the New Deal. During the thirties, the Du Pont family and other wealthy interests organized an assortment of 'Liberty League' front groups to try to defeat New Deal agenda items and repeal President Roosevelt's Social Security program."[68] For many decades now, big capital has created various advocacy groups and networks that are popular and democratic—"grassroots"—in name and rhetoric but harshly regressive corporate and authoritarian in reality. In his masterly volume *Who Will Tell the People?* William Greider told the story of the leading Washington, DC, lobbyist firm Bonner & Associates, an influence-peddling company that "packages democratic expression and sells it to corporate clients—drug manufacturers and the cosmetic industry, insurance companies and cigarette makers and the major banks." Besides pumping out facts and data to support their clients' policy cases, Bonner & Associates specialized in creating the illusion of mass support for elite industry agendas. "You want opinion polls? It hires polling firms to produce them. You want people— live voters who support the industry positions? Jack Bonner delivers them." When the U.S. Senate debated clean-air legislation in 1990, the company rallied numerous grassroots groups like the Big Brothers and Sisters of the Mahoning Valley and the Paralyzed Veterans Associations to contact senators and tell them inaccurately that new air pollution standards (designed in fact to "conserve energy and reduce the carbon-dioxide pollution that is the main source of global warming") would "make it impossible to manufactures any vehicle larger than a Ford Escort or a Honda Civic. . . . Vans and station wagons, small trucks and high-speed police cruisers, [legislators] were told, would cease to exist. The National Sheriffs Association was aroused by the thought of chasing criminals in a Honda Civic. The Nebraska Farm Bureau said rural America would be 'devastated' if farmers tried to pull a trailer loaded with livestock or hay with a Ford Escort."[69]

This was and remains a standard Washington story before and since the time Greider wrote. Beneath all its claims to novelty and antiestablishment identity, the Tea Party walks in deep historical, plutocratic, and false-popular footsteps.

4

Tea Party Racism

Tea Party activists and supporters react with rapid and pronounced hostility to the slightest hint and/or serious indication that their "movement" has anything to do with racism. In September of 2010, for example, Tea Party backers attacked Kate Zernike, the main reporter responsible for covering the Tea Party at the *New York Times* and the author of a book on the topic, *Boiling Mad*. The book was largely sympathetic to the Tea Party, framing it as a grassroots movement that opposed Washington-based establishment politics and corruption on Wall Street.[1] However, Zernike's rather meek discussion of racial prejudice among some segments of the Tea Party drew conservative ire.

The right-wing Media Research Center (MRC) was the first to attack Zernike for suggesting that racism had any role at all to play in the Tea Party phenomenon. In September of 2010, the center assaulted her "unfair" book for exuding a liberal "race obsession." At the heart of the critique was the following mild passage from Zernike's reporting on a national Tea Party rally that Glenn Beck held at the Lincoln Memorial in Washington, DC, on (a source of no small affront to black civil rights leaders) the forty-seventh anniversary of Dr. Martin Luther King's famous "I Have a Dream" speech (delivered on the same exact spot in 1963):

> Still, the government programs that many Tea Party supporters call unconstitutional are the ones that have helped many black people emerge from poverty and discrimination. . . . Even if Tea Party

members are right that any racist signs [held up by protesters at Tea Party demonstrations] are those of mischief-makers, . . . it would be hard to quiet the argument about the Tea Party and race.[2]

During early 2010 protests of health care "reform" in Washington, DC, McClatchy Newspapers released a report based on direct testimony that Tea Party demonstrators outside the U.S. Capitol, angry over the Democrats' proposed health care bill, shouted "nigger" at Representative John Lewis, a Georgia congressman and civil rights icon. Protesters shouted obscenities at other members of the Congressional Black Caucus, spitting on at least one black lawmaker, McClatchy reported. By Lewis's account, the protests were accompanied by an atmosphere of rabid racism he had not seen for decades: "They were shouting, . . . harassing. . . . It reminded me of the 60s. It was a lot of downright hate and anger." One of Lewis's colleagues said that protesters initially shouted at Lewis, demanding that he "kill the bill." When Lewis indicated that he supported "health care reform," the chant changed to "Kill the bill, then the nigger."[3]

The right-wing group Accuracy in Media (AIM) immediately attacked the reporting of this ugly incident by McClatchy and other "race-obsessed" organs of the "liberal media." Simply dismissing the on-the-ground facts, AIM insisted there was "no evidence" that racial slurs had been expressed. It proclaimed that "the mainstream press should make it clear to the public that this is only hearsay at best and reflects their own bias against the Tea Party movement."[4]

Right-wing attacks on the "liberal media" for spotlighting Tea Party racism are largely misplaced. Although there have been some strong criticisms of Tea Party racism in the dominant media, those criticisms have tended—inaccurately in our opinion—to portray the majority of Tea Partiers as nonracist. Zernike's book is an excellent example. The MRC's critique notwithstanding, *Boiling Mad* largely exonerates Tea Partiers from the racism charge. It treats racists turning out for Tea Party rallies—including "birthers" who insist that President Obama is a Muslim born in Kenya—as "fringe elements." Zernike explains that race plays "some part" in Tea Party opposition to Obama and faults Tea Party leaders for failing to ostracize the "movement's" racist "fringe."[5] But she fails to understand that the Tea Party's racism is not confined to the sort of open and explicit bigotry that a small number of extremists exhibit at rallies. Beneath the failure to fully exclude such noxious elements lies a deeper problem: *Most Tea Partiers do harbor racist opinions*—though often in a more subtle, implicit, and outwardly "color-blind" way than the more extreme racists at their rallies. And Tea Party racism—largely implicit and "color-blind" in relation to blacks and Latinos—is explicit and full blown when it comes to Muslim Americans.

Media Marginalization of Tea Party Racism

Consistent with this criticism of Zernike's book, we find that the Tea Party's racism has received superficial and inadequate coverage in the mass media. The topic gained attention in the news during mid- and late 2010 when the National Association for the Advancement of Colored People (NAACP) released a report that criticized individual Tea Party activists for being racist (while claiming that "the majority of Tea Party supporters are sincere, principled people of good will") and called for the Tea Party to take "steps to distance themselves from those . . . leaders who espouse racist ideas, advocate violence, or are formally affiliated with white supremacist organizations."[6] While right-wing media coverage and commentary predictably exonerated Tea Partiers from the charge,[7] the liberal cable news station MSNBC was critical of Tea Party prejudice in the wake of the NAACP study. MSNBC's Ed Schultz criticized "Tea Party leaders [who] haven't had the character to tell the racists or the people who promote violence in their party to knock it off."[8] Keith Olbermann attacked the Tea Party for "condescension and arrogance" in response to the NAACP.[9] Olbermann and Rachel Maddow targeted overtly racist elements within the Tea Party. Chris Matthews took issue with racist signs appearing at Tea Party rallies.[10] But none of the MSNBC hosts seemed aware that (as we will show in this chapter) racism was a deeply rooted problem afflicting most Tea Partiers beneath and beyond explicitly bigoted statements and signs on the part of a few "fringe" elements. Schultz's statement suggested that Tea Party leaders had the responsibility to repudiate racism in their group—implying that it remained a problem among only a small number of Tea Partiers. Matthews broadcast an interview in which NAACP president Ben Jealous explained that "we aren't taking issue with the Tea Party itself. What we're taking issue with is the perpetual tolerance for racist statements by [a certain small number of] their own folks." This position is contrary to our finding that racism, deeply understood, is endemic within the ranks of the Tea Party.

The "liberal" print media have been just as willing as cable television to exonerate the Tea Party from the charge of racism. Of twelve editorials and op-eds on race and the Tea Party that appeared in the *Washington Post* from January through September 2010 (when charges of racism in the run-up to the midterms were gathering steam), nine did not identify the group with racism in any meaningful way. In the *Post*, Michael Gerson called the NAACP's statement that "we don't think the Tea Party is racist" "encouraging" and described the NAACP's discussion of photographs showing openly racist placards at Tea Party rallies as "a pretty thin indictment" of the group.[11] Gerson criticized "the left" for its "political interest in defining the broad backlash against expanded government as identical to the worst elements of the Tea Party movement—birthers and Birchers, militias and nativists, racists and conspiracy theorists."[12] While noting (accurately in our opinion) that "racially charged rhetoric has been part of the [Tea Party's] stock-in-trade all along," *Post* columnist Eugene Robinson thanked the Tea Party for expelling a noted racist organizer as "a start to disowning and discarding this [racist] element" from the group. Robinson expressed concern that "some fraction of the Tea Party's energy is drawn from racism."[13] The *Post*'s right-wing editorialist Charles Krauthammer lambasted the "mainstream media's scurrilous portrayal of [the Tea Party] as a racist rabble of resentful lumpenproletarians," while the liberal E. J. Dionne Jr. acknowledged only that there were some "racist elements in the Tea Party."[14] Of all the *Post*'s columnists, only two suggested that racism might comprise a large and even defining part of what the Tea Party represented. The notion that the Tea Party was fundamentally racist was left to Colbert King, who described Tea Partiers as "legacies of the late Alabama governor George Wallace in that they, like his followers, are smoldering with anger out of fear that they are being driven from their rightful place in America."[15]

Commentary in the *New York Times* was even softer. A small number of *Times* editorials—just three—addressed the topic of the Tea Party and racism. *Times* columnist Charles Blow criticized the Tea Party for protesting "too much" over the NAACP's report,[16] but he argued that

> there is no way to know how many Tea Party supporters—or supporters of any group—are motivated by racism, or to what degree. . . . What is clear is that technology and social media have empowered the least sane among us and amplified their voices. Thus, a random racist at a Tea Party rally suddenly becomes the face of a group of people who are, on the whole, decent, law-abiding citizens with legitimate concerns about government expansion and the inherent erosion of individual freedom.[17]

Not a single op-ed writer at the *New York Times* was willing to consistently make the claim that the Tea Party is fundamentally racist.

The Tea Party and Interpersonal Racism

We have encountered numerous Tea Party supporters who insist that the notion that they are racist is little more than an ad hominem attack designed to direct attention away from their real concern with economic issues. Tea Party organizers at meetings we observed consistently made it a point to claim that they were "not racists" and that prejudice toward African Americans or other minorities had nothing to do with their "movement."

Nevertheless, it is clear that many Tea Partiers harbor deeply racist positions. As the NAACP accurately noted in its relatively unimpressive and aforementioned study on the eve of the 2010 midterm elections, "Confederate battle flags, signs that read 'America is a Christian nation,' and racist caricatures of President Obama have been an undeniable presence at Tea Party events in both local communities and in Washington, D.C. The venom (and spittle) directed [by some Tea Partiers] at African American Congressmen during the health care debate carried an unmistakably racist message."[18]

Some of the most virulent racist comments have come from Tea Party leaders themselves. At the 2010 Nashville Tea Party conference, for example, Republican representative Tom Tancredo lamented the election of the nation's first African American president, blaming the country's troubles on the lack of a civics literacy test (prominent in the Jim Crow South) as a requirement to vote. As Tancredo complained, "People who couldn't even spell the word 'vote' or say it in English put a committed socialist ideologue in the White House. His name is Barack Hussein Obama."[19] Tancredo's statement—consciously invoking Obama's entire "foreign-sounding" name, appeals to Tea Partiers and other reactionaries of the "birther" persuasion, who claim that Obama is not a U.S. citizen and represents a fifth column foreign threat. Tea Partiers and their supporters commonly refer to the president as "Barack Hussein Obama." This use of his entire "foreign-sounding" name reflects a racialized sense of the nation's chief executive as a non- and un-American—an alien and illegal *other*.

Other Tea Party attacks on Democratic policies have been less overtly racist but carried strong racist implications. Rand Paul's now-infamous discussion with MSNBC host Rachel Maddow is an important case in point. Paul suggested that the 1965 Civil Rights Act, which required the desegregation of public and private institutions, was acceptable only when it came to ending segregation in public institutions. Paul said "Yes" when Maddow asked, "Do you think that a private business has the right to say we don't serve black people?" Paul qualified his answer, explaining that he did not personally support racial discrimination; he merely supported the right of racist private business owners to decide whether or not they should be able to discriminate against minorities.[20] Paul's distinction between his support for the "right" to discriminate and his opposition to racism more generally was likely lost on those who quite reasonably saw the Civil Rights Act as a landmark victory in the struggle against public and private racism.

We witnessed a considerable amount of implicit racism on the part of Tea Party activists in the Chicago area. Those activists organized what they claimed was a broad-based popular movement in areas that were disproportionately minority populated with virtually no minorities evident at rallies and meetings. The Tax Day Protest in downtown Chicago on April 15, 2010, is a revealing example. The rally was 99 percent white in a city where 62 percent of the residents are black or Hispanic. Speakers at the rally continually repeated that Tea Party was not "about race"—a message that received roars of approval from the nearly 100 percent Caucasian crowd. John O'Hara, a spokesman for the right-wing Illinois Policy Institute and a leading national figure in the Tea Party "movement," spoke to the Chicago demonstrators. O'Hara proclaimed that he knew the Tea Party was winning the fight for the public mind because "*the right people are angry.*" One needed to look no farther than the crowd of white, affluent protesters at the city's downtown Daley Center to see who O'Hara thought "the right people" were. Although O'Hara hardly meant to state explicitly that only white was "right," he was nonetheless speaking almost exclusively to affluent whites in a city that continues to suffer from extreme levels of residential and educational racial segregation and massive related racial disparity. His comment reflected significant racial indifference at the very least. Many of the Chicago area's blacks and Latinos/as would certainly have been insulted by O'Hara's implicit identification of the region's white populace as the only fitting and proper people—especially at a rally claiming to represent the poor and downtrodden who have suffered under the economic crisis.

The Tea Party's Color-Blind Racism

But perhaps the most important dimension of the Tea Party's racist attitudes toward black Americans takes on a "color-blind" form. Liberal antiracist commentator Tim Wise highlights a pattern whereby "a steady drumbeat of racially coded conservative propaganda concerning government programs for those in need" contributes to "white racial resentment, which is regularly manipulated by reactionary commentators and politicians." Attacks on blacks are expressed through "implicit racial biases (which often exist side-by-side with an outwardly non-racist demeanor and persona)." These attacks "frequently influence the way we view and treat others. . . . Colorblindness, by discouraging discussions of racial matters and presuming that the best practice is to ignore the realities of racism, makes it more difficult to challenge those biases, and thus increases the likelihood of discrimination."[21]

Our sense of the Tea Partiers as color-blind racists arises largely out of their assumption of black laziness and black self-sabotage within a conceptual framework that denies persistent deep structural and institutional barriers to black advancement and racial equality.[22] Nowhere is the group's color-blind racism clearer than in an early 2010 University of Washington poll of Tea Partiers and the general public, which found deep-seated animosity toward blacks and immigrants. Table 4.1 reproduces data from the poll, which found that Tea Partiers were particularly prone to seeing black Americans as indolent, stupid, and untrustworthy. Seventy-three percent of Tea Party supporters (compared to just 33 percent of Tea Party opponents and 56 percent of all whites) surveyed by the University of Washington believed that black laziness explained existing economic disparity between blacks and whites. Just 35 percent of Tea Party supporters (as opposed to 55 percent of Tea Party opponents and 40 percent of all whites) agreed with the description of black Americans as hardworking. Eighty-eight percent of Tea Party supporters (compared to 70 percent of all whites) agreed with the following statement: "Irish, Italians, Jewish, and many other minorities overcame prejudice and worked their way up. Blacks should do the same without special favors." Seventy-two percent of Tea Party supporters (compared to 28 percent of Tea Party opponents and 58 percent of all whites) disagreed with the idea that "generations of slavery and discrimination have created conditions that make it difficult for blacks to work their way out of the lower class," and 83 percent of Tea Party supporters (compared to 48 percent of opponents and 72 percent of whites) disagreed with the idea that black Americans had gotten less than they deserved in recent years. (These poll results were consistent with two findings from the previously mentioned 2010 CBS/*New York Times* survey, which determined that [a] nearly three-fourths [73 percent] of Tea Party supporters thought that "white people and black people have about an equal chance of getting ahead" in American society and [b] more than one-half of Tea Party supporters [52 percent] thought that "in recent years too much has been made of the problems facing black people.")[23]

TABLE 4.1

Beliefs About Black Americans and Racial Inequality	Tea Party Opponents N = 66	Never Heard of Tea Party N = 157	All Whites N = 511	Tea Party Supporters N = 117
Irish, Italians, Jewish, and many other minorities overcame prejudice and worked their way up. Blacks should do the same without special favors. (Agree)	56%	66%	70%	88%
It's really a matter of some people not trying hard enough; if blacks would only try harder, they could be just as well off as whites. (Agree)	33%	55%	56%	73%
Generations of slavery and discrimination have created conditions that make it difficult for blacks to work their way out of the lower class. (Disagree)	28%	65%	58%	72%
Over the past few years blacks have gotten less than they deserve. (Disagree)	48%	73%	72%	83%
Blacks are hardworking. (Agree)	55%	41%	40%	35%
Blacks are intelligent. (Agree)	59%	51%	49%	45%
Blacks are trustworthy. (Agree)	57%	50%	47%	41%

SOURCE: University of Washington Institute for the Study of Ethnicity, Race, and Sexuality, "2010 Multi-State Survey on Race and Politics," at http://depts.washington.edu/uwiser/racepolitics.html.

Available evidence strongly contradicts the notion that black character flaws or laziness is to blame for black-white inequality. Surveying existing studies, leading public opinion scholar Martin Gilens concluded that "the empirical data available offer no evidence that there is a 'kernel of truth' to the belief that blacks are less committed to the work ethic than are whites. Both in the attitudes they express in surveys, and in their behavior with regard to work, black Americans display the same commitment to work as their white counterparts."[24] At the same time, a rich body of scholarly and journalistic evidence and readily observable black experience demonstrates the persistence of steep structural- and institutional-racist barriers to black employment and advancement and racial equality beneath and beyond the real but limited victories of the civil rights movement. Those barriers include the following:

- Endemic racial bias in real estate and home lending that reflects and empowers the reluctance of whites to live next door to blacks. Racial discrimination in lending is systematic and occurs regularly.[25]
- Unequal incomes between black and white families, with black workers earning sixty cents for every dollar made by whites.[26] Past research demonstrates that this inequality has nothing to do with black "laziness."[27]
- Systemic racial residential and school segregation.[28]
- A critical shortage of affordable housing in predominantly white opportunity-rich communities and the systematic, historic efforts on the part of lenders, white communities, and the government throughout the post–World War II period to deny black families access to affluent, nonsegregated suburban living.[29]
- The disproportionate flight of capital and jobs from predominantly black communities, which has eroded former industrial urban cores and caused the rise of the "jobless" black inner-city neighborhood.[30]
- Historic and widespread public and private underinvestment in black communities.[31]
- Historic and persistent endemic racial discrimination in hiring and job training.[32]

- The radical growth of mass incarceration and the criminalization of adult black males, one in three of whom is marked for life by the crippling stigma of a felony record, a reflection of profound antiblack bias in the waging of the "war on drugs" inside the United States.[33]
- The refusal of many employers to hire people with felony records and the widespread employer assumption that black job applicants are felons, which together amount to an employment death sentence for millions of black Americans.[34]
- The aggressive pursuit of prison construction by many rural white communities and legislators in the promotion of a form of "economic development" that depends on black criminalization.[35]
- The funding of schools largely on the basis of local property wealth, which perpetuates existing race-based inequalities in the realm of school and teacher quality.[36]
- The hyperconcentration of black children in troubled, high-poverty, and underperforming schools.[37]
- The extensive reliance on high-stakes standardized tests and related zero-tolerance, quasi-militarized disciplinary procedures in predominantly black schools.[38]
- Endemic metropolitan sprawl, funded by massive state and national government subsidies that help create harshly race- and class-segregated patterns of development pitting affluent white suburbs against poorer and blacker inner cities and "inner-ring" suburbs.[39]
- The predominantly white nation's refusal to remotely address the problem of reparations (at the very least by expanding social welfare directed at disadvantaged minority peoples) for more than two and half centuries of black chattel slavery and nearly a century of Jim Crow terror, both of which provide essential historical context for the persistence of a massive wealth gap between black and white American households.[40]

As this abbreviated list strongly suggests, racial inequality is inextricably linked to the persistence of racial segregation. Social and economic opportunities are not distributed evenly across and between space and community. The geography of American opportunity is heavily racialized. Nobody has stated the core problem posed by the persistent residential segregation of African Americans more concisely than University of Pennsylvania sociologist Douglas S. Massey, who notes:

> Housing markets are especially important because they distribute much more than a place to live; they also distribute any good or resource that is correlated with where one lives. Housing markets don't just distribute dwellings, they also distribute education, employment, safety, insurance rates, services, and wealth in the form of home equity; they also determine the level of exposure to crime and drugs, and the peer groups that one's children experience. If one group of people is denied full access to urban housing markets because of the color of their skin, then they are systematically denied full access to the full range of benefits in urban society.[41]

We are concerned here with something different and deeper than the examples of open bigotry highlighted in occasional mainstream media discussions of explicit Tea Party racism. The bigger problem is a persistent "state-of-being," or structural, racism that generates racially disparate results even without racist intent ("state-of-mind" racism) on the part of white actors.[42] Racialized social processes work in routine and ordinary fashion to sustain racial hierarchy and white supremacy often and typically without explicit white hostility or purpose.[43]

Tea Partiers are hardly alone in their indifference to the persistence of institutionalized racism in American life. They and other right-wing conservatives are simply more extreme in the extent to which they accept a "postracial" narrative that is pervasive in white America. The widely available evidence demonstrating the persistence and even deepening of racial separatism and racial oppression is deemed largely irrelevant in a "post–civil rights" (and hardly "postracial") era when the leading architects of policy and opinion have declared "race" over as a barrier to black advancement. Avoiding race and racism has become the order of the day in an officially "colorblind" neoliberal era when conventional wisdom ascribes people's status and wealth to purely private and personal success or failure in adapting to permanent realities of inequality in a "free-market" system of reactionary corporate rule to which "there is no alternative." In the dominant public discourse of this new era, the nation's "pervasive racial hierarchies collapse," in the words of prolific social critic Henry Giroux, "into power-evasive strategies such as blaming minorities of class and color for not working hard enough, refusing to exercise individual initiative, or practicing reverse racism." Even as an entrenched, increasingly invisible racism "functions [as] one of the deep and abiding currents in everyday [American] life," this discourse works "to erase the social from the language of public life so as to reduce all racial problems to private issues [of] . . . individual character and cultural depravity." This "neoliberal racism," as Giroux calls it, "can imagine public issues only as private concerns." It sees "human agency as simply a matter of individualized choices, the only obstacle to effective citizenship being the lack of principled self-help and moral responsibility" on the part of those most victimized by structural oppression and the amoral agency of superempowered actors atop the nation's interrelated hierarchies of class and race. Under its rule, "human misery is largely defined as a function of personal choices," consistent with "the central neoliberal tenet that all problems are private rather than social in nature."[44] Government efforts to meaningfully address and ameliorate (not to mention abolish) sharp societal disparities of race and class are deemed alternately futile, counterproductive, and inappropriate. Government's actions are progressively concentrated (in political scientist Adolph Reed Jr.'s words) on "making war," "enhancing opportunities for the investor class," "suppressing [already declining] wages for everyone else," and "suppressing dissent."[45]

Cathy Young's Attempted Exoneration of Tea Party Racism

One right-wing response to the University of Washington poll attempted to divert attention from Tea Partiers' racism. On RealClear Politics, leading Tea Party advocate Cathy Young (of the right-wing Media Research Center) offered a curious defense. She highlighted the survey's finding that racism also existed among Tea Party opponents and whites more generally. Young tried to further exonerate Tea Party prejudice by noting that many black Americans agree "that the black community's problems are partly rooted in damaging behavioral and cultural patterns."[46] Her argument finds some support in existing survey data showing that both blacks and whites agree that personal factors and individual behavior contribute to the problems faced by black families. But Young deleted the fact that most blacks also see the persistence of racist structural and cultural barriers to black equality imposed by the white majority society—factors that Tea Partiers and indeed most white Americans deny—as equally, if not more, relevant. The notion that both blacks and whites concur on the "laziness" of the African American community is misleading. Black Americans may quite logically believe that their communities would more likely prosper if more black individuals would stop using drugs, tried harder to find employment, and more closely adhered to religious values, but they are far more likely than whites to recognize the structural forces that impede black progress in the United States.[47]

Segregation and Mediated Racism

Antiblack Tea Party attitudes likely spring in part from Tea Partiers' lack of direct experience with black Americans and their related reliance on the mass media in forming race-related opinions. "One of the most important, though most subtle and elusive aspects of white supremacy," notes prolific black race theorist Charles Mills, "is the barrier it erects to a fair hearing. It is not merely," Mills writes, that nonwhites are "trying to make case for the economic and juridico-political injustice of their treatment; it is that they are additionally handicapped in doing so by having to operate within a white discursive field" wherein "dominant white patterns of structured ignorance" and "overt or hidden white normativity" make the basic factual "claims of people of color . . . seem absurd" and "radically incongruent" with dominant notions of history and society. It does not help, Mills adds, that "the physical segregation of white and nonwhite populations" creates "a segregation of experience" that "reinforces radically divergent pictures of the world" based on the fact that "typically black and typically white realities—in terms of everyday experience with government bureaucracies, the police, and the job market, housing, and so forth—are simply not the same."[48]

Most Tea Party supporters are white (89 percent) and hail disproportionately from rural areas where relatively fewer blacks live, or from metropolitan suburbs, which are occupied primarily by affluent whites (91 percent of Tea Partiers live in rural and suburban areas).[49] Tea Partiers' sense of black and Latino/a life and experience is thus particularly mediated, with their racial attitudes shaped and informed largely by the dominant mass media, often at the subconscious level. And as much recent media research demonstrates, media outlets promote subtle racist messages in relation to issues of welfare, poverty, crime, and urban living. Contemporary color-blind racism is fed by a steady stream of mass media messages that link urban minorities with crime, indolence, drug addiction, moral failure, welfare dependency, and other undesirable behaviors and personal traits. The most effective and typical forms of media racism are expressed softly and indirectly, rather than through explicit portrayal of minorities as lazy, dangerous, and otherwise lacking in personal virtue. Curiously enough, dominant U.S. media tend to portray social welfare programs that are more traditionally associated with whites (such as Social Security) as benefiting those who have engaged in hard work and earned legitimately gained rewards. In contrast, other forms of social welfare (primarily food stamps and family public cash assistance) associated with the poor and with minorities are typically linked in dominant media to "laziness" and "perverse incentives."[50]

The Tea Partiers' racial attitudes reflect a heavily mediated corporate-neoliberal ideology that denies the role of *any* forms of structural oppression in the creation of black misery, while fanning a white rural and suburban "moral panic" over supposedly depraved behavior and welfare dependency in the black inner city. At the same time, such toxic media imagery feeds heavily on modern racial apartheid's role in rendering much black experience invisible and unintelligible to the politically dominant white majority. As media scholar Stephen Macek notes, "The geographical and cultural distance separating ghetto residents from white suburbanites predispose[s] the latter" to accept dominant "nightmare" representations of the black inner city "at face value."[51] Racial segregation of experience is certainly part of why so many Tea Partiers—a very disproportionately suburban, exurban, and rural group—are easy prey for the dominant media and broader political culture's vicious and victim-blaming "common sense" on race issues.

Tea Party Xenophobia and Anti-immigrant Racism

As we observed Tea Party gatherings in the Chicago area in 2009 and 2010, we encountered numerous participants who strongly advocated "cracking down on illegal immigration." At an anti-immigration protest in the suburb of Naperville, Tea Partiers demonstrated in favor of a draconian Arizona bill (Senate Bill 70) that granted law enforcement expanded powers to detain any individual merely suspected of being an illegal immigrant. Local Tea Partiers said the law targeted only "illegals" and described it as simply a means to enforce already-existing laws against unauthorized immigration. The highly controversial Arizona bill was backed by 88 percent of Tea Party "true believers" polled by the University of Washington in the spring of 2010.[52]

The Tea Party has opposed the proposed moderate federal immigration reform called the Dream Act. The act (reintroduced in the House of Representatives in 2009 and supported by 60 percent of Americans in October of 2010) would have changed existing immigration law by granting amnesty to a select number of unauthorized immigrants living in the United States.[53] The bill would allow young people whose parents brought them here as children access to military service and higher education. If they finish high school, show "good moral character," and serve at least two years in the military or earn a college degree, they could earn citizenship.[54] The bill's condition that its beneficiaries be of "good moral character" excludes immigrants who have been convicted of drug dealing or committed any other felonies. The Dream Act was designed to circumvent traditional conservative attacks on "liberal amnesty legislation."

Tea Partiers across the country came out to organize against the bill. Local chapters were unequivocal in their opposition, denouncing the legislation as "pro–illegal alien," attacking it for allegedly forcing states to give taxpayer-funded financial aid to illegal immigrants and claiming (against the evidence) that it would put millions of Americans out of work.[55]

Tea Partiers claim that their call for harsher measures against immigrants is simply about "following the letter of the law." But the Tea Party's fundamental problem is with the notion that any currently unauthorized immigrants (even those without a criminal record and with a history of hard work) should *ever* be granted citizenship. The Public Religion Research Institute found in October 2010 that 61 percent of Tea Partiers oppose any policy that would allow "undocumented immigrants who have been in the U.S. for several years to earn legal working status and an opportunity for citizenship in the future."[56] It is no surprise that openly racist and xenophobic, far-right nativist groups like the Minutemen and Numbers USA have formed connections with local Tea Party chapters across the country.[57]

Keeping with the Tea Party's blunt, black-and-white, gut-level approach more generally, the Tea Party activists we spoke with and observed were no more interested in the nuances of the immigration issue than they were in the complexities of structural racism. Our efforts to engage them on the role of U.S. trade and foreign policy in creating immigration pressures by fueling Central and Latin American poverty and repression, for example, met derision and stone-faced rejection. Beneath the Tea Partiers' outwardly race-neutral claim to be interested merely in upholding the "letter of the law" lay a deep indifference to the real-life circumstances faced by Central and Latin American immigrants and their children. The Tea Party's harsh anti-immigrant sentiment appeared to be the product of an instinctively reactionary mind-set linked to racist and xenophobic worldviews.

Targeting Muslim Americans

Tea Party racism has often been quite explicit and open when it comes to Muslims. Sharron Angle, the Tea Party Republican senatorial candidate from Nevada in 2010, was asked at a Tea Party rally in the run-up to the midterm elections about the danger posed by "Muslims [who] want . . . to take over the United States." Angle responded by warning that certain localities in America were facing a "militant terrorist situation" whereby Muslims were seeking to subvert American values: "My thoughts are these, first of all, Dearborn, Michigan, and Frankford, Texas, are on American soil, and under Constitutional law. Not Sharia law. And I don't know how that happened in the United States. . . . It seems to me there is something fundamentally wrong with allowing a foreign system of law to take hold in any municipality or government situation in our United States."[58] The notion that any American local governments were falling under "Sharia law" was paranoid and bizarre.

The Tea Party's anti-Muslim racism was on special display during the dispute surrounding the "Ground Zero mosque." In the late summer and fall of 2010, an explosion of right-wing media and political commentary portrayed a planned Muslim community center (it was not a mosque, nor was it on Ground Zero) in lower Manhattan as an egregious insult to those who had lost their lives during the jetliner attacks of September 11, 2001, and as a symbol of an Islamic fundamentalist threat to U.S. national security.[59] The Tea Party weighed in heavily against "Cordoba House,"[60] proposed by Iman Faisal Abdul Rauf, a self-described "moderate Muslim" cleric who had reached out to the American public in rejection of Islamic fundamentalism and Islamist terrorism after 9/11. The project was so nonthreatening that New York City mayor Michael Bloomberg voiced his support for it. When controversy over the center erupted, Bloomberg defended it in a speech delivered with the Statue of Liberty in the background. A mother of a 9/11 victim publicly supported the center. And in early May of 2010, the city's Community Board voted unanimously to approve the project.[61]

A chapter of Brooklyn New York Tea Partiers voiced opposition to the proposed center as "a threat to American cultural values." John Press, the president of the Brooklyn Tea Party, was enraged by Rauf's attempt to find common ground with non-Muslims. Press rejected the notion "that all cultures are our friends," explaining that "that's why we've got to replace multiculturalism with culturalism."[62]

Echoing the Brooklyn Tea Party's views, New York Senate candidate (and also a Tea Partier) Gary Bernstein announced his strong opposition to the Muslim community center. Bernstein opined that "this looks like a foreign effort to put something there. . . . It will be a magnet for militants. Militants will be driven to that mosque."[63] Similar attacks against the Muslim community center came from Tea Party leader Mark Williams. Williams's comments on his blog in May of 2010 were explicitly racist and incendiary:

> The animals of Allah for whom any day is a great day for a massacre are drooling over the positive response that they are getting from New York City officials over a proposal to build a 13 story monument to the 9/11 Muslims who hijacked those 4 airliners.
>
> The monument would consist of a Mosque for the worship of the terrorists' monkey god and a "cultural center" to propagandize for the extermination of all things not approved by their cult.[64]

Right-wing blogger Pamella Geller, who calls herself a Tea Party person, posted a reflection titled "Monster Mosque Pushes Ahead in Shadow of Islamic Death and Destruction." Geller's entry warned that "this is Islamic destruction and expansion. The location is no accident. Just as Al-Aqsa was built on top of the Temple in Jerusalem." Her group, Stop Islamization of America, quickly launched "Campaign Offensive: Stop the 9/11 Mosque," premised on the claim that Muslims are scheming to overthrow American democracy. As media scholar Deepa Kumar notes, "Geller is a fan of the far-right [and anti-Muslim] Dutch politician Geere Wilders . . . and an admirer of open fascists and street gangs such as the English Defense League that routinely attack Muslims and immigrants." Notorious Islamophobe Wilders was a featured speaker at a 2010 September 11 rally against Cordoba House called by Tea Party activists. He told his audience to "defend itself against the powers of darkness, the force of hatred and the blight of ignorance."[65]

Geller, like many Tea Partiers, is a "birther." Claiming that President Obama's birth certificate is a forgery, she has called Obama a "third worlder and a coward" who's "appeas[ing] his Islamic overlords." She has insistently advanced the myth that Obama is Muslim.

She has even argued that Barack Obama is "the illegitimate child of Malcolm X."[66]

The assault on the Manhattan community center was one component of a larger campaign against Muslim sites and institutions. Tea Party protests of mosques or Muslim community centers took place across the country in mid-2010.[67] Plans to build a mosque in Temecula, California, were met by Tea Party claims that "mosques are monuments to terrorism." One Tea Party protestor in Temecula warned that "in 20 years with the rate of the birth population, we will be overtaken by Islam, and their goal is to get people in Congress and the Supreme Court to see that Sharia is implemented. My children and grandchildren will have to live under that."[68] Geller spoke at the Tennessee Tea Party convention in May 2010, lending support to a campaign of anti-Muslim intimidation (including violent assaults on an Islamic center in Murfreesboro) in that state.[69]

Anti-Muslim racism was evident when Tea Party Republican Lou Ann Zelenik, running for Congress in Tennessee in 2010, criticized local Muslims' plans to build a mosque in a suburb outside Nashville. Zelenik denounced the proposed "Islamic training center" as part of a larger effort "designed to fracture the moral and political foundation of Middle Tennessee. . . . Until the American Muslim community finds it in their hearts to separate themselves from their evil, radical counterparts, to condemn those who want to destroy our civilization," Zelenik intoned, "we are not obligated to open our society to any of them."[70]

Tennessee is also the state where Lieutenant Governor Ron Ramsey ran on a promise to block "Sharia law's" alleged threat to America. Ramsey called Islam "a cult" and "a violent political philosophy." He was endorsed by more than twenty Tea Party groups.[71]

Anti-Muslim bigotry was also in evidence at Fox News, where Tea Party inspirational leader Glenn Beck verbally assaulted Keith Ellison (DFL-MN)—the first Muslim American to be elected to Congress. Beck's infamous interview began with the demand that Ellison "prove . . . you are not working with our enemies." Beck assumed—along with many Tea Partiers—that Ellison's Muslim background justified automatic suspicion that he was colluding with terrorists.[72]

Beck's battering of Ellison was seconded by Tea Party Nation founder Judson Phillips. He called for conservatives to throw Ellison out of Congress because "he is the only Muslim member of Congress."[73] The Tea Party–affiliated Resistnet group called for Ellison to be removed from Congress "to insure [that] these Islamic sympathizers disguised as Democrats get booted out of our government."[74] Tea Party attacks grew in light of Ellison's connections to the moderate and civil-liberties- and human-rights-oriented Council on American-Islamic Relations (CAIR, which has condemned the 9/11 terrorist attacks and worked with the FBI on antiterrorist investigations), and despite Ellison's call for an end to the violence between Israel and the Palestinian Islamist group Hamas, which controls the government of the Gaza Strip.[75]

Our local observations of the Tea Party confirm that the group's supporters harbor deeply racist opinions toward Muslims and Arabs at home and abroad. At an April 2010 Chicago Tax Day rally, Tea Partiers made repeated references to Obama as a "noncitizen." A sample of signs displayed at this and other Tea Party rallies includes the following: "Somewhere in Kenya, a Village is Missing its Idiot"; "Barack Obama: Illegal Alien"; "The Zoo has an African Lion, and the White House has a Lyin' African"; "Where's the Birth Certificate?"; "Impeach the Muslim Marxist"; and "No Birth Certificate = Barack Hussein Obama." At the Chicago April 15, 2010, rally, one such placard warned of the ominous "Barry Hussein Obama," with "Barry" referring to Obama's alleged alter ego "Barry Soetoro." Soetoro is the last name of Obama's stepfather, who was a citizen of Indonesia, and who—according to one version of the birther theory—adopted Obama, ensuring that he lost his citizenship. Birther conspiracies have long been accepted by right-wing elites like Rush Limbaugh, Michael Savage, Lou Dobbs, Sarah Palin, and Michele Bachmann—despite the complete lack of evidence that Obama was born outside the United States.[76] Reflecting, in part, the influence of such right-wing personalities, the April 2010 CBS/*New York Times* poll found that 59 percent of Tea Partiers thought either that Obama was "born in another country" or that they could not be certain that he was a U.S. citizen.[77]

Statistical surveys of Tea Partiers find a consistent pattern of anti-Muslim prejudice. Polling from the University of Washington in early 2010 found that 73 percent of Tea Party supporters disapproved of Obama's supposed policy of "engaging with Muslim countries." Sixty three percent of Tea Party supporters disagreed with the idea that "we should not single out Muslims or Middle Easterners for airport security drops"[78]—a practice that leading human rights groups have reasonably challenged as racist, unconstitutional, unproductive, and contrary to basic human rights.[79]

Tea Party chapters have called for laws that would differentiate Muslims from non-Muslims, legally disfranchising individuals based upon their religion.

Tea Partiers in Florida attracted controversy when they invited Brigitte Gabriel, an anti-Muslim speaker from the nativist group Act! for America, to address them. Gabriel argued that Muslims should never be allowed to run for or hold a public office and that an American Muslim cannot be a loyal citizen because Islam is the "real enemy."[80]

We observed a Tea Party–supported Act! for America seminar in the Chicago suburb of Palatine in mid-2010. The event's leaders warned of the supposed fifth column threat of Islam to America's cultural identity and national security. Speakers raised the alarm about "a religion and philosophy of destruction put in place by the laws of Islam." The imposition of "Sharia law" and "violent Jihad" were said to be around the corner, with Sharia representing "a Trojan horse that, if introduced, will destroy the American economy." The speakers were transparently paranoid, depicting Muslims as members of a one-dimensional group that believes "the world belongs to Islam." Presenters at the Palatine meeting complained that Obama was a "secret Muslim" who was "coordinating a conspiracy to turn the U.S. into a "Muslim nation." Act! for America organizers we observed warned of alleged plans to build a local mosque. They echoed Tea Party leader Newt Gingrich's argument that no more mosques should be built in the United States until Saudi Arabia allows Christian churches. They exhibited a victims' mentality, expressing fears of a supposedly dangerous alliance between "the left" and "Jihadists" and lamenting the possibility that "if I say something bad about Muslims, I might get killed." At the end of the seminar, one speaker called for violence against the Muslim "fifth column" to "start taking our streets back."

Tea Partiers' perceptions of Muslims reveal profound ignorance, which they appear to view as a virtue in light of their refusal to consider more nuanced (and more accurate) portrayals of Islam. Public opinion research shows that Muslim Americans are highly assimilated into American society and believe that Muslims coming to the United States should try to adopt American customs. The Pew Research Center reports that support for Islamic extremism among Muslim Americans is quite low, especially when compared with Muslims around the world.[81]

Tea Partiers and others on the right exhibit little grasp of the meaning of concepts like Jihad and Sharia. As a religious philosophy, Jihad is defined simply as a spiritual struggle against the evil that is a part of all people. Jihad is considered a duty of all Muslims striving to live by the laws of God.[82] Right-wing pundits and Tea Partiers have stripped away any intellectual understanding of the term in favor of a representation that views Jihad as exclusively terrorist. In a similar vein, Tea Partiers' blanket assault on the supposed danger of Sharia reveals ignorance of differences among Muslims on precisely how Sharia (Islamic law) should be applied in Muslim countries and over whether it has any legitimate place in government.[83]

Tea Partiers' obsession with Islam's supposed threat to Judeo-Christian values and American democracy is rather strange in light of Muslims' tiny presence in the United States. There is no comprehensive data, such as a Census Bureau count, on the number of Muslims in the United States. The most authoritative research on the topic, carried out by the Pew Research Center in 2007, put the number at 2.3 million, less than 1 percent of the populace. Two-thirds of U.S. Muslim adults are immigrants, born outside of the nation. Of this group, 24 percent were born in Arab countries, 18 percent in South Asia, and 8 percent in Iran. Half of the nation's native-born Muslims are black Americans, and 20 percent of the nation's Muslims are black Americans. More than three fourths (77 percent) of U.S. Muslims are American citizens.[84]

Where do Tea Partiers get their misguided conceptions of Islam and its alleged threat to America? Tea Partiers admit that they rely heavily on right-wing media, with 6 in 10 Tea Partiers listing Fox News as their "trusted" source of news.[85] Fox notoriously disseminates racist messages against Muslims, as has been demonstrated in a number of studies.[86]

But Fox is not the only source of American ignorance regarding Islam. The U.S. media as a whole have long spread racist images and messages against Islam.[87] The late Edward Said famously warned against the danger of distortion inherent in Western "Orientalism," which obliterates the Arab-Muslim "other's" humanity through "highly exaggerated stereotyping and hostility" enabled by "the absence . . . of a long standing cultural attention to Islam."[88] The U.S. movie industry has been "awash with offensive images of Arabs and Muslims for a century"—images that encourage a "pervasive, and unapologetic degradation and dehumanization of a people."[89] Individuals who rely primarily on the mass media for their information about Islam are significantly more likely to hold racist, anti-Arab, and anti-Muslim attitudes.

After controlling for a variety of demographic variables, our analysis of recent Pew Research Center data reveals that those who are more likely to hold racist beliefs against Islam include conservatives, Protestants, Republicans, whites, and older Americans.[90] All of these groups are disproportionately represented in the Tea Party's ranks. Three other vital factors that explain racist views: lower levels of education, lack of acquaintance or friendship with a Muslim, and increased reliance on the mass media for one's information about Islam. Right-wing media pundits—the primary source of information for Tea Partiers—have played a critical role in fomenting the anti-Muslim, anti-Arab paranoia that is so disturbingly prevalent in the Tea Party.

Concluding Lessons

In a critical piece on the Tea Party, *Rolling Stone* journalist Matt Taibbi argued in the fall of 2010 that "it would be inaccurate to say the Tea Partiers are racists. What they are, in truth," Taibbi argued, "are narcissists"—people concerned to slash social programs that help less-advantaged others but determined to preserve programs that serve their own interests.[91] We believe that Tea Partiers are both racist *and* narcissistic. A strong majority of Tea Partiers, like much of the general public in the United States, is racist, along the "color-blind" lines described in this chapter. Implicit, rather than explicit, racism is clearly the order of the day in contemporary American political culture, at least in relation to discussions of blacks and illegal immigrants. The Tea Partiers are no exception on the whole. A more brazen form of racism is clearly at work, however, in Tea Party conduct and statements regarding Islam and Muslim Americans. As the Tea Party's conduct during and after the spring 2010 media drama over the proposed Cordoba Center in lower Manhattan suggests, moreover, the Tea Party seems to have taken a page from the European right. It has learned that racism and the politics of scapegoating can help it reach a wider audience in the midst of an economic crisis.

5

Return of "the Paranoid Style in American Politics"

Authoritarianism and Hyperignorance in Tea Party Nation

This so-called climate science is just ridiculous. . . . Some people say I'm extreme, but they said the John Birch Society was extreme, too.
—*Kelly Khuri, founder of the Clark County Tea Party Patriots, Clark County, Indiana, October 20, 2010*[1]

The Paranoid Style

In his classic 1964 essay, "The Paranoid Style in American Politics," historian Richard Hofstadter traced reactionary ideologies back through much of America's past. He warned specifically of post–World War II right-wing fundamentalism, which assaulted its political opponents with "heated exaggeration, suspiciousness, and conspiratorial fantasy." The hysterical, anticommunist, and right-wing mind-set of the 1950s and early 1960s was characterized by "systematized delusions of persecution," which depicted nonconservative political forces as part of an insidious "one world socialistic government."[2] Hofstadter was writing at a time when McCarthyism was considered mainstream and the reactionary right was consumed by conspiracy theories based upon warnings about a sinister "international communist conspiracy" headquartered in Moscow—a plot that McCarthy-era paranoids claimed to have discovered in the upper reaches of U.S. government.

The conspiracies imagined by the John Birch Society and other sections of the reactionary American right have changed over the years, but the paranoid style remains. The Tea Party is the latest and best example. Contemporary right-wing paranoia and extremism within the Tea Party are manifest in warnings about the dire menaces to liberty posed by "radical professors," "socialist" Democrats and liberals, and international schemes by scientists to dupe the public into fearing the (most Tea Partiers think) nonexistent problem of climate change. These are just some of the conspiracies that Tea Party America claims to have uncovered. Apocalyptic warnings about the momentous and imminent dangers they pose to American freedom and prosperity permeate Tea Party discourse.[3]

Consistent with Hofstadter's reflections half a century ago, the delusional Tea Party mind-set is fed by remarkable willful ignorance, reinforced by openly expressed disdain for critical empirical inquiry, falsifiable hypotheses, and ideological pluralism.[4] Paranoia and ignorance are accompanied by an abject authoritarianism that is deeply consistent with liberal journalist David Niewert's warnings about growing antidemocratic sentiments on the American right. In his chilling book *The Eliminationists: How Hate Talk Radicalized the American Right* (2009), Niewert observes the right's practice of promoting fringe ideas and framing the world in binary terms—in black-and-white, all-or-nothing language. Rightist authoritarianism tends to gain prominence, Niewert warns, during periods of economic uncertainty and social chaos. Niewert worries that a "fascistic" threat could emerge in the United States if American "conservatives" continue their pronounced rightward shift in coming years.[5]

The Archauthoritarian Drift

Despite leftist evocations of the memory of Weimar Germany and warnings of a "real fascist movement in this country,"[6] we do not yet see much threat of fascism in the Tea Party phenomenon. The true historical fascism of the interwar years involved fanatical support for charismatic dictatorial rulers explicitly dedicated to the overthrow of parliamentary institutions. It mobilized a mass of adherents in frequently violent, archmasculinist, and hyperracist movements wedded to extreme nationalist militarism and the despotic use of expanded and repressive state power against minorities, the poor, leftists, liberals, and trade unionists. It arose in response to genuine fears of an organized and radical left—something that does not really exist to any serious degree in the contemporary United States.[7]

The neoliberal, individualistic, and "free-market"-oriented Tea Party is not fascist in the classic sense. Still, the Tea Party represents an *authoritarian* brew, with the potential to become more extreme if, say, the economy worsens to the point of producing social instability. Proto-fascistic aspects in the Tea Party phenomenon should not be ignored. Many Tea Partiers seem willing to blame blacks, immigrants, workers, and the poor for their own disadvantaged position while letting the nation's rich and powerful off the hook. The harsh, deeply ignorant, and paranoid-style authoritarianism of the Tea Party takes numerous other chilling forms, including the following:

- Regular demonization of the Progressive Age, the New Deal era, the Great Society, and all other moments of reform in American history as episodes of totalitarian socialist creep.[8]
- The insistent claim that the Obama administration is "socialist," "Marxist," and the "most radical and left-wing presidency" in U.S. history.
- The regular claim that "radical Left activists" (a category that in Tea Party discourse seems to range from relatively conservative corporate Democrats like Obama to actual leftists) are "polarizing" America and "driving the country over the cliff" with extreme and anti-American values.
- An embrace of deeply reactionary, racist, and conspiratorial theories on the president's alleged alien origin and Muslim identity.
- A belief that political goals can be attained through violence against the government.[9]
- The regular practice among Tea Party–supporting Fox News pundits of verbal bullying, coupled with hints of physical coercion.[10]
- The notion that every participant at Tea Party meetings could be a plant sent out by liberal agents to derail the "movement."[11]

- Tea Partiers' fundamental distrust of multiparty politics, reflected in melodramatic rhetoric painting the Democratic Party as a radical threat the country can no longer endure.

The Radical Threat Posed by the Democratic Party?

Consistent with their near-universal opposition to Obama (96 percent) and their almost unanimous belief that Obama is a socialist,[12] Tea Partiers exhibit an absolutist mind-set that sees Democrats, liberals, and their purported radical Left allies as the cause of all of America's problems and far-right Republicans and unregulated business power as the only solution. It has been disturbing to hear this extreme way of thinking voiced over and over in the Tea Party gatherings we have attended. Over many years on the left, both of us have observed that progressive contempt for the Republican Party as well as the corporatist Democratic Party is widespread. We have heard and in some cases advanced left warnings about the erosion and eclipse of functioning democracy under corporate and imperial rule.[13] But none of our experiences on the radical left prepared us for the extremism of Tea Party organizers' regular claims that the Democrats constituted an immediate threat to the survival of the American republic and to democracy itself. No one we knew on the left has insisted that American democracy would be destroyed once and for all if George W. Bush was not removed from the presidency or if Republicans were allowed to remain in Congress for even a few more months.

This was a regular assertion about Democratic Party power in the White House and Congress in the Chicago-area Tea Party chapters we observed. One Chicago organizer warned that the tax increases supposedly occurring under Democrats *"could mean the end of America as we know it."* A Tea Partier in the Chicago suburb of Palatine claimed that the rapid acceleration of the national debt was soon reach "the tipping point" as a result of the Democrats' runaway spending, which could be ended only by right-wing efforts to "take back America." The "tipping point" of which Tea Partiers spoke reflected their perception that they were being taxed to fund President

Obama's "secret socialist agenda"—this despite the fact that Obama and the Democrats actually lowered taxes for the vast majority of Americans, and despite the president's clear commitment to business agendas, as seen in the Obama administration's rescuing of Wall Street investors, in the 2008 Troubled Asset Relief Program and 2009 auto bailouts, in the corporate-friendly health care reform, and in Obama's deference to British Petroleum (BP) following that company's epic oil spill in the Gulf of Mexico during the spring and summer of 2010.[14] In the case of the oil disaster, Obama consistently reiterated his support for a market-based solution to the crisis, claiming that BP was capable of containing the damage and coordinating the cleanup. This deference continued even as it was clear that the crisis was escalating beyond BP's control.[15]

Tea Partiers' insistence that American democracy is at risk of radical leftist takeover by Obama and his progressive allies is at once deeply paranoid and stunningly ignorant. Whatever their promises to progressive voters during the 2008 election cycle, Team Obama and the Democrats have governed by trying to find middle ground with Republicans. Obama campaigned on a platform of postpartisanship.[16] The Democratic health care reform bill was conservative. It relies on "market solutions" in the form of state-based insurance exchanges, thus bowing to right-wing arguments about the need for decentralization and state empowerment. It requires Americans to buy insurance, to be provided not by the government but by private companies, and to rely on privately provided medical care, medical equipment, and hospital services.[17] In fact, the Democratic health care legislation that passed in March of 2010 was substantively similar to the 1993 Republican health care reform proposal, consistent with Obama's repeated call for a bill that would please both Democrats and Republicans.[18] Republicans rejected Obama's proposal for a bipartisan summit on health care. They employed extremist rhetoric absurdly attacking Democrats for advancing the "government takeover" of medical care, claiming that the bill called for "death panels" and "government rationing of care"—all the while refusing to consider any of the market-based reforms Obama and the Democrats supported.[19] Republicans were opposed in principle to the notion that government should do anything to make health care affordable or more easily obtainable by the poor and uninsured. Supported by conservatives and Tea Partiers, Republican officials openly admitted that their goal was obstruction rather than compromise. Republican senator from South Carolina and Tea Party hero Jim DeMint announced that Republican efforts to block a vote on health care were intended to embarrass Democrats and provide Republicans with a political advantage: "If we're able to stop Obama on this [health care reform] it will be his Waterloo. It will break him."[20]

The best scholarly analyses of recent ideological polarization in U.S. politics show that congressional Republicans have moved to the right at a dramatically faster rate than Democrats have moved to the left.[21] Self-designated Republican activists shifted away from the political center at a rate twice as fast as Democratic activists moved to the left during the last forty-five years. Although Democratic activists continued to grow more liberal from the mid-1960s through the late 1980s, their shift left subsided from the mid-1990s onward as they began to move slightly back toward the center after 2000. In contrast, Republican activists grew steadily more conservative throughout the *entire* period.[22] The Republican Party and particularly its far-right elements—the Tea Party today—are the main cause of the growing, much-bemoaned polarization of the national political system. Sadly, however, the right wing, including the Tea Party, has—with no small assistance from right-wing and mainstream media—convinced much of the American public that ideological extremism in government is the result of the Democratic Party's supposed radical faith in the expansion of big and leftist government.

"The Most Left-Wing Presidency in American History"

Tea Partiers' claim that the Obama White House is the most left-wing presidency in American history is obviously false. Franklin Roosevelt promoted a major expansion of the welfare state in the 1930s through New Deal initiatives establishing a minimum wage, a legal right to unionize, and a social security program. By contrast, Obama appointed a bipartisan national committee to consider reducing Social Security benefits. The Obama administration abandoned prolabor initiatives such as the Employee Free Choice Act (EFCA), which it never seriously considered. Obama's market-based health care package is nowhere near as progressive as the successful efforts of Lyndon Johnson to create the Medicare and Medicaid programs. A progressive equivalent to Johnson's accomplishments would have required at the very least passage of the public option (or perhaps even universal health care), which the Democratic Party never seriously considered. Obama's relatively conservative politics and policies are exactly what should have been expected in light of his centrist and neoliberal rhetoric and beliefs, clearly evident to those willing to look beneath fake-progressive campaign imagery.[23] One who was willing to peer behind the left illusion was *New Yorker* reporter Larissa MacFarquhar, who interviewed and examined the future president in great detail in late 2006 and early 2007. In a May 2007 essay titled "The Conciliator: Where Is Barack Obama Coming From?" MacFarquhar (no leftist) noted:

> In his view of history, in his respect for tradition, in his skepticism that the world can be changed any way but very, very slowly, Obama is deeply conservative. There are moments when he sounds almost Burkean. He distrusts abstractions, generalizations, extrapolations, projections. It's not just that he thinks revolutions are unlikely: he values continuity and stability for their own sake, sometimes even more than he values change for the good. Take health care, for example. "If you're starting from scratch," he says, "then a single-payer system"—a government-managed system like Canada's, which disconnects health insurance from employment—"would probably make sense. But we've got all these legacy systems in place, and managing the transition, as well as adjusting the culture to a different system, would be difficult to pull off. So we may need a system that's not so disruptive that people feel like suddenly what they've known for most of their lives is thrown by the wayside."[24]

Obama the Marxist

Tea Partiers' almost ritual claim—explicitly advanced by right-wing media personalities like Glenn Beck and Mark Levin—that Obama and the Democrats are Marxists, socialists, communists (even some-times Marxist-Leninists), epitomizes paranoid-style hyperignorance. This preposterous belief reveals an epic lack of knowledge not just about Obama and the corporate-captive Democrats (once aptly described by Kevin Phillips as "history's second most enthusiastic capitalist party"), but also about socialism, communism, and Marxism. Karl Marx called for a radical workers' revolution leading to the creation of a postcapitalist society.[25] Marx and Friedrich Engels called for the "the proletariat" to "use its political supremacy to wrest, by degrees, all capital from the bourgeoisie, to centralize all instruments of production in the hands of the state."[26] As it seems almost embarrassing to note, the militantly state-capitalist and corporate-neoliberal Obama administration and the Democratic Congress (2009–2010) made no movements in these directions. As a political leader of the capitalist class himself, Obama has long expressed great approval of the corporate capitalist system, and there is, of course, no record of him condemning owner-worker relations under capitalism.[27] He has never called for a mass movement of "the proletariat" to overthrow capitalism. Nor has he acted to mobilize the left (such as it is) for strong reforms in favor of worker rights. Instead, Obama has *demobilized* and discouraged U.S. labor by abandoning reforms that would make it easier for workers to unionize.[28]

Some Tea Partiers will interject that the Obama administration seized a majority stake in General Motors (GM) when the company was forced into bankruptcy in 2009.[29] Obama presided over a plan that granted partial ownership of the company to the United Auto Workers (UAW). Contrary to Tea Party and Fox News propaganda, however, these initiatives were not remotely socialist. Government majority ownership of General Motors is not synonymous with government control over the company and expropriation of its productive capacity so that it can be used to promote the public good. Obama announced after the "takeover" that he had no interest in running GM, contradicting the core socialist principle that government and worker ownership of industry is intended to advance the public welfare and democratize the economy.[30] The administration then ordered a profits-friendly taxpayer-subsidized downsizing of many workers.[31] The White House's auto bailout wiped out tens of thousands of livable wage union jobs and led to a wave of wage and pension cuts for current and retired auto workers. Incredibly enough given the prolabor sentiments he expressed during the campaign and the strong union support he got before and during the election, the bailout also subsidized GM efforts to move yet more jobs abroad. As William Greider explained in May 2010:

> So this is how the auto bailout will work. American taxpayers pump tens of billions into rescuing General Motors from bankruptcy. Then GM pays us back by shipping more jobs overseas—the equivalent of four assembly plants. The federal money will directly subsidize more imports from abroad, enabling GM to double its car production in Mexico, South Korea and China and selling the cars into the U.S. market.
>
> . . . GM's restructuring plan envisions a doubling of the vehicles it will import from overseas factories, from 372,000 to 737,000, in the next four years. GM's imported cars—already 15.5 percent of its domestic sales—will rise to 23.5 percent. . . . The president is sticking with Rubinomics.[32]

Obama's betrayal of American auto workers reached levels that struck Noam Chomsky as "surreal." In the summer of 2009, the business press reported that Obama's transportation secretary traveled abroad in pursuit of contracts with European manufacturers to construct high-speed rail projects with federal funds designated by Congress for U.S. economic stimulus. Taxpayer funding for badly needed domestic infrastructural development would perhaps go to European corporations. "At the same time," Chomsky noted, "Washington is busy dismantling leading sectors of U.S. industry, ruining the lives of the workforce, families and communities. . . . Surely," Chomsky reflected, "the auto industry could be reconstructed, using its highly skilled workforce to produce what the country and the world needs—and soon, if we are to have some hope of averting major catastrophe. It has been done before, after all. . . . But all such matters are off the agenda."[33] Under the terms of the bankruptcy deal that the Obama White House and its "Car Czar" Steven Rattner worked out with General Motors at the end of May 2010, the company was permitted to grab workers' pension funds to pay off Wall Street.[34]

Obama promised that government would not interfere with managerial prerogatives or play a leading role in GM's major restructuring (including workforce downsizing) or other business decisions once the bailout was complete.[35] Furthermore, as soon as the Obama administration got into the business of owning a stake in GM, it was looking to get out. As Edward Whitacre, the CEO of GM, explained, GM plans in early 2010 were to "quickly arrange a public stock offering that would allow taxpayers to cash out their 60 percent ownership stake in the automaker," thereby absolving the government of any responsibility for the beleaguered auto giant in the future.[36] Most importantly, Obama's partial nationalization of GM did not strip Wall Street of its failed investment in the company. It directly assaulted the legal property rights of auto workers. Obama, aided by the national court system, blatantly violated the legal contracts of GM workers by seizing workers' pension funds in order to pay for $6 billion in loans to General Motors from banks such as Citibank and Morgan Stanley.[37]

Looking back on the White House auto deal in the fall of 2009, *New York Times* chief financial columnist Floyd Norris marveled at how the Obama administration was *"teaching capitalism to the carmakers."* Back "in the bad old days, when supposed capitalists were running Detroit," Norris wrote, the auto industry relied on expanding volume through price cuts and "sweet lease deals," all designed to maintain cash flows and preserve market share. But, faced with a powerful union (the UAW), the big three automakers failed in Norris's view to focus on capitalist profitability, which would have required closing plants and firing workers. The situation was corrected by the Obama administration, falsely accused of "socialism," in Norris's opinion. "The result," Norris noted, "was a lot of job cutting, not something you might have expected from an administration elected with union support. The unions lost their generous pay for laid-off workers. To be sure, the union health plans were not treated as harshly as some creditors were, but in the end creditors and workers all paid for the sins of past managements" (emphasis added).[38]

In the Obama administration's version of state capitalism as applied to the auto industry, the state was *more ruthlessly capitalist than the capitalists themselves.* Its actions were a far cry from "socialism," notwithstanding Tea Party diatribes about Obama's Marxist take-over of private industry. The same point holds for the administration's tepid corporate-friendly health care and financial "reforms," its environmental policies, and much more.[39] The hysterical Tea Party call for the United States to "move away" from "socialism" and "Marxism" is preposterous. It is widely documented that big business has long been the most privileged actor in American politics (across Democratic and Republican regimes), and that capitalist-based business elites and service professionals dominate the campaign contribution and lobbying processes, exerting their power among officials throughout the entire political system and on both parties.[40]

Black-and-White Thinking and the Fox News Box

Hyperignorant black-and-white thinking distorts political debate and consciousness in dangerous ways. We observed a disturbing pattern in our discussions with, and observations of, Tea Partiers throughout the Chicago area. They regarded evidence challenging their positions as unworthy of consideration and routinely ridiculed those promoting more liberal policy views, considering them beneath respectful consideration and engagement.

This mind-set is characteristic of right-wing groups and individuals. Individuals who score high on polling questions measuring authoritarianism are considerably more likely to identify themselves as conservatives (as do the great majority of Tea Party supporters) and generally share a low commitment to exploring the complexities and nuances of public policy issues.[41]

The Tea Partiers' deeply reactionary mind-set is reinforced by their extreme reliance on right-wing media. National polling data reveal that Tea Partiers view Fox News channel as their most trusted source of political information. Those who depend on Fox News are increasingly uninterested in consulting *any* other sources. Our analysis of Pew Research Center data from 2004 through 2009 demonstrates that Fox News viewers (specifically those who rely on Fox above all other sources for their news) are unwilling to consider other television

FIGURE 5.1

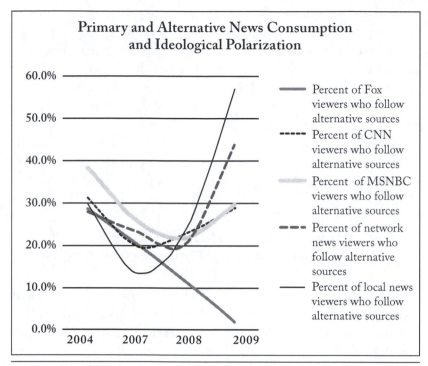

SOURCE: Pew Research Center, polls on media consumption from 2004 through 2009.

media outlets.[42] As Figure 5.1 shows, a majority of primarily Fox News viewers (along with all other television viewers) were already unlikely to turn to alternative sources during the Bush years. This pattern grew more extreme, however, during the 2004–2009 period. Although primary viewers of MSNBC and CNN (often framed as "liberal" in their politics) grew less likely to consult alternative sources from 2004 to 2007–2008, their consumption of other outlets did eventually increase by 2009. By contrast, Fox News viewers' consultation of alternative sources fell radically from less than one-third of viewers in 2004 to just a few percent of viewers by 2009. Conservative media audiences thus became more narrow in their media usage precisely at a time when they were attacking liberals and "the left" for close-mindedness, extremism, and dogmatism.

Anti-intellectualism and the Myth of a Leftist Academy

Ignorance is a virtue in the Tea Party worldview. The vast majority of Tea Partiers we observed in our Chicago area case study exhibited a chilling lack of interest in empirical evidence and exuded contempt for those who seek open and fact-based discourse. Those we spoke with proclaimed that Fox and like-minded right-wing sources were the only voices providing them with the truth on important political subjects. "We're not just against something, the men and women I speak to," one Tea Partier told *New York Times* reporter Kate Zernike in 2009. "It's not just 'Obama, yuck.' . . . We're well informed, well educated."[43] But Tea Partiers' definition of well educated had nothing to do with consulting and weighing divergent sources and evidence. Instead, it seemed to mean that Tea Party activists were strongly interested in politics and followed political stories in the right-wing media they trusted.

Those who speak for the Tea Party "movement" at the national level harbor a deep distrust for higher education as inherently elitist and liberal. Tea Party heroine Sarah Palin encapsulated this view well as she announced during the 2008 presidential campaign that "we need a commander-in-chief, not a professor of law."[44] Right-wing media regularly assault liberal and leftist academics. Conservative talk radio icon Rush Limbaugh regularly attacks "radical liberalism in academia." At Fox News, Tea Party cheerleader Sean Hannity frets over college students being indoctrinated by their liberal professors. Hannity claims to provide his viewers with the tools needed "to combat the liberal hijacking of higher education."[45] Fox's national Tea Party icon Glenn Beck chastises university educators for "indoctrinating our youth [with an] onslaught of progressive lies,"[46] a rather ridiculous take on contemporary American higher education. As the venerable Princeton political scientist Sheldon Wolin explained a couple of years ago, American academia has undergone "effective integration . . . into the corporate state." Furthermore, "through a combination of governmental contracts, corporate and foundation funds, joint projects involving university and corporate researchers, and wealthy individual donors, universities (especially so-called research universities), intellectuals, scholars, and researchers have been seamlessly integrated into the system. . . . The Academy has become self-pacifying."[47]

Neo–John Bircher Glenn Beck as "an American Educator"

Beck has spearheaded Fox's assault on supposedly leftist academia. In the summer of 2010, Beck established the online, for-profit "Beck University" (BU). It offers courses like Faith 102, which argues that "revisionists and secular progressives" are wrong about the separation of church and state, and Hope 102, which assaults an activist federal government.[48] Beck University provides the "true" history of America with guests who claim that the United States was founded as a Christian nation, that "free markets" are superior to government regulation of business, and that America has been under internal "socialist" assault since the early-twentieth-century Progressive Era. During a summer 2010 show dedicated to "restoring history," Beck pointed to a stack of history textbooks and pronounced them all the products of "malicious progressive intent." Vile "progressives," he explained—"liberals, socialists, Communists, the broad conflated spectrum of 'the left'"—"knew they had to separate us from our history to be able to separate us from our Constitution and God." Dressed as a mock professor and surrounded by charts and figures, he told a chilling story of once-virtuous America's long collapse into Obama-era totalitarianism. The degeneration, Beck claimed, started with the Progressive Era and above all with the Woodrow Wilson presidency, when both the Federal Reserve System and the graduated federal income tax (both "socialist") came into being. "Wilson," Beck told his radio audience, "just despised what America was."[49]

As bizarre as this sort of historical "education" may be, it has found a wide audience among Tea Party activists and sympathizers. "At the movement's Freedom Summit in Washington," Princeton historian Sean Willentz notes, "one activist told a reporter, 'The election between Teddy Roosevelt and Woodrow Wilson in 1912 was when it started going downhill.'" Similarly, a furious member of the Tea Party Patriots group from aptly named Cape Fear, North Carolina, claimed on the group's website that "the very things you see happening in this country today started with the Wilson Administration." We have repeatedly heard self-identified Tea Partiers call right-wing talk radio shows to advance Beck's strange claim of socialist-imposed decline initiated during the Progressive Era.

Interestingly enough, Beck's curious neo-McCarthyite views on American history and society are directly linked to the paranoid right-wing politics of the 1950s John Birch Society. As Willentz notes:

> Calling Obama a socialist in the tradition of Woodrow Wilson is audacious enough to seem like the marker of a new movement. . . . In fact, it marks a revival of ideas that circulated on the extremist right half a century ago, especially in the John Birch Society and among its admirers.
>
> Beck's [Woodrow Wilson–obsessed] version of American history relies on lessons from his own acknowledged inspiration, the late right-wing writer W. Cleon Skousen, and also restates charges made by the Birch Society's founder, Robert Welch. The political universe is, of course, very different today from what it was during the Cold War. Yet the Birchers' politics and their view of American history— which focused more on totalitarian threats at home than on those posed by the Soviet Union and Communist China—has proved remarkably persistent.
>
> After Senator Joseph McCarthy's fall, in 1954, many of McCarthy's followers felt bereft of a voice, and Welch seemed to speak for them; by the mid-sixties, his society's membership was estimated to be as high as a hundred thousand. Welch, exploiting fears of what McCarthy had called an "immense" domestic conspiracy, declared that the federal government had already fallen into the Communists' clutches.
>
> . . . Wherever he looked, Welch saw Communist forces manipulating American economic and foreign policy on behalf of totalitarianism. But within the United States, he believed, the subversion had actually begun years before the Bolshevik Revolution. Conflating modern liberalism and totalitarianism, Welch described government

as "always and inevitably an enemy of individual freedom." Consequently, he charged, the Progressive era, which expanded the federal government's role in curbing social and economic ills, was a dire period in our history, and Woodrow Wilson "more than any other one man started this nation on its present road to totalitarianism."[50]

The neo-Bircher Beck holds great sway among those who call themselves Tea Party supporters and activists. An opinion poll released by Democracy Corps in the summer of 2010 showed that he was "the most highly regarded individual among Tea Party supporters." Tea Partiers saw him "not merely as entertainer, like Rush Limbaugh," Willentz notes, "but as an 'educator.'"[51]

Constitutional Originalism

Tea Partier Christine O'Donnell's campaign for a U.S. Senate seat in Delaware was regularly marked by controversy, ranging from her admission that she had dabbled in witchcraft to her complaints about masturbation. More significant from a policy perspective was her religiously inspired worship of the Constitution, expressed during the run-up to the Delaware senatorial race (in which she was running as the Republican candidate). *Newsweek* reported her militantly archaist understanding of the Constitution as a covenant from God:

> The Founders' masterpiece, O'Donnell said, isn't just a legal document; it's a "covenant" based on "divine principles." For decades, she continued, the agents of "anti-Americanism" who dominate "the D.C. cocktail crowd" have disrespected the hallowed document. But now, finally, in the "darker days" of the Obama administration, "the Constitution is making a comeback." Like the "chosen people of Israel," who "cycle[d] through periods of blessing and suffering," the Tea Party has rediscovered America's version of "the Hebrew Scriptures" and led the country into "a season of constitutional repentance." Going forward, O'Donnell declared, Republicans must champion the "American values" enshrined in our sacred text. "There are more of us than there are of them," she concluded.[52]

A Chicago Tea Party rally we attended in Morton Grove included a speech from the wife of congressional Republican candidate and Tea Partier Joel Pollak. Mrs. Pollak informed her audience of her determination—made after having recently studied the U.S. Constitution in her effort to become an American citizen—that any powers exercised by the national government beyond those specifically listed in the Constitution were "blatantly unconstitutional."

The Tea Party's legal philosophy claims to reflect the original intent of the Founding Fathers, stressing legislators' duty to act in strict accord with exact guidelines laid out in the Constitution. This approach, often called constitutional originalism, condemns political officials for stepping outside the powers allowed by the national government's charter document. It calls for a return to small government, as purportedly envisioned by the Founders. Originalism became particularly popular among Tea Partiers as they claimed that attempts to expand national health care (specifically through a public option or through a strengthening of Medicaid) were unconstitutional because not specifically allowed in the Constitution.[53]

Tea Partiers pointed to the enumerated powers of the Constitution—those capacities they claim government cannot go beyond according to the rules laid out by the Founders. They drew attention to the Tenth Amendment, which establishes that "the powers not delegated to the United States by the Constitution, nor prohibited by it to the States, are reserved to the States respectively, or to the people." Citing this amendment, Tea Partiers maintained that policy initiatives such as health care reform were the province either of the states or of "the people," to be provided either through state funding or through private charity.

Historian Jill Lepore rightly criticizes the Tea Partiers' constitutional originalism as a form of "anti-history" that "exist[s] outside of argument and ha[s] no interest in evidence. . . . Set loose in the culture, and tangled together with fanaticism," Lepore writes, "originalism looks like history, but it's not; it's historical fundamentalism, which is to history what astrology is to astronomy, what alchemy is to chemistry, what creationism is to evolution."[54]

Consistent with this judgment, the Tea Party's claim that the 2010 health reform bill was unconstitutional is based on extreme ignorance.

It ignores the passage in the Constitution (Article I, Section 8) that provides the federal government with the power to implement policies needed to provide for the general welfare. This clause is purposely vague in terms of what powers are granted to the federal government. Indeed, this imprecision has helped the Constitution remain relevant over the years, as Americans' understandings of the legitimate roles of government have expanded to include majority support for a system of national taxation (not provided in the Constitution), the outlawing of slavery (which was tolerated in the original document), the granting of basic labor protections (such as the forty-hour work week, the minimum wage, and a prohibition on child labor), the extension of basic consumer and environmental protections through national legal and bureaucratic-regulatory initiatives, and the extension of a number of welfare protections (such as Social Security, an extensive public education system, and health care programs such as Medicaid and Medicare).

The notion that American government can and indeed must undertake policies that are not explicitly and specifically established in the Constitution is hardly new. James Madison (who supported a national government strong enough to veto state laws) opposed the idea that the delegated national powers described in the Constitution were to be the only capacities granted to the federal government because "there must necessarily be admitted powers by implication" as well.[55] Though it was not originally included in the Constitution, Thomas Jefferson called for the establishment of a progressive federal tax system directed at the wealthy, one that would ensure that "the farmer will see his government supported, his children educated, and the face of his country made a paradise by the contributions of the rich alone, without his being called on to spend a cent from his earnings."[56] The nation's great state capitalist pioneer Alexander Hamilton established a national bank, though the power to do so was not remotely mentioned in the Constitution. In broadly interpreting government powers under the Constitution, Hamilton saw the bank as necessary for coordinating national economic growth and establishing a single currency to help pay the Revolutionary war debts of the states. The Supreme Court sided with Hamilton in the landmark *McCulloch v. Maryland* case (1819). The High Court ruled that Hamilton's bank was permitted under the Constitution's "Necessary and Proper Clause" (in Article I, Section 8), which grants the federal government very broad capacities required for developing, expanding, and protecting the nation. Equally important is the "General Welfare" clause, which provides the national government with significant power to promote all types of policy initiatives deemed necessary for ensuring the common good.[57] Numerous Supreme Court decisions have supported the national government's capacity to advance the common good by engaging in activities beyond the original enumerated powers (e.g. *Helvering v. Davis* [1937] and *United States v. Butler* [1936]).[58]

This legal history was unknown and of no interest to those we listened to and spoke with at the Tea Party rallies and meetings we attended. The Tea Partiers we met depicted the Constitution in militantly archaist, inflexible, and black-and-white terms that revealed remarkable ignorance. Nevertheless, they expressed their determination to "get into high school civics classrooms" to wrest control from liberals perverting youthful minds about the true intent of the Founding Fathers.

Capitalist Originalism

National Tea Party activist Keli Carender (falsely credited by Tea Party elites with organizing the first Tea Party protest in 2009) explained in 2009 that her "free-market" opposition to the Obama administration was inspired by her reading of the Founding Fathers in addition to such leading modern capitalist theorists and propagandists as Thomas Sowell, Ayn Rand, and Milton Friedman.[59] Carender was advancing another key form of the historical ignorance, manipulation, and amnesia so prevalent in the Tea Party. A consistent Tea Party theme holds that the United States was founded as a free-market capitalist state—a sacred origin that has been perverted by dastardly and totalitarian progressives in the twentieth and twenty-first centuries.

This curious capitalist originalism is fundamentally mistaken on two levels. First, as a long empirical and scholarly record reveals, no true free market—a purely private economy bereft of government interference—has ever existed in American history or in any capitalist system. Governments have always played critical roles in establishing the conditions required for modern capitalist processes to function (such as government recognition of corporate property rights).[60] The Tea Party notion that free markets can and should rule is little more than a propagandistic fiction—a tool of top-down class warfare used by business leaders in their assault on positive government action for social welfare and the common good.

Second, there is no evidence that the Founders sought to build a capitalist society—free market or otherwise—in the United States. The word "capitalism," it is worth recalling, was not in common usage in the United States or the broader Atlantic world at the time of the American republic's emergence. It appears in neither the Declaration of Independence nor the Constitution. At the same time, the Founders exhibited no small degree of what might today be called anticapitalist sentiment. The nation's early republican originators shared a sense that a society made up of a few employers and many employees—a hallmark of modern capitalist society—could never function in a way consistent with principles of popular government. "Free men," they felt, did not rent themselves out to others except on a very temporary basis. Permanent wage earners could never live as free citizens.[61]

Jefferson warned explicitly and stridently against the "insidious power" of the "banking institutions and money incorporations." If these selfish interests of concentrated private wealth were not "curbed," Jefferson worried, "they would become a form of absolutism that would destroy the promise of the democratic revolution." He hoped to "crush in its birth the aristocracy of our moneyed corporations, which dare already to challenge our government to a trial of strength and bid defiance to the laws of our country."[62] Jefferson shared with Aristotle the belief that widespread poverty and concentrated wealth cannot exist side by side in a democracy (as they do, by definition, under capitalism). Observing the rise of early industrial capitalism, Jefferson in his later years drew what Noam Chomsky calls a "distinction between 'aristocrats' and 'democrats.' . . . The aristocrats of his day," Chomsky notes, "were the advocates of the rising capitalist state, which Jefferson observed with rising dismay, recognizing the obvious contradiction between democracy and capitalism—or, more accurately, really existing state capitalism, linked closely to state power."[63]

James Madison worried early and seriously about capitalist takeover of policy and opinion, warning by the 1790s against the rising class of business elites that were becoming at once the "the tools and tyrants" of government. Madison warned against unchecked capitalist (corporate) power, "which ought to be guarded against." Capitalist efforts to pursue "the indefinite accumulation of property" were to be strictly limited because "the growing wealth acquired by them" was "a source of abuses."[64] Madison also warned that "incorporated companies . . . are at best a necessary evil."[65] The giant capitalist conglomerates that predominate today[66]—natural outcomes of the development of so-called free market capitalism—would surely appall Madison.

The Founders were precapitalists, imbued with a traditional aristocratic spirit of noblesse oblige that led them to abhor the so-called free market's tendencies to turn government into a mechanism for the upward distribution of wealth and to deepen the chasm between the rich and poor, the propertyless many and the wealthy few.

Systematic Ignorance

Many other examples of Tea Party hyperignorance—often combined with a significant degree of conspiracist paranoia and religious fundamentalism—deserve mention:

- The Tea Party claims that the 2009 stimulus had no effect, despite extensive evidence that it prevented further economic deterioration and despite estimates that unemployment would have been significantly higher without it.[67]
- The Tea Party claims that the Democrats are to blame for the poor state of the economy and that the economy will improve significantly if only Republicans are returned to power, despite the fact that past support for deregulation of Wall Street (one of the main causes of the 2008 economic crash) was a bipartisan phenomenon.[68]

- The Tea Party blames Obama and Democrats for "unsustainable" deficits and debt, despite the fact that nearly all of the debt taken on over the last thirty years arose from Republicans' simultaneous commitment to cutting taxes on the rich and radically escalating military spending.[69]
- The Tea Party portrays the national debt as at its highest point in U.S. history, despite conclusive evidence that debt as a percentage of gross domestic product is significantly lower than at other points in our history, and despite economists' warnings that there is no significant relationship between debt and economic growth and vitality within wealthy nations.[70]
- Most Tea Partiers believe that Obama raised their taxes during 2009 and 2010, despite his extension of neoliberal tax cuts to most Americans and his support for further tax cuts to the majority of Americans (opposed by Republicans) in the run-up to the midterm elections.[71]
- The Tea Party claims that Democratic health care reform will radically increase the deficit and national debt, despite considerable uncertainty about any future budgetary and economic predictions produced by the Congressional Budget Office (CBO—estimates are always tentative, even if based on sound economic projections). The nonpartisan CBO estimates that the reforms supported by Democrats would not contribute to the debt and might even reduce it.[72]
- The Tea Party believes that tax cuts primarily for the rich are the only effective means of promoting economic stimulus, despite a vast quantity of empirical research to the contrary and the important fact that the Bush tax cuts were accompanied by one of the weakest economic recoveries in recent history.[73]

Especially disturbing in light of the increasingly grave existential threat posed to livable ecology by anthropogenic climate change,[74] most Tea Partiers believe that global warming either doesn't exist or that it will result in no serious impact, despite the consensus among climatologists that global warming *is* occurring, that humans share significant (even primary responsibility), and that the effects are potentially catastrophic.[75] As John M. Broder of the *New York Times* noted in mid-October of 2010, "Skepticism and outright denial of global warming are among the articles of faith of the Tea Party movement, here in Indiana and across the country. For some, it is a matter of religious conviction; for others, it is driven by distrust of those they call the elites. And for others still, efforts to address climate change are seen *as a conspiracy to impose world government* and a sweeping redistribution of wealth" (emphasis added). A large majority of Tea Party–supported House candidates doubted global warming science and opposed legislation designed to address it. A common Tea Party sentiment on the supposed global warming ruse was expressed to Broder by Lisa Deaton, a small-business owner in Columbus, Indiana, who started We the People Indiana, a Tea Party affiliate. "*They're trying to use global warming against the people*," Deaton told Broder. "*It takes away our liberty*. . . . Being a strong Christian," Deaton added, "I cannot help but believe the Lord placed a lot of minerals in our country and it's not there to destroy us" (emphasis added).[76]

The Return of the Paranoid Style

The Enlightenment Era was marked by the advance of critical, open-ended, scientific, and evidence-based investigation and discovery. As part of the reactionary and authoritarian drift in American politics, the Tea Party phenomenon assaults Enlightenment values. Tea Partiers and others on the right share a deep distrust of independent and open-minded inquiry. The increased unwillingness of the most committed rightists to consider alternative news sources, coupled with their profound extremism and ignorance, represents, we think, a dangerous development in American history.

The Tea Party phenomenon at once drives and reflects the ominous return of the right-wing paranoid style in American politics. High-profile personalities like Glenn Beck and Sarah Palin (both major leaders of the Tea Party) speak in all seriousness of a moderate, procorporate president of the United States, the business-friendly Democratic Party, and mildly progressive liberal activists and intellectuals as alien, socialist threats to American freedom and prosperity. Masses of registered and highly motivated right-wing voters and activists recycle fantastically ignorant notions, including the following ideas:

- The president is a Marxist and "radical leftist" and not a legal U.S. citizen.
- The United States has been undergoing deadly socialist-totalitarian creep since the supposedly America-hating presidency of Woodrow Wilson.
- The Federal Reserve and numerous other top federal agencies pose imminent "socialist" threats to democracy.
- The nation's universities and intellectual culture are under the dangerous control of anti-American radicals.
- The corporate media work for and are run by extreme liberals and leftists who loathe the nation's conservatives and democratic values.
- The Democrats' corporate-friendly 2010 health reform bill and much else in the Obama policy record reflect a Marxist agenda that stands outside the parameters of the U.S. Constitution.
- The nation's Founding Fathers were advocates of "free-market" capitalism devoid of any public regulation.
- The progressive income tax is a communist plot.

Numerous deeply ignorant, conspiratorial, and paranoid ideas have buzzed around the margins of the American right for decades, of course, before and since the McCarthy era that provided the essential backdrop for Richard Hofstadter's reflections. Such ideas have now resurfaced and gained legitimacy in the dominant political culture like no time since the 1950s. We see four basic reasons for this. First, the Republican Party continues to move rightward and no longer seems willing or able to rein in its more extreme elements. In the early 1960s, Willentz notes, "the [John] Bircher right . . . provoked deep anxiety among conservatives, who feared being perceived as paranoids and conspiracy-mongers." That fear seems to have disappeared on the part of much of the current Republican elite, which rushes in many cases to align itself with the Tea Party, which, according to one poll in the fall of 2010, garnered support from more than 70 percent of Republicans.

Second, top Democrats seem unwilling or unable to denounce the authoritarian threat on the right. In a 1961 speech in Los Angeles, Democratic president John F. Kennedy clearly denounced those "discordant voices of extremism" that "equate[d] the Democratic Party with the welfare state, the welfare state with socialism, and socialism with Communism." There has been no such clear and explicit denunciation of the new right paranoia from President Barack Obama or other top Democrats on the whole. As Willentz further notes, "Obama's White House [in October 2010] is still struggling to make sense of its enemies. In the absence of forthright leadership, on both the right and the left, the job of standing up to extremists appears to have been left to the electorate."[77]

Third, a powerful right-wing communications empire arose in the late 1980s and now holds major propaganda strongholds operating from within the very heart of mainstream media. Fox News and the vast talk radio network broadcast the delusions of hard-right propagandists and their false—and rancid—populist paranoia and rage.

Last, but not least, late-twentieth- and early-twenty-first-century America is dangerously bereft of a really existing relevant Left capable of countering right-wing stereotypes, pushing the Democrats to enact effective and progressive programs that might keep right-wing critiques at bay, and capturing legitimate popular anger that is dangerously seized and misdirected by right-wing activists and personalities. It's not a pretty story.

6

Astroturf to the Core
Reflections on a Mass-Mediated "Movement"

Push Republican principles; just don't ever actually concede to anyone you talk to that this is all about returning Republicans to office.
—*Chicago Tea Party organizer to a handful of*
local chapter members, April 2010

Worthy and Unworthy Protest

We have found the Tea Party to be a fundamentally top-down, elite-directed affair. Our investigations reveal that the Tea Party is not an independent social movement at all. Nevertheless, leading newspapers and electronic media have consistently portrayed the Tea Party as grassroots, popular, diffuse, leaderless, populist, anti-establishment, nonpartisan, and insurgent.[1]

The reigning corporate media have richly fueled the fable that the Tea Party is a popular movement. As left journalist Adam Bessie noted in September of 2010:

The Tea Party mythology—that it is a grassroots, "insurgent" movement bent on overthrowing the "establishment"—has taken root in the corporate and even independent liberal media. . . . The Tea Party PR fairy tale . . . has become a commonplace . . . "factual" way in which the media covers the election, as we see in the McClatchy . . . report "Tea Party, Palin Put GOP Establishment on Ropes in Florida, Alaska."

The headline—which introduces an "objective" news report—spreads this conservative manufactured myth, that the Tea Party is separate from the Washington establishment, that it is "fighting" the beltway. . . . The media—both corporate and independent—has unreflectively spread the manufactured myth that Tea Party candidates are outside of the political establishment. In simply reporting the Tea Party as a separate entity from the Republican Party, many media sources have helped perpetuate the false notion that its leaders represent a new political movement. In even using the brand "Tea Party" we perpetuate the idea that it is not the same old Republican Party.[2]

The media myth was reflected in an October 2010 Bloomberg News story according to which "Tea Party activists, once on the fringe of the Republican mainstream, are fueling the party's momentum in the midterm elections."[3] Similarly, the Associated Press reported in the run-up to the elections that the Tea Party was independent of electoral politics, as it "is a network of loosely connected community groups—not an established political party with official nominees."[4]

The media myth-making includes significant and selective exaggeration of the Tea Party's status as a bona fide social movement. The LexisNexis media database from April 9 to 15, 2010 (the week before the Tea Party's headline-garnering April 15th national tax protests) reveals that the Tea Party was referred to as a "social" and/or "protest movement" in more than 115 stories in newspapers across the United States. (Liberal and progressive commentator and Web sites have repeated the same description to no small extent.) The mainstream media's depictions of the Tea Party stood in sharp contrast to its treatment of the antiwar movement at its height more than seven years ago. In the week prior to the February 15, 2003, global protests against the imminent U.S. invasion of Iraq—in which the BBC estimated that between 6 and 10 million turned out nationwide and internationally[5]—the protests were recognized as a "movement" in just twenty-four newspaper stories, op-eds, editorials, and letters across the nation. An estimated 100,000 people marched in New York City alone on February 15, 2003. Nevertheless, the Tea Party protest of mid-April 2009 was seen by the mass media as more than four times worthier of "movement" status—this even though the Tea Party's national turnout was in the tens of thousands.

Marginalization of progressive social movements in favor of reactionary ones—real or imagined—comports well with what Howard Zinn called "the unreported resistance." Genuinely popular oppositional activity, Zinn observed, tends to be deleted from dominant media coverage because it challenges existing domestic and imperial hierarchies and refuses "to surrender the possibility of a more equal, more humane society."[6] The forgotten and censored social movements of past and present might be labeled "unworthy protests," following the dichotomy drawn between Noam Chomsky and Edward Herman's "worthy" and "unworthy" victims of U.S. violence. In laying out their "propaganda model," Chomsky and Herman were concerned with how foreign people killed and injured by U.S. and U.S-allied violence went mostly unreported and unmourned in the mass media, whereas the victims of officially designated "enemy" state violence—real or imagined—received extensive attention that was the subject of considerable moral outrage.[7] We would designate the anti–Iraq war demonstrations as officially unworthy protests (when compared to the coverage received by Tea Partiers) in dominant media—a reflection of their challenge to U.S. militarism, which has long garnered approval in the nation's reigning bipartisan American political and media cultures. Authentic popular struggles that confront concentrated wealth and power receive short shrift in American corporate media. Fake social movements that conform to the needs and views of the rich and powerful receive much more extensive and favorable coverage and commentary. The Tea Party is a graphic example of a "movement" that falls within the spectrum of officially acceptable (worthy) protest.

Consistent with this analysis, the media-monitoring group Fairness and Accuracy in Reporting (FAIR) noted in September 2010 that significant left protests and gatherings had been pushed to the margins by media preoccupied by the Tea Party. FAIR's Julie Hollar reported that a march on Washington, DC, in the fall of 2009 by tens of thousands of gay, lesbian, and bisexual activists received significantly less coverage than the smaller Tea Party protests of April 2010. Similarly, the February 2010 Tea Party Convention in Nashville received far more media attention than the Detroit meetings of the U.S. Social Forum, a large convention of leftist and socialist activists. The Social Forum drew 15,000 to 20,000 attendees, compared to 600 at the Tea Party convention, but the sizable left gathering received just 1.5 percent of the coverage given to the Tea Party in a sample of ten national news outlets.[8] The lesson is clear: A top-down phenomenon like the Tea Party—whose messages were promoted by the Republican Party—was seen by the leading media corporations as significantly more discerning of description as a legitimate social and protest movement than were rank-and-file protests and movements of the left.

Establishment Leaders, Weak Local Organization, and Uniform Message

There is little evidence that the Tea Party is either diffuse or grass-roots. On the contrary, it is fundamentally dependent upon the Republican Party. Its most prominent leaders are all leading and heavily corporate-connected Republicans. The progressive antiwar and social justice movements consider dissidents like Noam Chomsky, the late Howard Zinn, Amy Goodman, Ralph Nader, and Cindy Sheehan as among their most visible leaders. None of these figures are political officials or representatives of corporate America; they often work with actual grassroots and local organizations to advance peace, social equity, and democracy. By contrast, the Tea Party's most notable public figures have included prominent members of Republican officialdom, such as Dick Armey, Sarah Palin, and Michele Bachmann. All three occupy key political positions, have extensive ties with corporate America, and have blatantly violated their own rhetorical support for free markets by granting massive public subsidies to corporate interests.[9] The highly visible Tea Party inspirational leader Glenn Beck is, of course, a major player in the very "mainstream media" that Tea Partiers routinely denounce and is highly connected in elite Republican and business circles.

The Tea Party's organization is weak at the local level, suggesting that the "movement" lacks vigor and mass-based sustainability. One of our first encounters with the Tea Party was with the most visible chapter in Chicago, the Chicago Tea Party Patriots, following an antiwar talk we gave at Columbia College on April 13, 2010. In an upscale South Loop tavern, we ran across a grand total of four people who had responded to the chapter's call for supporters to create signs for the April 15 rally in the city's downtown Daley Plaza. For all intents and purposes, the bar was empty. The meager turnout made us curious about just how much popular participation the group enjoyed.

National polling figures from the *New York Times* in the spring of 2010 suggested that the local activism of the Tea Party was sizable; 21 percent of the public reported knowing of a local Tea Party chapter that was politically active in their community.[10] Our survey in the wake of the April 2010 national tax rallies suggested, however, that this number was far too high. Turnout for various Tea Party protests we observed was also radically smaller than what one would expect if the 4 percent of Americans who classified themselves as activists for the "movement" were actually participating in demonstrations. The April 15 Tea Party protest in the Chicago suburb of Joliet brought out just 300 demonstrators in a city of 152,000. A turnout of 4 percent of the city's population would have numbered more than 6,000. The turnout of 1,500 at the April 15 rally in Chicago represented just .05 percent of the city's population.[11] If just 1 percent of the city's population had turned out for the rally (one-fourth of those who claim to be Tea Party activists), there would have been nearly 30,000 demonstrators. Either the vast majority of the 4 percent of Americans who called themselves Tea Party activists are exaggerating the extent of their involvement or a vast majority of these individuals thought they could be activists without bothering to show up for the most important Tea Party protest to date.

There is little evidence of sustained Tea Party activity on the local level—a prime ingredient of any successful social movement. We attended local Tea Party meetings throughout Chicago and its suburbs to find out exactly who made up this "movement." We read the Web sites of Chicago area chapters to learn when they met. There was only one problem: Virtually no meetings were listed. The "local chapters" of the Tea Party did not exist except for a single contact name listed for each group. The majority of the chapters (thirteen of the twenty examined) had no Web site of their own and were coordinated through a central national Web site (the Tea Party Patriots).

We found little evidence that regular local meetings even took place. To the extent that any of these local Web sites listed ways to "get involved," they suggested signing online petitions, attending the April 15 rally, and attending local Sarah Palin and Michele Bachman visits. Very few of the local Web sites we examined provided information about regular local chapter meetings taking place prior to the April 15 demonstration. Only three of the twenty groups provided information for meetings for the roughly 5 million people living in the Chicago suburbs. In the future, such meetings were to be centrally located in the Hyatt Chicago Place in the affluent suburb of Schaumburg and in two other locations. At the time of our analysis, the allegedly decentralized Tea Party had virtually no base of regular local participants (except for those who passively received e-mail updates) and retained a highly centralized meeting system (with only one meeting per month) in just 3 of 264 municipalities in the Chicago metropolitan area.

We also found no history of regular activism at the local level in our national review of Tea Party chapters. We surveyed more than 150 cities that claimed a Tea Party rally on April 15, 2010, and learned that less than 50 percent of those cities showed any evidence of even having a Tea Party Web site to help organize local activities.[12] We found that 92 percent of these cities showed no indication of regular local Tea Party meetings. We quickly found out why when we attended the very few meetings and events that did take place in the city of Chicago and in Chicago suburbs such as Morton Grove, Schaumburg, Naperville, and Palatine. Tea Partiers did not believe they should be expected to organize anything outside of a few basic public relations events (rallies in particular) that were intended to draw in media attention in time for the 2010 election. The thinking was clear: Send out an e-mail blast just before a planned rally; invite high-profile, corporate-backed Republicans to the rallies in the hope of getting a mass turnout; and sit back and watch as hundreds (or at best a few thousand) turn out for the photo op. We heard a regular complaint from the few Tea Partiers who did attend local planning meetings (seldom more than five to twenty-five people). Many people they knew said they supported the Tea Party, but "no one wants to actually do anything about it." Organizers at the Palatine Tea Party meetings complained that holding meetings was hard work (even just one a month) and that they could not be expected to carry the burden by themselves anymore, after having organized three or four meetings following the April 15 rally.

When more than four or five people did show up at meetings, never more than a handful actually said anything or offered to do anything before the gathering ended. Many of these weekend warriors felt compelled to do little more than show up at a small gathering once a month (at most) to voice disgust at the "decline of American society" resulting from the Democratic Party's "extremism" and "socialism." In all the meetings we attended, it was clear that the members had no commitment to participatory politics. Meeting organizers rarely permitted attendees the time needed to speak, and whenever time was allowed, few participants advanced concrete or coherent ideas for how to "take [our] country back." If this was a social movement, then the term itself was truly vacuous.

The central tenets driving local Tea Party meetings were so uniformly consistent across all the events that they could not possibly have been manifestations of a diverse, grassroots social movement. No organic, decentralized movement could have such dramatic uniformity of language and ideology across so many chapters. This rhetorical uniformity appears to be largely the result of the heavily mass-mediated nature of the "movement." The major principles driving the Tea Party originate from the right-wing media machine and filter down to the general public and Tea Party supporters.

At the Tea Party events and meetings we attended, we heard the same shopworn conservative catchphrases over and over again. The regular recurrence of specific arguments could only have been the result of a centrally organized and directed campaign, coordinated by Republican Party operatives working through the mass media to manufacture a Tea Party "movement" from the top down. Obama and his moderate efforts at business-friendly health care reform were routinely condemned as reflecting a "socialist" agenda for the "big government takeover of health care." The president was consistently demonized for "reckless spending" and for "bankrupting our children's futures" with unsustainable debt. His labor support base was unfailingly linked to "union thugs" intimidating American workers and Tea Party organizers. Tea Partiers regularly spoke of the importance of supporting their sacred trio—free-market capitalism, the Founding Fathers, and the Constitution (understood in archaist and originalist terms). The claim that Obama's health care bill was "unconstitutional" was repeated again and again. The claims that the Tea Party was mainstream and nonpartisan permeated meetings, despite the fact that most Tea Party members who bothered to speak up indicated that they ritually watched the militantly Republican Fox News, loathed Democrats and Obama (routinely accused of destroying America), and desperately wanted to see the Republican Party return to power in the fall of 2010. Another common theme was the claim that the Association of Community Organizations for Reform Now (ACORN) was seeking to infiltrate the movement and destroy the election process—a charge promulgated by Beck and other right-wing media pundits for nearly a year.

The Chicago protest on April 1, 2010, left us with an even stronger impression that the Tea Party was not a social movement but rather a façade for the Republicans' 2010 electoral push. The Chicago rally was very different from the antiwar protests in Washington, DC, from 2002 through 2007, where a large number of local groups congregated in the capital, tabling and leafleting. The Chicago Tea Party rally had none of these. We were able to collect only one flyer, and the only table we saw sold Tea Party T-shirts.

The speakers' list for the Chicago rally cemented the Tea Party's status as a covert Republican operation. Five of the fifteen speakers were candidates running for Congress; all were Republicans. The speakers were careful *never* to reference these candidates as running for the Republican Party. Over and over again, they claimed that this "movement" had nothing to do with partisan politics and that it was a genuinely grassroots phenomenon advancing "leaderless resistance." The crowd booed as a number of speakers complained that some "conspiracy theorists" saw the Tea Party as "a front for corporate power and Republicans." Nevertheless, the speakers consistently echoed core super-Republican themes, celebrating free markets and complaining about the inherent corruption of big government. A leading Tea Party figure from the archreactionary Illinois Policy Institute promised a "revolution" but then fell back on shopworn Republican rhetoric demonizing congressional Democrats and Obama's supposed socialism and defending middle-class taxpayers' right to keep more of their own money. By the end of the rally, the message was clear: All one really needed to do was to vote the right way in November—for power-serving Republicans masquerading as unaffiliated popular rebels.

This Is All About Returning Republicans to Office

The consensus at Tea Party meetings we attended was that Tea Partiers simply needed to find a way to return Republicans to office in 2010, not to build a long-term movement. At one meeting, a Chicago Tea Party organizer spent nearly three hours reading a PowerPoint presentation instructing activists how to canvass local communities (with the help of databases provided by the Republican Party) to get Republicans into office in the midterm elections. Tea Party canvassers were told to "push Republican principles; just don't ever actually concede to anyone you talk to that this is all about returning Republicans to office." This sham has continued since the April 2010, rallies. Local Tea Partiers we met regularly claimed that their "movement" had nothing to do with the established parties, but they privately conceded that the real goal was to get the Republican Party back in power and then push it even further to the right.

Our investigation of the Tea Party raises interesting questions for those progressives who criticize "the left" for failing to be more like the right in our activist campaigns. It would be easy to say that progressives have been incredibly successful *if* their only goal had been to return Democrats to power in 2008, making use of massive subsidies from corporate America and benefiting from all the institutional resources of the Democratic Party in pursuing that endeavor. In contrast, the true progressive left seeks to fundamentally reshape society from the bottom up over and against the corporate elite and the reigning big money political parties and beyond periodic election spectacles. Election victories within the business-dominated, two-party political system are the main goal of the Tea Party, which has provided little indication of any sort of plan for changing society outside of returning Republicans to power in late 2010.

Asking whether the Tea Party and Republican Party will join forces (as many mass media reporters and pundits have done) is similar conceptually to wondering whether General Motors and the automotive industry are planning to join hands. The premise of the question is inappropriate because the two entities already overlap so fundamentally that the notion of them merging is absurd.

A Missing Story: Organizational Failure on the National Scale

Developments in the fall of 2010 suggested that the Tea Party was nothing like the powerful, autonomous, and popular "movement" that the dominant media described. The "movement's" meager level of participation made it impossible for the Tea Party to organize successfully on a national scale in the run-up to the national elections. This failure was evident in the collapse of the National Tea Party Convention in Las Vegas. Originally planned for July, the convention was postponed, allegedly due to the unforgiving summer heat. Organizers promised that the convention would take place in mid-October immediately before the midterm elections, although reporting in September concluded that the entire event had been canceled.[13]

This cancellation was not the first time that the Tea Party suffered from a lack of participation at the national level. The first national Tea Party rally in Nashville in February 2010 was poorly attended, with just 600 representatives from across the entire country. Exorbitant costs ($549 to attend, plus food, travel, and lodging) were a factor behind this weak showing, but the Tea Party–organized LibertyXPO event was also an abject failure, even though attendance was free. LibertyXPO, a national organization seeking to galvanize

Tea Partiers, saw the collapse of its planned September 10, 2010, convention in Washington. It was timed to coincide with the right-wing, heavily Tea Party–affiliated 9–12 Rally, in Washington, which also suffered from lackluster participation. LibertyXPO was plagued by incredibly low attendance, and the organization failed to raise even the $40,000 it originally sought to cover conference expenses, despite spending almost an entire year networking with local Tea Party leaders and groups.[14]

The 9–12 event drew just a few thousand protesters.[15] (In contrast, the left bemoaned the decline of the peace movement in late 2007 when tens of thousands of antiwar demonstrators rallied in Washington, DC.)[16] At a time when massive attendance and activism at national conventions and rallies seemed urgent, Tea Partiers declined to engage in the sort of action that would bring about a genuine mass movement.

The failure of the Tea Party to organize local chapters into a national force stands (we think) in telling contrast to the massive turnout for mass-mediated rallies and events that claimed the Tea Party banner even as they were clearly manufactured from the top down. A stark example is the August 2010 Glenn Beck–Sarah Palin "Restoring Honor" rally, which—much to the understandable irritation of black civil rights activists and officials (given the Tea Party racism documented here in Chapter 4)—coincided with the anniversary of Martin Luther King's "I Have a Dream" speech. Turnout at this Washington rally was reported as 100,000 or more—the only Tea Party rally in 2010 that even came close to the hundreds of thousands of antiwar protesters who regularly appeared in Washington between 2003 and 2005.[17] The impressive attendance at Beck's rally suggests that the Tea Party phenomenon has been largely a media creation. Tea Partiers could not be bothered to show up in large numbers for their own conventions and other national rallies when those gatherings failed to headline prominent national figures such as Beck and Palin. The Las Vegas Tea Party convention and the LibertyXPO rally required sustained and mass-based local activism (coordinated at the national level) to draw a mass turnout, whereas Beck and Palin merely needed to employ their megaphone at Fox News to attract demonstrators.

The national media have played an important role in exaggerating the power of the Tea Party in relation to other social movements but also in masking the Tea Party's failures when they raise serious questions about the group's power as an independent social movement. National reporting largely ignored the collapse of the LibertyXPO convention. A LexisNexis search finds that neither the *New York Times* nor the *Washington Post* ran a single story on the meeting's failure in September 2010, but directed strong attention to the more successful, if lightly attended Nashville conference earlier in the year. Additionally, the failure of the October 2010 Tea Party convention in Las Vegas was almost completely ignored. Reporters preferred the narrative of an ascendant and insurgent Tea Party—rising up from the grassroots against establishment politics. The breakdown of the Las Vegas convention was covered in just one story in the *New York Times* and one story in the *Washington Post* in the last two weeks of September, when the story was originally reported by alternative media.

Mediated Consciousness: Tea Partying with Fox News

If there was little sustained local or national organizing, then what drove the Tea Party "movement" in 2009 and 2010? Part of the answer can be found in the crucial importance of elite right-wing interest groups—including FreedomWorks, Americans for Prosperity, and America Deserves Better—in coordinating and funding the Tea Party phenomenon at the national level. Another and equally significant part can be found in the mass media, which have proven critical in disseminating to a giant public audience both the Tea Party myth (of a popular, independent, nonpartisan, grassroots, and antiestablishment sociopolitical "movement") and super-Republican Tea Party ideology. Tea Party messages are main staples of the right-wing communications empire, including reactionary talk radio and Fox News—the leading source of political information for Tea Party members.[18] The consumption of right-wing media by Tea Party supporters and other rightists helps create a chilling hall-of-mirrors effect whereby listeners/viewers/readers' preexisting right-wing views are perpetually reinforced and media consumers are prevented from considering evidence that challenges their worldviews.[19]

We analyzed Fox News coverage and commentary in depth in a critical sample period covering July 2009 through July 2010, in the run-up to the debate over health care and in the wake of Democrats' passage of new reforms. Tea Party themes were the norm in Fox's overage and editorializing. False right-wing deference to the Founding Fathers was ubiquitous. A close link between the nation's founders and the virtues of "free markets" was a regular Fox staple. Such references to the Constitution or the Founding Fathers were found in more than 620 news stories, or on average more than 50 per month. Stories discussing the Founding Fathers or the Constitution alongside positive discussion of capitalism or "free markets" appeared in more than 160 stories, an average of 14 per month.

Prominent Fox pundit Sean Hannity regularly attacked Obama for "shredding our Constitution" by passing health care reform.[20] Glenn Beck lamented that "the truth about the Founding Fathers" (as understood by reactionaries) "is not being taught in schools."[21] Tea Party candidates and leaders regularly appeared on Fox to bolster right-wing agendas and promote the Tea Party "insurgency." Joe Miller, the Alaskan Republican Tea Party candidate running for the Senate, was headlined on *Fox News Sunday*, informing viewers that the Constitution "does not provide for this all-encompassing power that we've seen exercised over the last several decades." Miller warned that "the entitlement mentality" represents a "disingenuous" understanding of the Constitution, providing citizens with the terrible (in Miller's view) impression that "it's the federal government's role to get in there and provide for the general welfare, to basically provide for the solvency particularly of states and other entities"[22]— a remarkable statement.

Fox's discussions were linked to the common Tea Party misperception that the Democrats' expansion of Medicaid was unconstitutional. Sarah Palin proclaimed on Hannity's program that Tea Partiers and other Americans needed to "take our country back" from the "socializing of America that Obama had promised." To "those who love America and who don't want to see that kind of transformation of America into some kind of socialized country," Palin said, "let's go on our high horse and do all we can to provide more education to voters so we can undo what happened to America last night" (when Obama signed his health care bill into law).[23] Glenn Beck's attack on the welfare state included an all-out assault on the New Deal, which he called unconstitutional.[24] The "socialism" frame dominated Fox programming in the period we examined. References to Obama alongside discussions of socialism, communism, and Marxism appeared in 580 Fox stories, or an average of 48 per month (1.5 stories every day).

Consistent with the Tea Party's strong theme that the "undeserving poor" should not get assistance from the government, Hannity maintained that "capitalism has lifted more people out of the grinding misery of poverty, has created more wealth, more success, more prosperity than any other economic system. And by the way, is the most fair and the most compassionate."[25] Bill O'Reilly blamed the welfare state for perpetuating poverty. He explicitly linked Obama (a supporter of the neoliberal assault on public family cash assistance known as "welfare reform") to the "big government" welfare state's alleged enablement and preservation of poverty.[26] Beck advanced a similar perspective, portraying the poor as complacent slackers coddled by Barack Obama's "socialist welfare state."[27]

Other indications of Tea Party ignorance (discussed in Chapter 5) include the false claim that tax cuts are the only legitimate way for policymakers to stimulate the economy, as well as the unwarranted dismissal of the notion that the stimulus eased the recession and created jobs, and the false assumption that Obama and the Democrats were almost exclusively responsible for creating the skyrocketing national deficit and debt. Such slanted discussion supporting tax cuts appeared in 318 Fox stories during our one-year sample period, 27 stories per month. Similarly, items either explicitly or implicitly associating tax cuts with stimulus appeared in 201 Fox stories, 17 per month. Beck deceptively portrayed the Democrats' proposal that the Bush tax cuts for the wealthy be allowed to expire as a socialistic "Obama hike"—"one of the largest tax hikes in American history."[28] He rejected out of hand any data suggesting that Keynesian stimulus spending promotes growth, proclaiming that "innovation, growth, lowering taxes, smaller government, cutting federal spending, that's what leads to recovery. History shows it to us over and over again."[29] Sean Hannity and his guests regularly framed tax cuts as the only effective way to encourage growth while faulting the stimulus as a complete failure.[30]

References to Obama appeared alongside discussion of the deficit and debt in nearly 1,100 Fox stories in our sample period analyzed, approximately 90 stories per month (3 a day). References to Bush appeared in just 320 reports discussing the deficit (27 a month). Obama appeared in more than three times as many news items addressing debt and deficits, despite the fact that the Bush administration was far more responsible for the expansion of deficit spending and the massive growth of the national debt (a reflection of its combination of giant tax cuts for the wealthy with massive unfunded spending on foreign wars) since 2001. The number of Fox stories linking Obama to the debt and deficit spiked to an all-time high in March 2010, precisely at the time when health care reform legislation was being passed and after the Congressional Budget Office (CBO) released a report demonstrating that the bill passed by Democrats would not raise the national debt and might even help reduce it.[31]

Fox viewers in the wake of the CBO report were exposed to a litany of attacks designed to discredit the report without citing any evidence that the bill that would cost more than the CBO estimated. Bill O'Reilly simply rejected the CBO figures by saying that *"Republicans don't believe those numbers,"* and he implied that the CBO was operating as a partisan organization by providing Democrats "with cover" to pass health care reform.[32] Hannity decried the "budgetary gimmicks and tricks" used by the CBO and Democrats, but he provided no hard evidence that costs would be larger than the estimates suggested, relying instead on speculation to discredit health care reform.[33] Beck criticized Congress for having "jam[med] health care through," deceptively citing the CBO as validating his attacks on health care reform as fiscally unsustainable.[34]

False Populism from the Top Down

When viewed clearly, the Tea Party begins to look less like any kind of genuine social movement and more like a covert, heavily mass-mediated campaign to protect privilege and return Republicans to congressional power in the midterm elections. It was and is not a not a social movement at all; rather, it is an elitist interest group that amounts largely to a rebranding effort for the Republican Party. This rebranding campaign amounts to an implicit concession from the party that it lacks credibility with most of the electorate—a logical outcome of the fact that its evermore right-wing agenda is opposed by most Americans. Public distrust of both parties has recently approached an all-time high, and the Republicans' approval rating has been as dismal as that of the Democrats.

The Tea Party's claim to be a mass, independent, and popular social and political movement is offensive to those of us who believe and have participated in such movements. The Tea Partiers' anti-government rhetoric amounts largely to a selfish call for a government that sustains their own class and race privileges while slashing services and programs for the disproportionately nonwhite lower and working classes. This does not mean that all those who sympathize with the Tea Party's policy positions are affluent elitists, or that their grievances regarding a stagnating economy and the growing suffering of many Americans are without merit. Gallup polling in the spring of 2010 indicated that those who generically considered themselves Tea Party supporters were not much more affluent than the American public in general.[35] Many comparatively advantaged Tea Partiers express some legitimate grievances: They are understandably angry over having to work harder and longer while accumulating greater personal debt as they watch the national economy collapse and then stagnate around them.

But rage at the opulent few has not been terribly evident in the Tea Party "movement," which favors the deregulation of big business, opposes Wall Street regulation, and calls for the continuation of George W. Bush's plutocratic tax cuts. Tea Partiers' anger is directed more at those beneath them in the nation's steep and interrelated hierarchies of class and race. Reflecting a partisan, "super-Republican" essence, moreover, the Tea Partiers have directed their ire only at Democrats, failing to acknowledge the ferocious role of the Republicans, Wall Street, and corporate America in attacking middle- and working-class living standards over the last four decades. Such selective anger suggests that the majority of Tea Partiers share little real understanding of the larger macroeconomic and political problems—and the related top-down class warfare waged on working Americans by economic elites—that have plagued the United States in the neoliberal era. Without such an understanding, Tea Partiers' legitimate rage over national economic decline will never move beyond a vague, misinformed anger over fictitious "socialist" takeovers and Democratic "treachery" in "borrowing away" future prosperity through "reckless spending" and "unsustainable" borrowing. This worldview can only help return to power Republicans, whose regressive and deregulatory policies are guaranteed to exacerbate the economic crisis the Tea Party claims to oppose. Far from representing a legitimate popular movement, the Tea Party is more accurately described as a top-down conglomeration of elite interest groups led by national and local political officials and financed by corporate America. It is what left journalist Jeremy Scahill calls a classic "Astroturf movement"—a "fake grassroots movement" that is "run by the lobby of big corporations [which is] taking advantage of the stupidity of a lot of people who regularly vote against their own self interest on economic policy."[36] Scahill's reference to the stupidity of the "movement" is apt. The Tea Party's rank-and-file members strongly support Medicare and Social Security (for good, self-interested reasons), while the "movement's" leaders, such as Dick Armey, lead the Republican campaign to gut both programs in the name of self-reliance, freedom, and free-market capitalism.[37]

The militantly proestablishment Tea Party has received tremendous "movement"-inflating media attention because it purports to be a mass movement outside of and against establishment politics. The attention is inauthentic, a reflection of the corporate media's commitment to and enmeshment in the existing system. The Tea Party phenomenon has received massive and largely favorable and misleading coverage as a popular and antiestablishment force precisely because its politics, structures, and worldview are favorable to the rule of the many by the few and situated *within* the narrow, business-friendly, bipartisan spectrum of American establishment opinion (albeit on the most extreme rightward side of that spectrum). Political communication scholars have long documented a trend in American media reporting whereby groups and individuals who exist outside the constricted bipartisan sphere of acceptable debate are systematically ignored while those within this sphere receive significant attention.[38] The right-wing Tea Party is a perfect example of what the American ruling class considers to be a "worthy" popular protest "movement"—meaning no popular protest movement at all.

7

Elections 2010

The Democrats' Midterm Disaster, the Tea Party, and the Challenge to Progressives

The Right-Wing Comeback

It had been fairly clear for some time—certainly since Massachusetts Republican Scott Brown's Tea Party–assisted election to the U.S. Senate in January of 2010—that the Democrats would take a serious beating in the November 2010 midterm elections. For many months, leading political opinion surveys showed the Republicans tied with and leading the Democrats in likely voter preferences for congressional races. Quite ominously for Democrats, President Barack Obama had by the time of the elections become more unpopular than popular. In the late summer, pollsters found that 50 percent of Americans disapproved of his performance, compared to 45 percent who approved. A considerably larger percentage disapproved of the Democratic Party and the Democratic-majority U.S. Congress.[1]

To be sure, the Republican Party was actually less popular. But this did not seem to matter all that much given other factors and the limited choices afforded to voters under the American one-and-a-half-party system. For months, opinion pollsters, political commentators, and activists had reported a large "enthusiasm gap" between voters who planned to choose a Republican and those who planned to vote Democratic. That gap translated into a significantly larger mobilization and turnout of right-wing Republican voters, as exit polling demonstrated.[2] The nation's rightmost voters were "fired up, ready to go" (to use Obama's 2007–2008 campaign slogan, appropriated from the 1960s civil rights movement). The Democratic "base" was comparatively demoralized and indifferent, leading Obama, Vice President Joe Biden, and other leading Democrats in September and October to express frustration with progressive and other Democrats for failing to understand the stakes in the upcoming elections. It would be "inexcusable" for Democratic voters to sit the midterms out, Obama told *Rolling Stone* magazine and voters in a number of preelection rallies. "Don't compare [us] to the Almighty," Biden lectured disgruntled Democrats; "compare [us] to the alternative"—described by him as "the Republican Tea Party."[3] The harangues and pleas to the Democratic "base" were accompanied by revival of recently dormant movement rhetoric ("change only happens from the bottom up") and claims that Obama's sincere desire for progressive change had been blocked by special interests.

It didn't work. At the writing of this chapter a few days after the election, the Republican Party had picked up a remarkable sixty seats in the U.S. House of Representatives, well exceeding its gains in the so-called Republican Revolution of 1994. The outcome represented the largest loss in House seats for a party in more than sixty years. In addition, the Republicans gained six seats in the U.S. Senate. Significantly, two-thirds of the victorious House Republicans and five of the six new Republican senators were what the *New York Times* considered to be "Tea Party candidates."* This super-Republican and significantly Tea Party–fueled right revival crashed House Democrats from the Northeast to the South and across the Midwest. "Even though it was predicted," noted *New York Times* columnist Maureen Dowd, "it was still a shock to see voters humiliate the spellbinding young president, who'd had such a Kennedy-like beginning" and

---

*The *Times* definition of "Tea Party candidates": "those who had entered politics through the movement, or are candidates receiving significant support from local Tea Party groups and who share the ideology of the movement. Many have been endorsed by national groups like FreedomWorks or the Tea Party Express, but those endorsements alone were not enough to put them on the list." New York Times Interactive, "Where the Tea Party Candidates Are Running," October 14, 2010, at www.nytimes .com/interactive/2010/10/15/us/politics/tea-party-graphic.html.

who the Republicans had succeeded in painting as "not American enough, not quite 'normal,' too radical, too Great Society. . . . No one gets to take America away from Americans," Dowd mused sarcastically, "not even the American president."[4] Among those ousted were a significant number of long-term Democratic officeholders, including Missouri representative Ike Skelton (chairman of the House Armed Services Committee) and three-term Wisconsin senator Russ Feingold. "We've come to take our country back," said leading Tea Party candidate Rand Paul—a politician who early in his campaign defended private business owners' right to practice the sort of racial segregation and discrimination outlawed by the landmark 1964 Civil Rights Act—in his celebration speech after being elected to the U.S. Senate by Kentucky voters.[5]

It was an epic defeat for the party of mainstream liberalism. Just two years following Obama's historic victory on behalf of hope and change, after the Republican right seemed to have completely disgraced itself during the Bush-Cheney era, the highly unpopular GOP had somehow staged a major comeback. A considerable portion of the electorate *seemed* to have embraced dubious right-wing claims that slashing the government deficit was more important than government programs for jobs and the unemployed; that Obama (perhaps not a U.S. citizen) was a radical-leftist advocate of socialism and big government and an enemy of freedom and the unfettered capitalism that alone could produce growth; that immigrants, unions, lazy minorities, and public-sector workers were to blame for the ongoing economic crisis.

So what if the biggest economic crisis since the Great Depression had "punctured all the neoliberal and conservative myths about the free market,"[6] and if most Americans disagreed with the radical antiworker and antipoor agenda and beliefs of the hard right? The Republicans were back, promising to deepen policies that would only make the crisis worse. The significant number of Tea Party candidates who won office promised to drive the Republicans further to the right, making them even more intransigent in Congress, consistent with the long-term rightward and authoritarian drift of the GOP.

Business Week noted an interesting victor the day after the election: elite corporations. "The Republican victory in the House," *Business Week* added, "helps companies from Goldman Sachs Group

Inc. to health insurer Wellpoint Inc. gain support in efforts to undermine what they consider Obama's antibusiness policies on taxes, health care and financial regulation. . . . Exporters such as Caterpillar Inc. and United Parcel Service Inc. say a Republican-controlled House would be more likely to work with Obama to approve pending free-trade agreements with South Korea, Colombia and Panama."[7] The *New York Times* business section reported that the midterm elections promised to leave "the most powerful executives in the banking industry [in] an even stronger position, blunting the most serious overhaul of financial regulation since the Great Depression."[8] As *New York Times* financial writer Nelson Schwartz explained, "The widely expected Republican takeover of the House of Representatives and possibly the Senate would be warmly welcomed by the banks, who want a break from the regulatory push of the last two years. Divided government makes it harder to pass new legislation and brings with it other benefits for the banks, like reducing the chances of an increase in corporate taxes." It was no wonder that 71 percent of the financial industry's campaign contributions went to Republicans in September of 2010.[9]

A Predictable Voter Statement on the Bad Economy

How did this happen? The first key to the outcome is the ongoing epic recession, characterized by a functional unemployment rate of 16 percent and a poverty rate projected to reach the same percentage in the near future.[10] No incumbent party sitting on such astonishing economic failure and related social misery amid the worst recession since the Great Depression could expect anything other than a thrashing at the midterm polls. A significant section of the Republican vote was certainly composed of "conservative diehards who hated Obama and the Democrats from the start," but the terrible economy cost the Democrats a vast swath of "swing voters"—those who go back and forth between the two dominant business parties.[11]

The Republicans' extraordinary gains did not reflect some massive swing in public opinion away from liberalism (supposedly represented by the Democrats) and toward free-market politics (purportedly embodied by the Republicans). Scholarly studies have long shown that public opinion is nowhere near as volatile as such a narrative suggests. Public policy preferences remain remarkably stable over time and change only in slow, incremental ways for most policy questions surveyed.[12] National voting studies strongly indicated that the 2010 election would turn heavily toward the Republican Party, as one of us predicted in the spring of 2009.[13] Studies of congressional and midterm voting have long shown that the fate of incumbents is heavily tied to two key factors: the popularity of the sitting president and the state of the economy.[14] When presidential popularity is falling (as it always does following the president's initial honeymoon period), and when the economy is in poor shape, the public punishes the party of the chief executive. It does not matter which party is in power; the Republicans were punished in 2008.

This simple and predictable pattern was born out in the midterm elections. ABC News exit polling found that the economy remained the most important issue for 62 percent of midterm voters. The supposed big government and socialist takeover of America by the Democrats—the Tea Party's leading (if fake) issue—was mentioned as their most important issue by just 19 percent of voters.[15] However, approximately 90 percent of voters in exit polling from the Associated Press (AP) saw the state of the economy as bad and expressed worry over the coming year, while nearly 40 percent explained that "their personal finances had grown worse under President Barack Obama. All of those people leaned strongly Republican."[16] The AP exit poll found that 54 percent of voters gave Obama a negative approval rating, with "similar numbers [worrying that] his policies will harm the country." Independents—a majority of whom supported Obama in 2008—now disapproved of Obama's job performance by a ratio of three to two.[17]

Voting clearly reflected the negative economic conditions across the country, as seen at the state level. The federal Bureau of Economic Analysis—a widely respected government authority on measuring the health of the economy—does not collect economic data at the congressional-district level, but it does provide state-level data, allowing for an interesting comparison of Democratic and Republican electoral performance in the Senate. Our analysis of the state-level numbers finds that states that saw the strongest declines and the weakest recoveries in personal finance between 2008 and 2010 were consistently more likely to turn out in favor of the Republican Party. Democrats were punished the most in states where personal income decline was strongest, faring best in states where rebounds in personal income were the strongest.[18] Such was the straightforward calculus that motivated many voters in the 2010 midterms. According to Associated Press reporter Al Fram the day after, "The basic math for Tuesday's Republican election triumph was simple: Most people think the economy is in awful shape, and those feeling that way voted solidly for the GOP."[19]

The Tea Partiers Who Won

Consistent with the notion that standard material and institutional factors, *not* some big rightward shift in public opinion, produced the 2010 outcomes, it was no particular guarantee of success for a candidate to be linked to the Tea Party. In and of itself, being a "Tea Party candidate" did *not* translate into an electoral advantage in the 2010 midterms. Tea Party challengers were statistically no more likely to win races in the election than non–Tea Party candidates.[20] Far more important in determining election outcomes was the disastrous economy followed by the timeworn electoral advantages conferred by incumbency and campaign contributions. Incumbents have long been far more likely to win elections than challengers, and this election was no different. The Democratic incumbent reelection ratio stood at approximately 3.5 to 1 and the Republican incumbent ratio at an astounding 75 to 1. Incumbents have long been better able to raise large campaign finance war chests, thanks to their standing in Congress and their greater name recognition among activists, lobbyists, and the public. The 2010 election was no different, with incumbents raising 2.25 times more than challengers in the House and 2.6 times more in the Senate.[21]

There is little truth in right-wing politicos and pundits' depiction of Tea Party victories as a grassroots triumph of underdogs. Differential campaign contributions appear to have played the major role in distinguishing between the majority of Tea Party challengers (61.4 percent) who lost their respective races and the minority (32 percent) who won.[22] Higher levels of campaign contributions played a major role in determining the strength of individual Tea Party candidates, as measured in local polls evaluating their prospects for victories in House races.[23] Lopsided campaign contributions provided privileged Tea Partiers not only with an electoral edge but also with consistent victories over less-well-funded Tea Partiers and other congressional candidates. The average amount raised by Republican candidates running in the House of Representatives in 2010 was $375,163. Of those Tea Party House candidates who raised more than the Republican average, a majority (approximately 55 percent) won their respective races (45 percent lost).[24] Money by itself did not guarantee victory for Tea Party challengers, but it greatly helped. Of those who raised less than the Republican average, not a single Tea Party candidate won a race. Those challengers who raised large amounts of campaign cash had a fighting chance to win; those who raised little to no money had no chance.

The campaign finance numbers contradict right-wing rhetoric about the Tea Party's "little guy" identity. Successful Tea Partiers look like incumbents in terms of financial advantage. The average Tea Partier raised more than the average Democrat or Republican running in the House and Senate, and the average competitive Tea Partier raised contributions that rivaled or were greater than those of the average Democratic and Republican incumbents running in the House and Senate (see Table 7.1). In the midterm elections, campaign contributions were a far bigger determinant of electability than a candidate's status as a right-wing Tea Partier.[25]

"They Just Don't Get It": The Democrats' Demobilization of Their Base

Another part of the explanation for the Republican/Tea Party victory lay in Obama and the Democrats' demoralization and demobilization of the Democrats' base over the first two years of Obama's

TABLE 7.1

Tea Party Campaign Fundraising in Comparison to Other Congressional Candidates		
Candidate Type	*House*	*Senate*
Average Republican	$451,331	$2,277,567
Average Democrat	$757,030	$2,793,116
Average Tea Party Republican	$805,583	$7,331,806
Average Republican incumbent	$1,319,802	$7,801,507
Average Democratic incumbent	$1,488,297	$10,660,022
Average competitive Tea Partier	$1,432,266	$7,331,806

SOURCE: Center for Responsive Politics/Opensecrets.org.

presidency. Progressive author and blogger Les Leopold put it well on the left-liberal Web site FireDogLake:

> It's open season on Obama, whom so many hoped would lead us out of the neoliberal wilderness. He was once a community organizer and ought to know how working people have suffered through a generation of tax breaks for the rich, Wall Street deregulation and unfair competition. When the economy crashed, he was in perfect position to limit the unjustified pay levels on Wall Street. . . . Instead we got a multi-trillion dollar bailout for Wall Street, no health care reform, no serious financial reforms whatsoever, record unemployment, and political gridlock that will be with us for years to come.[26]

Liberals and progressives had little basis for thinking that Obama would guide them out of the wilderness.[27] As one of us (Street) demonstrated in great detail in late 2007 and early 2008, U.S. senator and presidential candidate Obama was what left political commentator Lance Selfa called "more of a pro-business, 'centrist' politician than the radical conjured up in the fantasies of the likes of Glenn Beck."[28] Nevertheless, by the fall of 2010, a large number of Democrats and in-dependent swing voters surely agreed with Leopold that "Obama hasn't produced the reforms he promised, while embracing policies like Bush's 'war on terror,' and the Afghanistan war that they abhor."[29] For a large number of core Democratic supporters, mainstream Democratic liberalism had failed to live up its idealistic campaign rhetoric—a problem that the Obama political team tried to acknowledge in personalized October e-mail messages that essentially apologized for disappointing progressives while trying to resurrect the party and politician's hopeful and activist rhetoric of 2007–2008.* Right-wing

---

*One of us (Street) received the following e-mail from info@barackobama.com on October 8, 2010: "Paul—I come into this election with clear eyes. I am proud of all we have achieved together, but I am mindful of all that remains to be done. I know some out there are frustrated by the pace of our progress. I want you to know I'm frustrated, too. But with so much riding on the outcome of this election, I need everyone to get in this game. Neither one of us is here because we thought it would be easy. Making change is hard. It's what we've said from the beginning. And we've got the lumps to show for it. The fight this fall is as critical as any this movement has taken on together. And if we are serious about change, we need to fight as hard as we ever have. The very special interests who have stood in the way of change at every turn want to put their conservative allies in control of Congress. And they're doing it with the help of billionaires and corporate special interests underwriting shadowy campaign ads. If they succeed, they will not stop at making our work more difficult—they will do their best to undo what you and I fought so hard to achieve. There is no better time for you to start fighting back—a fellow grass-roots supporter has promised to match, dollar for dollar, whatever you can chip in today. I know that sometimes it feels like we've come a long way from the hope and excitement of the inauguration, with its 'Hope' posters and historic crowds on the National Mall. I will never forget it. But it was never why we picked up this fight. I didn't run for president because I wanted to do what would make me popular. And you didn't help elect me so I could read the polls and calculate how to keep myself in office. You and I are in this because we believe in a simple idea—that each and every one of us, working together, has the power to move this country forward. We believed that this was the moment to solve the challenges that the country had ignored for far too long. That change happens only from the bottom up. That change happens only because of you. So I need you to fight for it over the next 26 days. I need your time. I need your commitment. And I need your help to get your friends and neighbors involved. Please donate $3—and renew your commitment today: https://donate.barackobama.com/OctoberMatch. If we meet this test—if you, like me, believe that change is not a spectator sport—we will not just win this election. In the years that come, we can realize the change we are seeking—and reclaim the American dream for this generation."

and "mainstream" media contributed mightily to the perception of disappointment, but Obama and the Democrats would have been well advised to look at themselves to understand the disgruntlement of the Democratic "base." For they have acted all too perfectly in accord with former Richard Nixon strategist Kevin Phillips's onetime description of the Democratic Party as "history's second most enthusiastic capitalist party."[30] As Selfa explained in October 2010:

> The Democrats had large majorities in both houses of Congress, including, for a period of time, a 60-vote majority in the Senate. They had the potential to reset mainstream politics for a generation. Yet, with the Obama administration in the lead, they mainly assumed the role as savior of the corporate system that was teetering on the edge of the economic abyss in late 2008 and early 2009.
>
> Since then, the Obama administration has bent over backwards to placate business and its right-wing critics while ladling out thin gruel to its most fervent supporters. . . . The stimulus plan was too small to lift the economy out of its deep hole. And the administration trimmed it further in a largely futile attempt to win "bipartisan" support. . . . Unemployment continued to rise under Obama, feeding the public perception that "government," and "government spending," was ineffectual. If the crisis of 2008 had discredited neoliberal nostrums, the continued crisis of 2009 and 2010 appeared to discredit liberal, "big government" solutions.
>
> Today, the administration proclaims the necessity of "deficit reduction," "entitlement reform" (aka, cutting Medicare and Social Security), and austerity. This largely reflects the administration's attempt to carry out big business's agenda.[31]

One did not have to be a radical to be bothered by Obama's centrist, business-friendly betrayal of the Democratic Party's working-class and poor constituencies. *New York Times* columnist Bob Herbert—a long-standing Obama supporter—expressed his disgust with the Democrats after Scott Brown's Tea Party–assisted victory in an op-ed titled "They [the Democrats] Still Don't Get It." "The door is being slammed on the American dream and the politicians, including the president and his Democratic allies on Capitol Hill," Herbert wrote, "seem not just helpless to deal with the crisis, but completely out of touch with the hardships that have fallen on so many." Herbert wondered if "there is anything" that could ever again "wake [the Democrats] up to their obligation to extend a powerful hand to ordinary Americans and help them take the government . . . back from the big banks, the giant corporations and the myriad other predatory interests that put the value of a dollar high above the value of human beings."[32] The left-liberal political scientist Sheldon Wolin foretold this sorry Democratic performance in his chilling 2008 book, *Democracy Incorporated:*

> The timidity of a Democratic Party mesmerized by centrist precepts points to the crucial fact that, for the poor, minorities, the working-class, anticorporatists, pro-environmentalists, and anti-imperialists, there is no opposition party working actively on their behalf. And this despite the fact that these elements are recognized as the loyal base of the party. By ignoring dissent and assuming the dissenters have no alternative, the party serves an important, if ironical, stabilizing function and in effect marginalizes any possible threat to the corporate allies of the Republican. Unlike the Democrats, however, the Republicans, with their combination of reactionary and innovative elements, are a cohesive, if not a coherent, opposition force.[33]

Part of the problem for the Democrats was the outsized influence of dedicated, high-turnout segments of the electorate (Tea Party Republicans are a classic example) in midterm elections, when overall turnout is generally lower than in the quadrennial contests that include presidential candidates. In presidential elections, progressive commentator Robin Hahnel notes, young, poor, minority and independent voters are more likely to turn out. "But not so in midterm elections, which are dominated by the party bases. For this reason," Hahnel concludes, "a newly elected President needs to prioritize programs that please his party base, because only by energizing one's base can one expect to do well in midterm elections."[34]

Clearly, Obama and the Democrats failed miserably to energize their base. The Pew Research Center reported in mid-October 2010 that the Democrats were considerably behind the Republicans in terms of stirring voter engagement. The Democrats' base was becoming increasingly disengaged due to disappointment with the Democratic Party.[35] As the *Washington Post* reported in early October, 43 percent of Democrats described themselves as "very interested" in the elections, as compared to 57 percent of Republicans and 74 percent of Tea Party supporters.[36]

Consistent with these findings, American University's Center for the Study of the American Electorate (CSAE) found that the average vote in statewide primaries in 2010 was the lowest ever recorded for Democrats during midterm election cycles—a telling indication of what CSAE director Curtis Gans called "a distinct lack of enthusiasm among the Democratic rank and file." This permitted the Republican average statewide primary turnout to exceed Democratic primary turnout for the first time since 1930. Republican primary turnout, as a percent of the eligible electorate, was the highest recorded in four decades, surpassing the Democrats by more than 4 million votes.[37]

In the general midterm contest, the Democrats suffered from significant declines in voter participation on the part of segments of the electorate that had played key roles in their triumphs in the 2006 (congressional) and 2008 (congressional and presidential) election cycles. Union households (predominantly Democratic) made up 23 percent of the active electorate in 2006; in 2010 they were 17 percent. Their support for Democratic House candidates dropped from 64 percent in 2006 to 60 percent in 2010. Young people (eighteen to twenty-nine years olds) were 18 percent of voters in 2008, when two-thirds of them voted for Obama; in 2010 they made up just 11 percent of the electorate, and they voted 56 percent for Democratic candidates. Black voters (90 percent Democratic in the 2010 elections) fell from 13 to 10 percent of the voters between 2008 and 2010. By contrast, voters who identified themselves as "conservative" increased their share of the active electorate from 32 to 41 percent between 2006 and 2010. "Conservatives" were more enthusiastic about GOP House candidates last fall than in 2006, when 74 percent of self-identified conservatives supported Republicans. Last November, 84 percent did.[38]

The Democrats' demoralization and the stand-down of their own "base" were disastrous in light of broader developments in the electorate. As *Time* magazine reported, "Swing voters who flocked to Barack Obama two years ago turned against his agenda, electing a tidal wave of new Republican members of Congress."[39] Swing voting independents—including women, Independents, working-class whites, and white Catholics (among other groups)—leaned Republican in very significant ways.[40] Democrats also suffered from the mobilization of traditionally privileged demographic groups. Reporting in the run-up to the midterms suggested that whites, men, Independents, those sixty-five years and older, and white Catholics were becoming increasingly likely to vote Republican.[41]

What Exists of a Popular Left

The problem on the left has not just been the Democrats. The nation's relatively moribund liberal activist and policy infrastructure has responded to the social and economic crisis and the corporate and imperial direction of policy under nominal Democratic rule with remarkably little serious criticism and protest. As John Judis noted in the *New Republic* even before Obama's administration was more than one month old, "There is not a popular left movement that is agitating for [Obama] to go well beyond where he would even ideally like to go. . . . *Instead, what exists of a popular left is either incapable of action or in Obama's pocket*" (emphasis added). By Judis's analysis, the U.S. labor movement and groups like Moveon.Org were repeating the same "mistake that political groups often make: subordinating their concern about issues to their support for the [Democratic] party and its leading politicians."[42]

Little occurred in the first two years of Obama's presidency to seriously undermine the wisdom of Judis's judgment. The nation's liberal and progressive political and activist network has been unable and/or perhaps unwilling to channel legitimate popular and populist anger, while the political class acted in accord with the standard elite principle: government subsidy and protection for the rich and market discipline for the poor and working classes. The "progressive movement" has been missing in action, at once bedazzled and disciplined by the nation's first black president, whose former chief of staff, Rahm Emanuel, threatened egregious retaliation against those liberal Democrats and activists who dared to substantively challenge the corporate and militaristic direction of policy.[43] As progressive author and journalist David Sirota noted after White House Press Secretary Robert Gibbs launched a tirade against "the professional left" in the summer of 2010, "Much of the 'American Left' is organized around the Democratic Party and specifically around Obama. The professional Left," Sirota noted, "are all the major, well-funded liberal interest groups (what Jane Hamsher sometimes refers to as 'the veal pen') and [those groups]have repeatedly shown themselves to be more loyal to the Democratic Party and Obama than their alleged policy/ideological missions. . . . That kind of Left," Sirota added, "is not built like successful social movements of the past." It "doesn't have the structure, independence or stomach for oppositional politics."[44]

The left, such as it is, has been all too ready to surrender the mantle of populist rage to the dodgy, regressive, and authoritarian right represented by the Tea Party—the latest incarnation of the right-wing version of the paranoid style in American politics and the most powerful such embodiment of that version in more than half a century. As *Progressive* magazine editor Matthew Rothschild wrote prior to the elections:

> The very character of our country is at stake. . . . With economic pain at the highest level ever seen by most Americans, and with minorities especially hard hit, we're seeing a revolt not by people of color, not the unemployed, nor the foreclosed upon. *Instead, we're seeing a revolt by the white middle class.* It's a revolt against the very notion of a positive role for government in helping people. It's a revolt against Latin American immigrants. It's a revolt against Muslim Americans. And it's a revolt against our black president.[45] (emphasis added)

There's a telling contrast here with Europe. As millions of European citizens flooded the streets in major social movements and marches to resist public budget, wage, and pension cuts imposed by the global economic crisis last September and October, American progressives could muster only a modest turnout for the "One Nation" rally in Washington. This gathering functioned primarily as a preelection get-out-the-vote rally for the Democrats and not as a significant statement against the bipartisan elite.[46]

How Tea Party
Candidates Performed

Nevertheless, we should not discount the role played by the Tea Party phenomenon in creating the Republican midterm victory. Our findings that being a Tea Party candidate did not make a candidate statistically more likely to win in the midterms should *not* be taken as evidence that the Tea Party was unimportant. The Tea Party's contribution to the election outcome was significant on a number of levels, reaching well beyond the question of how specifically designated Tea Party candidates fared. Following the lead of the *New York Times*, MSNBC downplayed those candidates' performance the day after the election:

> For all the talk of the Tea Party's strength—and there will certainly be a significant number of their candidates in Congress—just 32 percent of all Tea Party candidates who ran for Congress won and 61.4 percent lost this election. A few races remain too close to call.
>
> In the Senate, 10 candidates backed by the Tea Party ran and at least five were successful (Race in Alaska has not yet been called).
>
> In the House, 130 Tea Party-backed candidates ran, and just 40 so far have won.[47]

MSNBC's numbers, however, were misleading in two key ways. First, MSNBC unnecessarily diminished the size of the Tea Party victory by ignoring Tea Party incumbents. The MSNBC/*New York Times* count deleted the 52 Tea Party candidates who were reportedly already congressional officeholders prior to the midterm elections—the members who were part of the existing, in-power Tea Party Caucus.[48] Including these incumbents (47 of whom ran for reelection and won) changes the composition of the House from 39 Tea Party winners among 129 Tea Party candidates (a winning percentage of less than 30 percent) to 86 victors (a winning percentage of 49 percent), equivalent to a very significant one-fifth of the U.S. House. MSNBC's deletion of the significant number of Tea Party candidates who were already in the House is a small but revealing indication of the mass media's habit of ignoring the strong establishment roots of the Tea

Party and falsely portraying it as an "outsider," "independent" and "insurgent" force.

Second, the MSNBC/*New York Times* count *overestimated* the Tea Party's failure by including hopeless candidates alongside those who had a real chance of winning. Many of those reported as Tea Party candidates merely ran protest campaigns in solidly Democratic districts. They had little-to-no shot at success and garnered little in the way of the campaign finance and other resources required to mount viable campaigns. These candidates should have been taken no more seriously than other Independents, third partiers, or Democrats and Republicans who had no chance of taking down incumbents.

The Broader Pro-Republican
Impact of the Tea Party

Beyond the question of exactly how many Tea Party candidates won their races, the Tea Party had a broader and significant across-the-board impact reaching into the more than 300 House and 30 Senate races where no such candidates competed. The Tea Party was highly relevant in light of its broader capacity to speak to the general public. This power should be seen as heavily mass mediated in light of our failure to uncover real activism at the local level in Tea Party chapters (as described in Chapter 6), but it is important nonetheless at a time when most Americans interact with political forces and phenomenon through the media rather than in person.

At the most general level, being a Tea Party supporter played a major role in galvanizing "conservatives" to vote in increased numbers during the 2010 midterms. As CNN political analyst David Gergen explained in anticipation of the election results, "If it were not for the Tea Party, the Republican margin in the House of Representatives would not be as high as it's going to be." In reporting Gergen's comment, CNN also highlighted the fact that a sizable 23 percent of voters said that "one reason for their vote was to send a message in favor of the Tea Party."[49] In the run-up to the election, 19 percent of Independents said that candidates being of the Tea Party would influence their vote.[50] Preelection polling by the *New York Times* found that 23 percent of regular voters viewed the Tea Party favorably.[51] Pew Research Center polling found that Tea Party supporters were nearly 10 percentage points more likely to be registered to vote than non–Tea Party supporters, while Gallup discovered that 71 percent of Tea Party supporters were "more enthusiastic" about voting, compared to 51 percent of all Americans who felt similarly.[52] Associated Press exit polling found that preelection statistics were reinforced in actual turnouts, with Tea Party supporters accounting for about 4 in 10 voters overall.[53]

Even when Tea Party candidates were not running in individual House and Senate races, the Tea Party phenomenon encouraged increased support for Republicans. Gallup found that Tea Party supporters were overwhelmingly more likely to be Republican, with 17 percent of the group being moderate or liberal Republicans, 62 percent being conservative Republicans, and a total of 79 percent being Republican in general.[54] Both the Gallup Poll and a Bloomberg poll in the run-up to the midterm found that four of five Tea Party supporters planned to vote Republican, regardless of whether there was a Tea Party candidate or not in their respective races.[55] Exit polls showed that *a remarkable two in every three Republican voters* "expressed support for the Tea Party." The Tea Party phenomenon clearly provided a voter turnout boon for the GOP. As Kate Zernike noted on the front page of the *New York Times* the day after the election, the Tea Party's "energy propel[led] the Republican sweep in the House and capture[d] the mood of a significant chunk of the electorate."[56]

At the same time, by seeming to transform, energize, and rebrand the highly unpopular Republican Party, the Tea Party phenomenon made it more difficult for Obama and the Democrats to claim that a vote for the Republican Party amounted to an embrace of "the past." As former Bill Clinton adviser William Galston noted prior to the election, "The Administration's ability to make that argument has been weakened by the very vociferous changes that have happened in the Republican Party."[57]

There was a deeper and different but related way in which the Tea Party—understood largely as a mass-mediated phenomenon—could be credited for the midterm outcomes. Beginning in February 2009, the largely corporate-crafted Tea Party "rebellion" provided the corporate media with a steady flow of images and stories to help advance the false narrative that the moderate, and business-friendly Obama administration was lurching off center and to the big government, deficit-fueling left in accord with its supposedly progressive ideological inclinations.[58]* The Tea Party became a critical part of this standard media and right-wing trope against Democratic presidents and legislators,[59] helping to energize right-wing voters and drive Independent and other voters into opposition to Obama and the Democrats.

Also significant, the media's recurrent and often favorable treatment of the supposedly great and popular grassroots Tea Party "movement" and the media's self-fulfilling inflation of the phenomenon helped the Tea Party become something of what Zernike called "a blank screen on which they have projected all kinds of hopes and frustrations—not always compatible or realistic."[60] The media-generated "blank screen" and related (false) novelty dividend—with vague and ephemeral branding trumping policy substance—are, it is worth noting, something that the Tea Party's bête noire Barack Obama benefited from to no small degree from late 2006 (some might even say from late July of 2004) through the presidential election of 2008.[61]

We noted earlier in this study that many Americans voicing support for the Tea Party have little or no understanding of its actual, hard-right ideological agenda. Many of those expressing sympathy and approval for the Tea Party reject its call for tearing down "big government" and favor federal job creation over the Tea Party's declared goal of deficit slashing. Contrary to the dominant media narrative suggesting that the Tea Party reflects some sort of popular and mainstream reaction against the supposed leftward shift of policy under Obama, the majority of Americans remain opposed to the right Republican political-economic agenda, opposing regressive right-wing tax proposals and supporting progressive policies such

---

*As shown in the postscript, this media narrative has, if anything, become more pronounced and strident in the corporate mass media's treatment of the midterm elections.

as government spending on public works.[62] The corporate media's role in overcoming the apparent contradictions here has been critical. The nation's leading news outlets have failed to provide an accurate picture of the Tea Party's reactionary and elite-directed, top-down, manipulative, and partisan ("super-Republican") essence and of the centrist, business-, and empire-friendly nature of the Obama administration.

The fact that the Tea Party made a significant contribution to policy-relevant outcomes in the midterm elections might seem paradoxical. The Tea Party we uncovered in our research is relatively small, privileged, far more right wing than the broad U.S. citizenry, significantly paranoid, and toxically racist. By our analysis, it does not qualify for classification as a social movement at all. The paradox disappears, however, when we factor in both the absence of meaningful progressive expressions for popular anger in U.S. political culture and corporate media's power to disseminate the image of the Tea Party as a significant and popular political force. The Tea Party exists as a very real political force despite its considerable social and organizational liabilities thanks primarily to those media that help manufacture socially acceptable dissent with their fundamental distinction between worthy protesters (those who uphold the existing corporate, imperial, and state-capitalist status quo) and unworthy protesters (those who oppose that status quo).

The Challenge to Progressives: Looking to 2012 and Beyond

We will not attempt here to predict either the Tea Party's political future or the policy results that will flow from its 2010 electoral successes. It seems clear, however, that the Tea Party phenomenon is here to stay for a bit longer as right-wing Republicans build to take the presidency—the real prize for right-wing politicos—in 2012. The possibility that Obama will be opposed in 2012 by a Tea Party presidential candidate—Sarah Palin perhaps—should not be discounted. Progressives, we are certain, will be contending with the Tea Party phenomenon for at least two more years. They would do well not to misunderstand it as some sort of genuine independent and grassroots, working-class social movement with genuinely popular and democratic potential. They should, however, remember that popular resentment abhors a progressive vacuum and will flow into dangerously authoritarian and regressive directions without real and serious alternatives and avenues of expression on the left. Genuine long-term social movement building and progressive policy activism from the bottom up—independent from a Democratic Party and presidency that can be expected to triangulate further to the right in the wake of the Republicans' significantly Tea Party–assisted midterm triumph—strikes us as the order of the day for the progressive left in 2010. Even if Obama wins reelection in 2012—something that might be enabled by a Republican Tea Party nominee like Palin—he can be expected to remain tied to a Republican-led, Tea Party–fed, antiprogressive agenda that further punishes victims, rewards the wealthy few, and continues to exacerbate grave social, economic, and ecological crises. Progressive social movements and perhaps oppositional left working-class politics will be required to capture the popular anger that will result under that scenario.

Independent left electoral action either within or beyond the Democratic Party does not strike us as an especially promising vehicle for progressive change under current political circumstances. The question of how much to prioritize work on electoral campaigns versus building social movements has long been a key point of contention among progressives. Those on the left who focus on elections have often been divided on whether to build a progressive party outside the Democrats, concentrate on running progressive candidates in Democratic primaries, or to engage in some sort of fusion strategy. We do not believe that any of these difficult issues have been remotely resolved. Nevertheless, we think that there is a key matter that all progressives electoralists should face: campaign finance reform and the undoing of the critical 2010 *Citizens United v. Federal Electoral Commission* Supreme Court ruling, which decreed that corporate funding of independent political broadcasts in candidate elections could not be limited under the First Amendment and which cleared the way for corporations and other special interest groups to spend unlimited amounts of money on elections—this without disclosure and accountability. Thanks in no small part to this decision, the 2010 context was far and away the most expensive midterm election in American history, with total spending coming in at nearly $4 billion.[63] Reforming this system is necessary if progressives expect to make real gains via electoral politics. In the 2010 midterms, Hahnel notes,

> huge quantities of invisible money from out of state aided Republican candidates running against Blue Dog Democrats. . . . It also targeted strongly progressive Democratic incumbents in 2010. While this was not sufficient to unseat most progressive stalwarts this year in districts that are solidly liberal, the threat and the trend line is obvious and ominous. Plotting progressive electoral strategy has become largely pointless absent an effective strategy for getting money out of elections.[64]

Another thing strikes us as abundantly clear: Chances for moving any part of a progressive agenda forward at the national policy level are going to be quite low for at least two years. If progressives were unable to significantly advance a serious, genuinely popular, and progressive agenda in 2009 and 2010—a period of Democratic Party control of both the White House and Congress—they most certainly will not be pushing the progressive policy ball forward in Washington in the wake of the super-Republican midterm triumph.[65]

Serious progressives would do well to heed the words of late radical historian Howard Zinn: "The really critical thing isn't who's sitting in the White House, but who is sitting in—in the streets, in the cafeterias, in the halls of government, in the factories. Who is protesting, who is occupying offices and demonstrating—those are the things that determine what happens."[66] The Tea Party pseudo-movement has thrown down a gauntlet of sorts, we think, to the true populist builders of genuinely social, democratic, and progressive movements: "Where are the progressives? Sulking is not an alternative. . . . The Tea Party may be pulling a fast one on the country. . . . But if it has more audacity than everyone else, it will, I am sorry to say, get away with it."[67]

Chapter 8

Prospects for a Progressive Revival

Good News and Bad News from The Middle East and the American Middle West

The left and progressive failure and the right–Tea Party triumph of 2009 and 2010 are in the historical record now, but the struggle continues, and progressive activists should keep in mind that most of the citizenry actually supports a progressive policy agenda. The revitalization and expansion of the genuinely popular progressive movement called for in this volume began to show real signs of life very shortly after the Midterm disaster began to sink in and just as the rest of the world began to erupt in a rush to democracy.

The potential progressive revival took off in Madison, Wisconsin (sometimes described as the birthplace of progressivism) in the third week of February 2011. It was sparked by the provocative anti-labor actions of that state's Tea Party–approved Republican Governor Scott Walker—a fiercely dedicated capitalist ideologue carried away with the sense of his own mission to inflict historic damage on the economic and political power of organized labor and the Democratic Party. One of many hard-right Republicans elected with Tea Party support at the state level in November of 2010, Walker made little effort to hide his militantly regressive, pro-business agenda in early 2011. He quickly hung a sign on the doorknob of his office that read "Wisconsin is open for business." He rejected $810 million in federal money that Wisconsin was getting to build a high-speed train line between Madison and Milwaukee. He turned the state's Department of Commerce into a "public-private hybrid" in which workers had to re-apply for their jobs. He joined with other Republicans to grant $117 million in tax breaks to businesses and others—this even as he planned major cuts in social spending and an assault on the supposedly high pension and medical benefit levels enjoyed by public workers in the state.[1]

The core "super-Republican" Tea Party premise behind his attack on public employees was that those workers were exorbitantly compensated (thanks to their powerful unions) at taxpayers' expense and that their "bloated" salaries and benefits were what was driving government deficits. This ignored the much larger role of business tax loopholes and tax breaks for the rich and corporate in producing state and federal deficits. The notion that public workers were excessively compensated compared to workers in the private sector was not born out by basic salary and benefit comparisons showing that private employees earned more in Wisconsin than their public sector counterparts at every educational level. It is a statistical illusion based on the fact that government employees tend to have higher levels of education than the general workforce, although they are generally paid *less* than their private sector counterparts after controlling for education as a factor.[2]

But something differentiated Wisconsin's new governor from the standard run of "fiscally conservative" state politicians. Walker, other Wisconsin Republicans, and their corporate backers from within and beyond the state were not content merely with center-right business as usual—with balancing their state budget on the backs of working people and the poor while handing out tax cuts to the wealthy. As right-wing extremists of the Tea Party variety, they saw a shining opportunity to make capitalist history by breaking the back of public sector unionism. Using his state's deficit as a pretext, Walker saw a chance to gratify his business backers by inflicting an historic defeat on the last bastion of union power in the United States: the government sector (home to half of the nation's remaining union members). With corporate-sponsored Tea Party–friendly Republicans in control of both its executive and legislative branches in the wake of the November 2010 elections, Wisconsin was a natural ground zero for advancing the right-wing business class's campaign to destroy the economic and political power of organized labor in the public sector.

On Friday, February 11, 2011, Walker advanced a "budget repair bill" that would not only have significantly reduced benefits enjoyed by the state's public sector workers but also effectively stripped those workers of their of their hard-won collective bargaining rights. The self-proclaimed Tea Partier Walker's effort to strip unions of collective bargaining rights in the name of reducing deficits reflected his longstanding militant opposition to unions, which extended back throughout his political career and predated the economic and budget crises of 2008–2011. The governor's talk of balancing budgets was "cover," the *New York Times'* editors noted, "for the real purpose of gutting the political force of middle-class state workers, who are steady supporters of Democrats and pose a threat to a growing conservative agenda."[3] Consistent with the notion that his bill was significantly about concentrating political power in Republican hands, Walker and other Tea Party Republican governors were simultaneously advancing new restrictive voter identification laws designed to significantly reduce the Democratic vote in future elections.[4]

Walker and other Republican governors' efforts to blame union bargaining for spiraling state deficits bore no relationship to policy reality. Their argument was thoroughly bogus. As the Center for Budget and Policy Priorities demonstrated in late February 2011, there was no correlation between collective bargaining rights and state budget deficits and states that bar collective bargaining actually suffered from higher deficits in 2011 when compared to those that allow bargaining.[5] Walker's efforts to cut pension and health care costs and to rescind collective bargaining would have saved the state a mere $30 million out of a larger state debt of more than $3 billion.[6]

Walker's campaign to crush labor power in Wisconsin was launched on a chillingly coercive and authoritarian note. It was prefaced by a curious early warning reported in the *New York Times*: Walker would *call out the National Guard* if there was any labor disruption in response to his assault on public workers.[7]

Consistent with Walker's identification as a Tea Party Republican, the billionaire brothers and leading Tea Party sponsors Charles and David Koch (both fierce union opponents) were among his biggest campaign contributors.[8] Koch Industries' political action committee gave $43,000 to Walker's campaign, and David Koch gave $1 million to the Republican Governors' Association, which funded ads attacking Walker's opponent in the November 2010 election. Americans for Prosperity (AFP), the leading Tea Party group financed by the Kochs, launched a $320,000 television ad campaign in support of Walker's bill on February 23, 2011.[9] "Even before the new governor was sworn in last month," AFP president Tim Phillips told *New York Times* reporter Eric Lifton on February 20, 2011, "executives from the Koch-backed group had worked behind the scenes *to try to encourage a union showdown* [emphasis added]."[10] Sordidly enough, Walker's "budget repair" bill permitted his administration to sell power plants that heat and cool state buildings to private companies without any bids. Critics understandably worried that this measure would permit the Koch brothers' business interest to purchase power plants on the cheap. The Associated Press reported that Koch Industries maintained "extensive business operations" in Wisconsin and "recently opened a lobbying office in downtown Madison a block from the Capitol. Seven lobbyists have registered in Wisconsin to lobby for various Koch Industries companies."[11] Walker was also significantly backed by the militantly anti-union, right-wing, and Milwaukee-based Bradley Foundation and by the AFP.[12]

Labor suspicions that the Tea Party backers—the Koch brothers—were a major force behind the proposed Wisconsin legislation were validated when the liberal, New York–based blogger Ian Murphy placed a call to Walker in which Murphy posed as David Koch. Murphy (as Koch) and Walker spoke for twenty minutes—a conversation in which the governor described several potential ways to pressure Democrats to return to the Statehouse and revealed that he and his allies had considered secretly planting people in pro-union protest crowds to stir up trouble. Walker likened his stand to that taken by President Ronald Reagan when Reagan fired the nation's air-traffic controllers during a labor dispute in 1981. "That was the first crack in the Berlin Wall and led to the fall of the Soviets," Walker claimed. Walker said he expected the anti-union movement to spread across the country, and that he had spoken with the governors of Ohio and Nevada. The blogger pretending to be Koch agreed, telling Walker, "You're the first domino." Walker responded affirmatively, saying, "Yep, this is our moment." When Walker said he was willing to negotiate with Democratic senators, Murphy told him to "bring a baseball bat." Walker laughed and responded that he had "a slugger with my name on it." At the end of the call, the blogger posing as Koch said, "I'll tell you what Scott, once you *crush these bastards*, I'll fly you out to Cali and really show you a good time." Walker replied that "that would be outstanding," adding that the standoff is "all about getting our freedoms back." The prank caller said, "Absolutely. And you know, we have a little bit of vested interest as well."[13] Clearly, Walker's battle with labor was driven by his ideological distaste for unions and his support for an unbridled, hyper-capitalist order.

Revealing a personal relationship with at least one of the Koch brothers, Walker's conversation with Ian Murphy was consistent with earlier comments from the brash new Tea Party governor. Six days into the protests, Walker told Fox News that he was "not fazed" and predicted that Wisconsin would trail-blaze "conservative" policy for other states by weakening unions, much like it did with so-called welfare reform (the abolition of poor families' entitlement to public family cash assistance) and the advance of school privatization vouchers in the 1990s. As the *Times* reported six days in, "Mr. Walker, 43, the son of a Baptist preacher, is an Eagle Scout. . . . His political heroes: Tommy Thompson, this state's former governor, and Ronald Reagan. . . . 'He didn't flinch,' Mr. Walker said of Reagan. 'Obviously, I take a lot of inspiration from that.'"[14]

Consistent with his Koch-fueled labor-smashing ambitions, Walker did not walk alone in assaulting organized labor at the statehouse level. Republican Tea Party lawmakers across the Midwest quickly joined him in using state budgetary deficits to attempt "to cripple the bargaining power of unions—and ultimately realize a cherished partisan dream of eradicating them."[15] They used fiscal crisis as an excuse to attack public sector workers and consolidate their political power, which they saw as threatened by the voting power of Democratic-leaning pubic sector unions. The existential attack on public sector unions' economic and political power was replicated by other right-wing governors, including others elected in the 2010 Tea Party wave. In Ohio in mid-February, Republican legislators, backed by Tea Party governor John Kasich (also elected in 2010 with significant support from the Koch brothers) introduced a bill to end collective bargaining rights for state employees, along with imposing budgetary givebacks. In Indiana, where the right-wing governor (cited by Walker as an inspiration) Mitch Daniels ended collective bargaining rights for state workers in 2005, Republicans pushed a bill that would make Indiana a so-called right-to-work state, meaning that workers could not be required to join public- or private-sector unions or pay dues.[16] New Jersey's hard-right, super-Republican governor Chris Christie (another Tea Party favorite) loudly supported Walker's authoritarian assault on Wisconsin's public workers and launched a campaign to balance his state's budget by making huge cuts in social programs and in public workers' wages and benefits. Collectively, the state bills amounted to the largest assault on labor's collective bargaining power in recent United States history.

"This Is Not a Tea Party"

Walker's Tea Party–inspired assault on labor was a game-changer. It was one thing to ask public sector unions (above all, the Wisconsin Education Association and the American Federation of State, Municipal, and County Employees) for short-term, fiscally prudent concessions that could be reversed at the bargaining table when state finances returned to greater health. It was another thing to combine the demand for concessions with an attack on the very existence of unions empowered to recoup benefits won through hard struggles over many decades. The attack was widely and quite understandably perceived by much of the state's working populace (especially, but not exclusively, its public sector workers) as an egregious top-down assault on their basic human and civil rights within and beyond the workplace.[17]

Walker expected to pass his bill quickly through both houses of the Wisconsin state legislature in mid-February. He was prevented from achieving this, however, when fourteen of Wisconsin's Democratic state senators left the state, blocking the upper legislative body from assembling the number of representatives required to vote on a budge-related matter. Amid the resulting paralysis of the legislative process, the Wisconsin State Capitol in Madison became the site of a remarkable three-week (as of this writing on March 2, 2011) labor protest that sparked support demonstrations across the country and even received statements of solidarity from Egypt (home to an inspiring democratic revolution in late January and February of 2011). From one day to the next, tens of thousands of public union members, activists, and supporters marched and rallied around and inside the Capitol Rotunda. In the first week of the protest, schools were closed within and beyond Madison as teachers and others public school employees flocked to the state capital to show their opposition to "Imperial Walker's" attack on labor rights.

One of us (Street) drove to Madison to observe this remarkable labor protest on its fifth day, Saturday, February 19, a day when Tea Party activists vowed to hold a rally in support of Walker. Street observed and joined a seemingly endless sea of smiling, chanting, whistling, drumming, joyous, clapping, hooting, and diverse pro-labor humanity surrounding a comparatively tiny group (500 to 1,000 people tops) of angry Tea Partiers (organized by the AFP) stuck on the eastern side of the Capitol. (It was quite an understatement for the *Chicago Tribune* to call the pro-Walker rally "smaller but equally strident"[18]). The Tea Party contingent was outnumbered by at least sixty to one—something that went unreported in Chicago's evening news broadcasts that night, which depicted the day in Madison as pitting two roughly equivalent protests against one another. DiMaggio also attended rallies in Madison, including one (on February 26, 2011) that attracted more than one hundred thousand demonstrators. No Tea Party protestors were visible at any time during his repeated visits to the Wisconsin state capitol.

It wasn't just size that differentiated the two sides from one another. Equally significant was their comparative spirit and mood. The billionaire-backed Walker forces were sour and haughty, seemingly irritated at the requirement to gather collectively and make noise—the stuff of social movements. They did not seem to be enjoying themselves very much. They spewed jealous accusations at the supposed reckless "socialism" of "radical left" big government Democrats such as (the center-right) Barack Obama and the state senators (dubbed the "Fab 14" by some labor supporters) who had "fled Wisconsin." Their mean-spirited message was clear to the workers and professionals who teach the state's children and plow its highways and clean the bathrooms of its state, county, and municipal buildings: "Shut the Hell up, go back to work, and be thankful for whatever we see fit to pay you and, indeed, for having any kind of job at all." Some Tea Partiers displayed posters depicting Obama as a Communist. When Street asked one such Tea Partier if he really believed that the president of the United States—the savior of Wall Street—was a Marxist, the rightist looked at his questioner with disgust and turned away in stone silence.

By contrast, the progressive, union, and pro-labor mass of surrounding the dwarfing the Tea Party group was a model of festive good humor. There was music and street theater, including a pro-union fife and drum corps in colonial-revolutionary garb (take that Tea Party), a man dressed as "Darth Walker," and the impressive bagpipes of kilt-wearing members of the firefighters' union. Joyful and supportive conversation was free and easy between and among participants, who laughed and took pictures of each others' many handmade posters and signs, many of which were crafted to combine struggle with good humor. Anti–Tea Party and related anti-Koch sentiments were quite pronounced in the protestors' signage, which included the following messages: "This is Not a Tea Party," "No Tea for Me," "Wississippi: The Walker Tea Party Agenda," "Don't Drink the Tea," "Union Blood Is Thicker Than Tea," "Koch-Suckers" (with words above pictures of Walker and the two top Republicans in Wisconsin state legislature), "Corporate Street Walker" (with words above a salacious picture of Walker)," "Wisconsinites Love Beer and Bratwurst—Nobody Ordered Tea."

Unlike the Obama-obsessed Tea Partiers, the union and pro-labor crowds in and around the Capitol Rotunda seemed completely uninterested in the question of who sat atop the national media-politics extravaganza. With tens of thousands of them circling the Capitol and thousands occupying the structure itself, it seemed as if they were channeling Howard Zinn's wisdom (quoted earlier in this book) on how the really important question isn't "Who is sitting in the White House?" but "Who is sitting in—in the streets, in the cafeterias, in the halls of government, in the factories."[19]

On February 22, the Madison-based ninety-seven-union South Central Labor Federation (representing forty-five thousand public and private-sector union members in southern and central Wisconsin) passed a resolution in considering support of a general strike if Walker's bill passed. The federation appointed a coordinating committee to contact European unions with experience conducting general strikes.[20]

The Fire Spreads

The fire of state-level labor rebellion spread to other states along with the top-down, right-wing Tea Party attack on union rights. The next battleground was Ohio, where another recently elected and Tea Party–backed super Republican governor John Kasich and his right-wing allies in the state legislature were determined to smash public sector unions. As the *Times* reported, "Several thousand pro-union protesters filled a main hall of the state courthouse in Columbus and gathered in a large crowd outside, chanting 'kill the bill,' waving signs, and playing drums and bagpipes."[21] As of early March, the Ohio Republicans' bill would ban public employees from striking—a death-blow to labor power that made it unacceptable to the state's public sector unions. Sailing through the Ohio state legislature in late February and early March 2011, the Kasich-GOP bill was arguably more draconian than Walker's, and it attacked a larger number of workers (350,000 in Ohio versus 175,000 in Wisconsin).[22]

In Indiana, labor protest entered the state capitol in Indianapolis as most Democratic members of the state's House of Representatives stayed away from a legislative session on February 22, 2011, to block a Republican bill designed to weaken collective bargaining. As Kate Zernike reported in the *Times*, "Thousands of agitated protesters in hard hats and work boots clogged the halls of the Statehouse, chanting and cheering in support of the Democrats, most of whom remained camped at a discount hotel in Urbana, Illinois. . . . In the

Statehouse in Indianapolis, the sound of the protests was similarly overwhelming."[23]

As the struggles in Wisconsin, Ohio, and Indiana received national attention, more union rights struggles (sold as "budget repair" battles by Republican governors and legislators) were expected to break out soon—in Oklahoma, where the state House was considering legislation that would strip municipal unions of collective bargaining rights, and in Tennessee, where Republicans had introduced legislation to ban collective bargaining between teachers' unions and local school boards.

On Saturday, February 26, 2011, labor rallies in support of Wisconsin's public workers and collective bargaining rights were held across the country in every state capital in the United States—an extraordinary development. The rallies, organized by MoveOn, put thirty thousand people in the streets across the country.

"The People Have Been Able to Find Their Own Voice"

The Tea Party right insisted that their great, supposedly socialist nemesis Barack Obama was intervening decisively on the worker's side in, and even sparking these historic, state-level uprisings. The charge was absurd. As *Wall Street Journal* reporter Jonathan Weisman observed in the second week of the Wisconsin protests, Obama stepped back from the state-level battles after initially seeming to support labor in Wisconsin. Top Democratic officials told Weisman that this was because Obama "is eager to occupy the political center . . . to forge a bipartisan deal on the nation's long-term finances that could strengthen his position heading into the 2012 election."[24] In early March, *New York Times* correspondent Jackie Calmes learned that the White House actually intervened in anger against the national Democratic Party's initial efforts to support the labor rebellion, which administration officials found as contrary to its happy and neoliberal message:

> The White House mostly has sought to stay out of the fray in Madison, Wis., and other state capitals where Republican governors are

battling public employee unions and Democratic lawmakers over collective bargaining rights. When West Wing officials discovered that the Democratic National Committee had mobilized Mr. Obama's national network to support the protests, they angrily reined in the staff at the party headquarters. . . . Administration officials said they saw the events beyond Washington as distractions from the optimistic "win the future" message that Mr. Obama introduced in his State of the Union address, in which he exhorted the country to increase spending for some programs, even as it cuts others so that America can "out-innovate and out-educate" its global rivals.[25]

Obama responded to the rank-and-file labor rebellion in the American heartland in much the same way as he responded to the right-wing coup in Honduras in June of 2009 and to the rise of the Egyptian revolution in January and February 2011: with initial statements of seeming support for popular democratic forces followed by conservative equivocation and caution meant to identify himself with democratic change without severing his accommodation to dominant hierarchies and elites.[26]

His failure to align himself strongly with the public workers and their fight within and beyond Madison was consistent with his centrist campaign pledge to be a "post-partisan leader" ready to take on his own party's union base. It matched: his support (over the opposition of teachers' unions) of charter schools and "performance-based" teacher pay; his recent advance of corporate neoliberal free trade deals opposed by labor; his recent public strengthening of ties with business leaders; his refusal to move in any meaningful way on campaign promises to reform the nation's management-friendly labor laws, and his federal workers salary freeze (a move that angered public sector union members).[27] Before the progressive labor rebellion broke out, Obama had already gone far down the path of joining business and the right in advancing the narrative that American prosperity was being undone by overpaid public workers and excessive government regulation, not by the real culprits on Wall Street, who recklessly crashed the global economy in 2008.[28]

The real energy in the Wisconsin public worker rebellion and its state-level offshoots came from the bottom up. It arose from the grassroots, not from the top down. As Wisconsin State Democratic

Senate Leader Mark Miller rightly noted when the *Wall Street Journal* queried him on Obama's role: "Really the people of our state, and the people of our country, have been able to find their voice in this battle. The voices of the people are the voices the governor needs to listen to."[29]

Consistent with Miller's sentiments, a *USA Today* Gallup poll conducted at the height of the union rights battle in Madison found that "Americans strongly oppose laws taking away the collective bargaining power of public employee unions." The poll found that 61 percent of Americans would oppose a law in their state similar to the law proposed by Walker in Wisconsin, compared with just a 33 percent who would favor such legislation.[30]

The Midwestern Labor Rebellion and the Argument of This Book

The state-level struggles that emerged over union rights in February 2011 matched this book's analysis of the Tea Party phenomenon on numerous interrelated levels. The spectacle of relatively small and Koch-organized Tea Party rallies in defense of in-power right-wing, pro-business, super-Republican governors and being dwarfed by much larger and more vibrant, genuinely popular and grassroots union protests is consistent with our portrait of the Tea Party as a fundamentally "astroturf," fake-populist, and corporate- and Republican-directed, mass-mediated, pro-establishment, and electoral phenomenon that is above all about getting hard-right Republicans (i.e., Scott Walker and John Kasich) into elected office—quite the opposite of its own self-presentation and the often flattering portrayal (as an independent, grassroots, populist, and anti-establishment "movement") it has received in dominant mass media. The state-level, super-Republican Tea Party governors' and legislators' clear and abject service to the right-wing business agenda is consistent with our analysis of the Tea Party as a significantly corporate-coordinated and top-down phenomenon meant to attack the "left hand of the state," strengthen the right hand of the state, and generally assault progressive and democratic institutions and values on behalf of concentrated wealth. The tendency of the mass media to report these struggles as battles between roughly equivalent movements of left and right is consistent with this study's critique of the dominant media's pronounced habit of elevating what it sees as the worthy protests of the pro-establishment right over what it sees as the comparatively unworthy protests of the more genuinely popular and progressive Left. Also matching the analysis presented in this book, the supposedly populist Tea Party position in support of the right-wing governors' and legislators' attack on union rights stands in opposition to actual popular policy opinion—in support of collective bargaining and union rights. Consistent with our analysis of Tea Partiers' numerous hyper-ignorant opinions in Chapter 5 of this study, finally, Tea Partiers support for right-wing attacks on union rights in the name of deficit reduction is tied up in hopelessly tangled, ideologically driven intellectual knots reinforced by right-wing media. There is, as noted above, no correlation between union collective bargaining rights and state budget deficit levels. We should also add that Tea Partiers' claims that state-level tax cuts for big business and the wealthy will help close deficits and grow the economy stand in total defiance of elementary historical evidence showing that precisely the opposite resulted in states that undertook these right wing policies in the 1990s and early twenty-first century.[31]

Toward a Progressive Tea Party

Our excitement over the public worker uprising of February and March 2011 does not come without qualification. The state-level labor rebellion that emerged in response to right wing provocations is in our opinion a most welcome development—no small step in the direction the nation's all-too hidden, under-reported, and under-mobilized progressive majority needs to take if political and social democracy and sane, balanced, and egalitarian policy are going to survive and advance in twenty-first-century America. Still, it is one thing for existing labor institutions and leaders (themselves heavily integrated into the nation's reigning state-capitalist order) to rally popular masses in defensive response to the worst policy outrages of the most reactionary politicians in the rightmost wing of America's corporate-ruled "one-and-a-half party system." It is another thing to wield and expand proactively and against the richly bipartisan neoliberal business agenda and to capture and act meaningfully on the legitimate popular anger that the Tea Party and the broader right has at times been able to exploit and misdirect. The political observer Chris Green raised a good question in a private communication with Street on February 22, 2011. "Is this progressive movement going to operate," Green asks, "within traditional limitations, especially those imposed by the union leadership? That is, are they only going to protest Republican governors and not pro-cut Democrat governors in places like New York, California, and Illinois? This will be the challenge, not to get co-opted by the Democrats." Indeed, the austerity party is not limited to the Republicans. The left commentator Doug Henwood offers some sage and sobering advice at the end of a generally quite favorable and optimistic take on the eruption of labor protest in Wisconsin:

> It may be that had Walker not gone for such a maximalist agenda, this sort of protest might not have happened. Other governors may take note and opt instead for the death by a thousand cuts instead of one giant machete chop. But of course, it's not just Republicans. Democratic governors like Jerry Brown and Andrew Cuomo also have it out for public sector workers, since, as everyone knows, you just can't tax the fatcats these days. And you do have to wonder how aggressive unions in California and New York will be in protesting Democratic governors.[32]

Henwood could have added comments about the corporate-friendly, center-right agenda of the national Democratic Party and the Obama administration. A progressive resurgence that confronts Democratic Party corporatism and militarism as well as the Republican variants of the same diseases will have to take place on the national as well as the state level if we are going to make meaningful popular-democratic progress against the unelected and interrelated dictatorships of money and empire that continue to rule America beneath and beyond the staggered, candidate-centered, big-money, big-media electoral extravaganzas that continue to define "politics" in the United States.

On that note, we are happy to record one promising development at the national level—the emergence of the national group U.S. Uncut that organized fifty protests outside Bank of America headquarters and branches on Saturday, February 26, 2011. Inspired by the British anti-austerity group UK Uncut,[33] this new organization targets corporate tax evasion and points out the unjust absurdity of government claiming to address fiscal deficits by slashing social programs and attacking public workers while failing to collect billions of dollars in unpaid taxes due from corporate giants ExxonMobil, GE, and Bank of America, each of which paid no federal income taxes in 2010. As the Government Accountability Office reported in 2008, a fourth of the nation's largest corporations pay no federal income tax. Bank of America, the beneficiary of $45 billion in federal bailout funds, hides its would-be tax dollars into no less than 115 offshore tax havens. Meanwhile, policymakers refer to budget deficits as justification for pay freezes for public workers and cuts to key social safety nets. As Carl Gibson, a U.S. Uncut founder, noted in a press release prior to the February 26 protests: "Because of overseas tax havens and other tax loopholes, U.S. corporations are making profits in America but barely paying taxes here. If we close those loopholes, we wouldn't have to be cutting back on firefighters, library hours and student loans." This basic observation helps takes the ground out from under the corporate- and Republican-coordinated Tea Party campaign to balance federal as well as state and local budgets on the backs of the poor, working people, and organized labor.[34]

By the hopeful account of the liberal commentator Jonathan Hari in the *Nation* in early February 2011, U.S. Uncut holds the promise of becoming the beginning of "A Progressive Tea Party":

Imagine a parallel universe where the Great Crash of 2008 was followed by a Tea Party of a very different kind. Enraged citizens gather in every city, week after week—to demand the government finally regulate the behavior of corporations and the superrich, and force them to start paying taxes. The protesters shut down the shops and offices of the companies that have most aggressively ripped off the country. The swelling movement is made up of everyone from teenagers to pensioners. They surround branches of the banks that caused this crash and force them to close, with banners saying, YOU CAUSED THIS CRISIS. NOW YOU PAY. . . .

Instead of the fake populism of the Tea Party, there is a movement based on real populism. It shows that there is an alternative to making the poor and the middle class pay for a crisis caused by the rich. It shifts the national conversation. Instead of letting the government cut our services and increase our taxes, the people demand that it cut the endless and lavish aid for the rich and make them pay the massive sums they dodge in taxes.

This may sound like a fantasy—but it has all happened. The name of this parallel universe is Britain.* As recently as this past fall, people here were asking the same questions liberal Americans have been glumly contemplating: Why is everyone being so passive? Why are we letting ourselves be ripped off? Why are people staying in their homes watching their flat-screens while our politicians strip away services so they can fatten the superrich even more?[35]

In the three weeks following the *Nation's* publication of Harri's essay, hundreds of thousands of Midwestern workers and citizens had determined to leave their homes and televisions behind to make history from the bottom up. The answer to E. J. Dionne's previously quoted question "Where are the progressives?" was found the streets and legislative halls of state capitols across the American heartland.

---

*There is rich historical irony in the notion of inspiration for "a progressive [American] Tea Party" coming from England, the one-time colonial power that provoked the original Tea Party, whose popular legacy the hard right ilk of Charles and David Koch and Dick Armey have crassly appropriated in service to the authoritarian agenda of concentrated wealth.

Notes

Prologue

1. Alfred Young, *The Shoemaker and the Tea Party: Memory and the American Revolution* (Boston: Beacon Press, 1999), 53.

2. Ibid., 102–103.

3. Paul Krugman, "Tea Parties Forever," *New York Times*, April 13, 2009, at www.nytimes.com/2009/04/13/opinion/13krugman.html. See also Jane Mayer, "Covert Operations: The Billionaire Brothers Who Are Waging a War Against Obama," *New Yorker*, October 30, 2010.

4. E. J. Dionne cites historian Jill Lepore on the Tea Party and the mass-mediated "hall-of-mirrors" effect in "The Tea Party Movement Is a Scam," RealClearPolitics, September 23, 2010, at www.realclearpolitics.com/articles/2010/09/23/the_tea_party_movement_is_ a_scam.html.

5. John O'Hara, *The New American Tea Party: The Counterrevolution Against Bailouts, Handouts, Reckless Spending, and More Taxes* (New York: Wiley, 2010).

6. Sheldon Wolin, *Democracy Incorporated: Managed Democracy and the Specter of Inverted Totalitarianism* (Princeton, NJ: Princeton University Press, 2008).

7. Paul Street, *Barack Obama and the Future of American Politics* (Boulder, CO: Paradigm Publishers, 2008).

Chapter One

1. Michael Brendan Dougherty, "Tea Party Crashers,'" *American Conservative*, April 1, 2010, at www.amconmag.com/article/2010/apr/01/00006/.

2. John O'Hara, *The New American Tea Party: The Counterrevolution Against Bailouts, Handouts, Reckless Spending, and More Taxes* (New York: Wiley, 2010), xxv; Pew Center for the People and the Press, "The People and

Their Government: Distrust, Discontent, Anger, and Partisan Rancor," April 18, 2010, at http://people-press.org/reports/pdf/606.pdf.

3. "51% View Tea Parties Favorably, Political Class Strongly Disagrees," Rasmussen Reports, April 20, 2009, at www.rasmussenreports.com/public _content/politics/general_politics/april_2009/51_view_tea_parties_favorably _political_class_strongly_disagrees.

4. Steven Kull, "Big Government Is Not the Issue," WorldOpinion.org, August 19, 2010, at www.worldpublicopinion.org/pipa/articles/brunitedstates canadara/665.php.

5. "Tea Party Outpolls Democratic, Republican Parties—Will Anger Fuel 2010 Elections?" *Los Angeles Times* Blog, December 17, 2009, at http://latimes blogs.latimes.com/washington/2009/12/tea-party-more-popular-than-republicans-or-democrats.html.

6. Pew Center, "The People and Their Government." Even more brazen was how CNN framed one of its questions in a February 2010 poll. "Now suppose the elections for Congress were being held today and a third candidate were running who was endorsed by the Tea Party movement. Which candidate would you vote for in your Congressional district? (1) Democratic Party's Candidate; (2) Republican Party's candidate; (3) Tea Party's candidate."

7. Scott Rasmussen and Doug Schoen, *Mad as Hell: How the Tea Party Movement Is Fundamentally Remaking Our Two-Party System* (New York: HarperCollins, 2010), 5.

8. Kate Zernike, "For G.O.P., Tea Party Wields a Double-Edged Sword," *New York Times*, September 5, 2010.

9. Kate Zernike, "For Tea Party, Sway Beyond Mere Numbers," *New York Times*, October 15, 2010.

10. Lisa Lerer, "Tea Party Economic Gloom Fuels Republican Momentum," Bloomberg News, October 13, 2010, at http://insurancenewsnet.com/article.aspx?id=230316&type=newswires.

11. The list includes O'Hara, *The New American Tea Party: The Counterrevolution Against Bailouts, Handouts, Reckless Spending, and More Taxes* (January 12, 2010); Dick Armey and Matt Kibbe, *Give Us Liberty: A Tea Party Manifesto* (August 17, 2010); *New York Times* reporter Kate Zernike, *Boiling Mad: Inside Tea Party America* (September 14, 2010); Harvard historian Jill Lepore, *The Whites of Their Eyes: The Tea Party's Revolution and the Battle over American History* (October 12, 2010); Scott Rasmussen and Douglass Schoen, *Mad as Hell: How the Tea Party Movement Is Fundamentally Remaking Our Two-Party System* (September 14, 2010); Newt Gingrich, *To Save America: Stopping Obama's Secular-Socialist Machine* (May 2010); Joseph Farah, *The Tea Party Manifesto* (July 4, 2010); reactionary propagandist Leland Baker, *Tea Party Revival: The Conscience of a Conservative Reborn* (October 24, 2009);

Washington Post reporter Dana Milbank, *Tears of a Clown: Glenn Beck and the Teabagging of America* (September 2010), Sharon Cooper, *Taxpayers' Tea Party: How to Become Politically Active and Why* (June 15, 2010, revised and expanded version of original 1994 volume); John Amato and David Neiwert, *Over the Cliff: How Obama's Election Drove the American Right Insane* (2010); Will Bunch, *The Backlash: Right-Wing Radicals, High-Def Hucksters, and Paranoid Politics in the Age of Obama* (2010); right-wing former arms dealer Charly Gullet, *Tea Party Handbook* (September 11, 2009).

12. O'Hara, *The New American Tea Party*, xxvi.

13. Ibid., xxvi, 13–14, 17, 206, 235.

14. *PBS NewsHour*, September 9, 2010, at www.pbs.org/newshour/bb/politics/july-dec10/armey_09–09.html.

15. Newt Gingrich, *To Save America*, 312.

16. Farah, *The Tea Party Manifesto*.

17. "Times Topics: The Tea Party Movement," September 15, 2010, at http://topics.nytimes.com/top/reference/timestopics/subjects/t/tea_party_movement/index.html.

18. Ben McGrath, "The Movement: The Rise of Tea Party Activism," *New Yorker*, February 1, 2010.

19. Kate Zernike, *Boiling Mad: Inside Tea Party America* (New York: Times Books, 2010), 4–5.

20. Rasmussen and Schoen, *Mad as Hell*, 5.

21. David Paul Kuhn, "R.I.P. Political Establishment," RealClearPolitics, September 21, 2010.

22. Michael Scherer, "It's Tea Time," *Time*, September 27, 2010, 27–30.

23. Susan Page, "Dems in Power Could Be in Peril," *USA Today*, September 3, 2010.

24. Zernike, "For G.O.P., Tea Party"; Amy Gardner, "Tea Party Picking Up Steam Nationwide," *Washington Post*, September 21, 2010.

25. Daniel Henninger, "The Tea Party and Its Demons," *Wall Street Journal*, September 23, 2010.

26. See, for example, O'Hara, *The New American Tea Party*, 14, 16–17, 62, 80–81, 194–195.

27. Christopher Hitchens, *No One Left to Lie To: The Values of the Worst Family* (New York: Verso, 1999), 17–18.

28. Lance Selfa, *The Democrats: A Critical History* (Chicago: Haymarket, 2008), 87–125.

29. David Rothkopf quoted in David Sanger, "Obama Tilts Toward Center, Inviting a Clash of Ideas," *New York Times*, November 22, 2008. See also Paul Street, "Obama's Violin: Populist Rage and the Uncertain Containment of Change," *Z Magazine*, May 2009.

30. William Greider, *Who Will Tell the People? The Betrayal of American Democracy* (New York: Simon and Schuster, 1992), 274–275.

31. John Dewey quoted in Noam Chomsky, *Hegemony or Survival: America's Quest for Global Dominance* (New York: Metropolitan, 2003), 15. See also Arundhati Roy, "Democracy's Fading Light," *Outlook India Magazine*, July 13, 2009, at www.outlookindia.com/article.aspx?250418; Noam Chomsky, *Failed States: The Abuse of Power and the Assault on Democracy* (New York: Metropolitan, 2006), 214–250; William I. Robinson, *Promoting Polyarchy— Globalization, US Intervention, and Hegemony* (Cambridge, UK: Cambridge University Press, 1996), 48–51; G. William Domhoff, *Who Rules America? Power, Politics, and Social Change* (New York: McGraw-Hill, 2006); Jeff Faux, *The Global Class War: How America's Bipartisan Elite Lost Our Future and What It Will Take to Win It Back* (New York: Wiley, 2006); Thomas Ferguson, *Golden Rule: The Investment Theory of Party Competition and Logic of Money-Driven Political Systems* (Chicago: University of Chicago Press, 1995); Elizabeth Drew, *The Corruption of American Politics: What Went Wrong and Why* (Secaucus, NJ: Birch Lane Press, 1999); Center for Responsive Politics, *A Brief History of Money in Politics* (Washington, DC: Center for Responsive Politics, 1995); Jamin Raskin and John Bonifaz, "The Constitutional Imperative and Practical Imperative of Democratically Financed Elections," *Columbia Law Review* 94, no. 4 (1994): 1160–1203; Charles Lewis, *The Buying of the President* (New York: Avon, 1996), 1–20; Kevin Phillips, *The Politics of Rich and Poor: Wealth and the American Electorate in the Reagan Aftermath* (New York: Harper, 1989); and Laurence H. Shoup, "The Presidential Election 2008," *Z Magazine*, February 2008.

32. Paul Street, *Barack Obama and the Future of American Politics* (Boulder, CO: Paradigm Publishers, 2008), 3–12; Jamin B. Raskin, *Overruling Democracy: The Supreme Court vs. the American People* (New York: Routledge, 2004), 91–142; Selfa, *The Democrats*, 11–38; Sheldon Wolin, *Democracy Incorporated: Managed Democracy and the Specter of Inverted Totalitarianism* (Princeton, NJ: Princeton University Press, 2008), 103–104, 110, 136, 149, 156, 157, 166, 195, 201, 202–203, 206–208, 286–287; Steven Hill, *Fixing Elections: The Failure of America's Winner Take All Politics* (New York: Routledge, 2002); Chris Hedges, *Empire of Illusion* (New York: Nation Books, 2009), 145, 146, 157, 159, 17, 168, 175, 176, 183; Paul D'Amato, *The Meaning of Marxism* (Chicago: Haymarket, 2006), 92–97; Phillips, *The Politics of Rich and Poor*, 32; Greider, *Who Will Tell the People?* 245–269.

33. Selfa, *The Democrats*, 13; Domhoff, *Who Rules America?*; Edward S. Herman, "Big Government, Deficits, Entitlements, and 'Centrists,'" *Z Magazine*, April 2010; Larry M. Bartels, *Unequal Democracy: The Political Economy of the New Gilded Age* (Princeton, NJ: Princeton University Press, 2008); Larry Bartels, "Inequalities," *New York Times Magazine*, April 27, 2008.

34. See Pierre Bourdieu, *Acts of Resistance* (New York: Free Press, 1998), 2, 24–44; John Pilger, *The New Rulers of the World* (London: Verso, 2002), 5, 116; Paul Street, *Empire and Inequality: America and the World Since 9/11* (Boulder, CO: Paradigm Publishers, 2004), xiii–xiv; and Chomsky, *Failed States*, 218.

35. Neil Postman, *Amusing Ourselves to Death: Public Discourse in the Age of Show Business* (New York: Penguin, 1985), 126–132.; Chomsky, *Failed States*, 221, 214–250; Noam Chomsky, "'Good News': Iraq and Beyond," *ZNet*, February 16, 2008, at www.zcommunications.org/znet/viewArticle/16522; Paul Street, "Bush, Kerry, and 'Body Language' v. 'Message': Notes on Race, Gender, Empire, and Mass Infantilization," *ZNet Magazine*, October 12, 2004; Paul Street, *The Empire's New Clothes: Barack Obama in the Real World of Power* (Boulder, CO: Paradigm Publishers, 2010), 1–8; Noam Chomsky, *What We Say Goes: Conversation on U.S. Power in a Changing World* (New York: Metropolitan, 2007), 52–54; Hedges, *Empire of Illusion*, 44–48.

36. Wolin, *Democracy Incorporated*, 56, 64, 140, 150, 194, 197, 239, 284–286; Noam Chomsky, *Interventions* (San Francisco: City Lights, 2007), 99–100; Murray Edelman, *The Symbolic Uses of Politics* (Urbana: University of Illinois Press, 1964); Murray Edelman, *Constructing the Political Spectacle* (Chicago: University of Chicago Press, 1988); Howard Zinn, "Election Madness," *The Progressive*, March 2008; Adolph J. Reed Jr., "Sitting This One Out," *The Progressive*, November 2007; Tariq Ali and Anthony Arnove, "The Challenge to the Empire," *Socialist Worker Online*, October 20, 2006; Street, *Barack Obama and the Future*, 193–197; Charles Derber, *Hidden Power* (San Francisco: Berrett-Koehler, 2005), 6–9, 97–101, 143–149, 223–241; Paul Street, "Labor Day Reflections: Time as a Democracy Issue," *ZNet Daily Commentaries*, September 3, 2002, at www.zmag.org/sustainers/content/2002–08/01street.cfm; Paul Street, "The Resistance Gap: On Media, Time, and the Curious Absence of Riots," *ZNet*, February 9, 2009, at www.zcommunications.org/the-resistance-gap-on -media-time-and-the-curious-absence-of-riots-by-paul-street.

37. Rick Shenkman, "How Ignorant Are We? Voters Choose but on the Basis of What?" *Raw Story*, July 3, 2010, at http://rawstory.com/rs/2010/ 0703/onequarter-gained-independence/.

38. Alex Carey, *Taking the Risk Out of Democracy: Corporate Propaganda Versus Freedom and Liberty* (Urbana: University of Illinois Press, 1997), 14– 16. These all-or-nothing, black-and-white symbols are potent "means of social control" on behalf of corporate rule and military empire. There is little room for anything progressive, social, popular, and democratic between or beyond these two polar opposites of (a) good/sacred/light/American/capitalist/ "free market" and (b) bad/satanic/dark/alien/socialist-communist/statist.

39. Wolin, *Democracy Incorporated*, 115–116, 120–122. The Bible and the Constitution are the two principal sacred texts in the American archaic mind-set.

In sharp contrast to scientific truths, which change in accordance with facts and paradigm shifts, American archaism's truths are seen as "fixed and impervious to evidence," linking the doctrines of "the framer's original intent" and "constitutional originalism" to the creationist denial of biological evolution. The leading form of political archaism that holds influence in the nation maintains that "the United States was blessed with a once-and-for-all-time, fixed ideal form, an original Constitution of government created by the Founding Fathers in 1787. The original Constitution is the political counterpart of the Bible, the fundamental text, inerrant, unchanging to, to be applied, not 'interfered with' by 'activist judges' and 'the liberal media' and liberal administrations abetted by their minions in Congress and by judges who 'legislate' instead of 'following the letter' of constitutional scripture. The nation is perceived as a wayward sinner who frequently wanders from the straight and narrow and needs to be sobered, returned to its sacred text, its Word." Wolin, *Democracy Incorporated,* 120–121.

40. Andrew Bacevich, *The New American Militarism: How Americans Are Seduced by War* (New York: Oxford University Press, 2005), 23–24. As noted military historian and veteran Bacevich observes, "In public life today, paying homage to those in uniform has become obligatory and the one unforgivable sin is to be found guilty of failing to 'support the troops.'" American global military supremacy "has become central to our national identity." Efforts on the left and right to "call attention to the potentially adverse consequences of becoming smitten with military power" (i.e., extravagant taxpayer expense and related social opportunity cost) are beyond the parameters of "the exceedingly narrow range of views deemed permissible" in mainstream politics.

41. Henry A. Giroux, *The Terror of Neoliberalism: Authoritarianism and the Eclipse of Democracy* (Boulder, CO: Paradigm Publishers, 2004), xiii–53; Henry A. Giroux, *The Abandoned Generation: Democracy Beyond the Culture of Fear* (New York: Palgrave-MacMillan, 2003), 1–70; David Nibert, *Hitting the Lottery Jackpot: Government and the Taxing of Dreams* (New York: Monthly Review Press, 2000), 187–205; Paul Street, "More Than Entertainment: Neal Gabler and the Illusions of Post-Ideological Society," *Monthly Review*, February 2000, 58–62; Paul Street, *Racial Oppression in the Global Metropolis: A Living Black Chicago History* (New York: Rowman and Littlefield, 2007), 25, 37–38, 40, 148, 162, 285–295.

42. Robert W. McChesney, *Corporate Media and the Threat to Democracy* (New York: Seven Stories, 1997), 5–7; Robert W. McChesney, *Rich Media, Poor Democracy: Communication Politics in Dubious Times* (New York: New Press, 1999); Edward S. Herman and Noam Chomsky, *Manufacturing Consent: The Political Economy of the Mass Media* (New York: Pantheon, 1992); Anthony DiMaggio, *When Media Goes to War: Hegemonic Discourse, Public Opinion, and the Limits of Dissent* (New York: Monthly Review Press, 2010); Street, "More Than Entertainment"; Paul Street, "Killing Us Softly: Politics

and Entertainment," *ZNet Magazine*, April 21, 2004, at www.zmag.org/content/showarticle.cfm?SectionID=21&ItemID=5372; Paul Street, "Who Controls the Present," *Z Net*, May 14, 2010, at www.zcommunications.org/who-controls-the-present-by-paul-street; Paul Street, "Reflections on Herbert Schiller's The Mind Managers," *ZNet*, April 4, 2009, at www.zcommunications.org/reflections-on-a-largely-forgotten-book-herbert-schillers-the-mind-managers-1973-by-paul-street.

43. Leonard Steinhorn and Barbara Diggs-Brown, *By the Color of Our Skin* (New York: Penguin, 2000); Sheryl Cashin, *The Failures of Integration* (New York: PublicAffairs, 2004); Derrick Bell, *Silent Covenants: Brown v. Board of Education and the Unfulfilled Hopes for Racial Reform* (New York: Oxford University Press, 2004), 77–78; Michael K. Brown, Martin Carnoy, Elliott Currie, Troy Duster, David B. Oppenheimer, Marjorie M. Shultz, and David Wellman, *Whitewashing Race: The Myth of a Color-Blind Society* (Berkeley and Los Angeles: University of California Press, 2003); Stephen Steinberg, *Turning Back: The Retreat from Racial Justice in American Thought and Policy* (Boston: Beacon Press, 1995); Street, *Racial Oppression*; Paul Street, "A Whole Lott Missing: Rituals of Purification and Deep Racism Denial," *Black Commentator*, December 22, 2002; Paul Street, "The Full Blown Oprah Effect: Reflections on Color, Class, and New Age Racism," *Black Commentator*, February 27, 2005, at www.blackcommentator.com/127/127_oprah.html; Paul Street, "Skipping Past Structural Racism: Center Trumps Left in Recent PBS Series in Race in America," *Black Commentator*, April 8, 2004, at www.blackcommentator.com/85/85_think_street.html.; Street, *The Empire's New Clothes*, 144–145; and Paul Street, "Is Barack Obama Bad for Racial Justice?" *Black Agenda Report*, October 6, 2010, at www.blackagendareport.com/?q=content/barack-obama-bad-racial-justice.

44. Jacob S. Hacker and Paul Pierson, *Off Center: The Republican Revolution and the Erosion of Democracy* (New Haven, CT: Yale University Press, 2005), 1–40 and passim.

45. Kathleen Hall Jamieson and James Cappella, *Echo Chamber: Rush Limbaugh and the Conservative Media Establishment* (Oxford, UK: Oxford University Press, 2008).

46. Hacker and Pierson, *Off Center*, 174–181.

47. Richard Hofstadter, "The Paranoid Style in American Politics," *Harper's Magazine*, November 1964, http://karws.gso.uri.edu/jfk/conspiracy_theory/the_paranoid_mentality/the_paranoid_style.html.

48. Jill Lepore quoted in E. J. Dionne Jr., "The Tea Party Movement Is a Scam," *RealClearPolitics*, September 23, 2010.

49. See Adele Stan's problematic essay, "The Tea Party Is Dangerous: Dispelling 7 Myths That Help Us Avoid Reality About the New Right-Wing Politics," *AlterNet*, July 1, 2010.

50. Jean Baudrillard, *The Gulf War Did Not Take Place* (Bloomington: Indiana University Press, 1995).

51. Noam Chomsky, "We Shouldn't Ridicule Tea Party People," YouTube, April 30, 2010, at www.youtube.com/watch?v=8JQiEya_Jks.

52. Noam Chomsky, "Worker Occupations and the Future of Radical Labor: An Interview with Noam Chomsky," *ZNet*, November 19, 2009, at www.zcommunications.org/worker-occupations-and-the-future-of-radical-labor-by-noam-chomsky.

53. Adolph Reed Jr., *"Class Notes": Posing as Politics and Other Thoughts on the American Scene* (New York: New Press, 2000), 64–69.

54. Christopher Hitchens, *No One Left to Lie To: The Values of the Worst Family* (New York: Verso, 2000); Street, *Barack Obama and the Future*; Street, *The Empire's New Clothes*.

55. Dionne, "The Tea Party Movement."

56. Especially Bunch's *The Backlash* and Zernike's *Boiling Mad*.

57. We are particularly distressed at how poorly the "arguments" are constructed in O'Hara and Armey's transparently biased pro–Tea Party volumes and in Rasmussen and Schoen's horrifically conceptualized and egregiously mistaken best-seller *Mad as Hell*, which bears glowing cover endorsements from far-right Republican talk radio personalities Rush Limbaugh and Sean Hannity and archreactionary activist and columnist Willam Kristol.

Chapter Two

1. Karl Marx, *The Eighteenth Brumaire of Louis Bonaparte* (Moscow: Progress Publishers, 1972 [1852]), 10.

2. This and the next seven paragraphs rely on Eric Foner, *Give Us Liberty! An American History*, vol. 1 (New York: Norton, 2005), 163–181; Gordon Wood, *The American Revolution: A History* (New York: Modern Library, 2003), 27–38; Benjamin Larabee, *The Boston Tea Party* (New York, 1964); and Edmund Morgan, *The Birth of the American Republic, 1763–1789* (Chicago: University of Chicago Press, 1993).

3. Alfred Young, *The Shoemaker and the Tea Party: Memory and the American Revolution* (Boston: Beacon Press, 1999), 94.

4. Ibid., 99–100.

5. Wood, *The American Revolution*, 38.

6. J. Frederic Jameson, *The American Revolution Considered as a Social Movement* (Princeton, NJ: Princeton University Press, 1968).

7. Young, *The Shoemaker and the Tea Party*, 100.

8. Ibid., 92, 161.

9. Ibid., 53, 99–100.

10. Ibid., 100.

11. Ibid., 101–104, 107.

12. Ibid., 106–107.

13. Ibid., 108–131.

14. Ibid., 145–154.

15. Ibid., 170.

16. Ibid., 160–161.

17. In the 1830s and 1840s, pro- and antiabolitionists and antieviction "downrent" activists in the Hudson Valley all appropriated the symbols, regalia, and tactics of the Tea Party in different ways (the Hudson Valley movement cited the tea action as a justification for "extra-legal action"). At centennial celebrations in Boston of what had by 1873 become a fully enshrined iconic event, leading advocates of social reform, racial progress, and women's suffrage (including Frederick Douglass, Wendell Phillips, William Lloyd Garrison, Thomas Wentworth Higginson, and Lucy Stone) claimed the Tea Party for the causes of social justice and political reform and against those who were trying "to prevent money from accumulating in the aristocratic class." Two and a half years later, during celebrations of the nation's centennial, Phillips spoke in defense of the preservation of the Old South Meeting House by noting that "it was the mechanics [the artisans and workers] of Boston that threw the tea into the dock; it was the mechanics of Boston that held the hand of Sam Adams; it was the mechanics of Boston, Paul Revere among them[, who] carried us through the revolution." In sharp contrast, the well-off attendees of elite Tea Party centennial celebrations heard a speech from Robert C. Winthrop, a long-time Massachusetts congressman and president of the Massachusetts Historical Society. Winthrop "all but disavowed the destruction of the tea," saying that "we are not here today to glory a mere act of violence, or a merely successful destruction of property." Winthrop warned against "lawless violence" and claimed falsely that "we know not exactly whether any of the patriot leaders of the day had a hand in the act." The left-right divide over the meaning of the Tea Party would continue into the twentieth century. See Young, *The Shoemaker and the Tea Party*, 147–148, 180–183, 186–191.

18. Ibid., 195–198.

19. John O'Hara, *The New American Tea Party: The Counterrevolution Against Bailouts, Handouts, Reckless Spending, and More Taxes* (New York: Wiley, 2010).

20. Kate Zernike, *Boiling Mad: Inside Tea Party America* (New York: Times Books, 2010), 13; Ben McGrath, "The Movement: The Rise of Tea Party Activism," *New Yorker*, February 1, 2010.

21. See Chapter 3.

22. Jane Mayer, "Covert Operations: The Billionaire Brothers Who Are Waging a War Against Obama," *New Yorker*, October 30, 2010.

23. Sharon Cooper, *Taxpayers' Tea Party* (Baen, April 1994).

24. Young, *The Shoemaker and the Tea Party*, 198.

25. Zernike, *Boiling Mad*, 33–35.

26. http://mysite.verizon.net/nathanielyao/index.html.

27. Matt Taibbi, "Tea and Crackers: How Corporate Interests and Republican Insiders Created the Tea Party Monster," *Rolling Stone*, October 15, 2010.

28. Zernike, *Boiling Mad*, 13–19.

29. "A 'Tea Party' to Protest Paterson's Taxes," *Your News Now*, January 24, 2009, at http://centralny.ynn.com/content/all_news/132356/a—tea-party—to-protest-paterson-s-taxes/.

30. Anemona Hartocollis, "Failure of State Soda Tax Plan Reflects Power of an Anti-tax Message," *New York Times*, July 2, 2010.

31. Jill Leopore quoted in E. J. Dionne Jr., "The Tea Party Movement Is a Scam," RealClearPolitics, September 23, 2010.

32. See Paul Street, *The Empire's New Clothes: Barack Obama in the Real World of Power* (Boulder, CO: Paradigm Publishers, 2010) for a detailed left critique.

33. For useful reflections on the Tea Party's egregious exploitation and manipulation of American history, see Greg Grandin, "Glenn Beck, America's Historian Laureate: The Tea Party's Guide to American Exceptionalism," TomDispatch.com, May 13, 2010.

Chapter Three

1. Kevin Zeese, "Can the Right and Left Work Together to Oppose War and Empire?" Antiwar.com, February 25, 2010; Katrina vanden Heuvel, "Could Progressives Find Allies in the Tea Party?" *Washington Post*, April 14, 2010, at www.washingtonpost.com/wp-dyn/content/article/2010/04/13/AR2010041302492.html; Medea Benjamin, "Peace Activists Extend an Olive Branch to Tea Party to Talk About War," Huffington Post, April 13, 2010, at www.huffingtonpost.com/medea-benjamin/peace-activists-extend-an_b_535772.html; Chuck Collins, "How to Talk to a Tea Party Activist," *The Nation*, April 14, 2010, at www.thenation.com/article/how-talk-tea-party-activist; John Nichols, "Bad Brew: What's Become of Tea Party Activism," *The Nation*, April 14, 2010, at www.thenation.com/blog/bad-brew-whats-become-tea-party-populism?page=full; David Rovics, "Breaking Ranks: Tea Parties, Espresso Snobs, Freedom, and Equality," *Counterpunch*, April 15,

2010, at www.counterpunch.org/rovics04152010.html; Jon Hochschartner, "I Don't See Much Difference: An Interview with Noam Chomsky," *Z Magazine*, April 2010.

2. See, specifically, the bipartisan commission appointed by Obama set up to recommend cuts to Social Security: Laura Meckler, "Social Security Cuts Weighed by Panel," *Wall Street Journal*, August 20, 2010, at http://online.wsj .com/article/SB10001424052748704476104575439792287255372.html.

3. Hochschartner, "I Don't See Much Difference."

4. Noam Chomsky and Diane Krauthamer, "Worker Occupations and the Future of Radical Labor: An Interview with Noam Chomsky," *Z Magazine*, February 2010, 22.

5. Noam Chomsky, "The Center Cannot Hold: Rekindling the Radical Imagination," Address to Left Forum, New York City, New York, March 21, 2010, at *ZNet*, April 20, 2010, at www.zcommunications.org/the-center-cannot-hold-rekindling-the-radical-imagination-by-noam-chomsky

6. CBS/*New York Times*, "Polling the Tea Party: Who They Are and What They Believe," *New York Times*, April 14, 2010, at www.nytimes.com/ interactive/2010/04/14/us/politics/20100414-tea-party-poll-graphic.html #tab=4.

7. For a statement of the left critique focused on the first year of the Obama presidency, see Paul Street, *The Empire's New Clothes: Barack Obama in the Real World of Power* (Boulder, CO: Paradigm Publishers, 2010).

8. Thomas Frank, *What's the Matter with Kansas? How Conservatives Won the Heart of America* (New York: Metropolitan, 2004). For a useful critique, see Larry Bartels, "Inequalities," *New York Times Magazine*, April 27, 2008.

9. Glenn Beck quoted in Adam Bessie, "Media Spreads Tea Party Leaders as 'Anti-Establishment' Myth," Media-ocracy, September 20, 2010, at www .media-ocracy.org.

10. Ben McGrath, "The Movement: The Rise of Tea Party Activism," *New Yorker*, February 1, 2010.

11. Steve Kull, "Big Government Is Not the Issue," World Public Opinion .org, August 19, 2010, at www.worldpublicopinion.org/pipa/articles/ brunitedstatescanadara/665.php?nid=&id=&pnt=665&lb=.

12. Ibid.

13. Pew Research Center, "Public Sours on Government and Business," Pew Research Center, October 25, 2005, at http://people-press.org/report/ 261/public-sours-on-government-and-business.

14. Anthony Oberschall, *Social Movements: Ideologies, Interests, and Identities* (Piscataway, NJ: Transaction, 1996), 22–23.

15. Ibid.

16. CBS/*New York Times*, "Polling the Tea Party."

17. Interviews with 1,023 adult Americans, including 954 registered voters, conducted by telephone by Opinion Research Corporation on February 12–15, 2010, at http://i2.cdn.turner.com/cnn/2010/images/02/17/rel4b.pdf.

18. Lee Fang, "The Tea Party Profiteers: How Republican Operatives Are Exploiting Economic Anxiety for Power, Cash," ThinkProgress, February 2, 2010, at http://thinkprogress.org/2010/02/02/tea-party-profiteers/; Janie Lorber and Eric Lipton, "GOP Insider Fuels Tea Party and Suspicion," *New York Times*, September 18, 2010, at www.nytimes.com/2010/09/19/us/politics/19russo.html; Stephanie Mencimer, "Tempest in the Tea Party," *Mother Jones*, December 30, 2009, at http://motherjones.com/politics/2009/12/tempest-tea-party; Adam Bessie, "Tea Party Leaders Are Not Anti-Establishment," Truthout, October 10, 2010, at www.truth-out.org/tea-party-leaders-are-not-anti-establishment64056; Lee Fang, "Maddow Exposes Oil Industry Backing of Astroturf Lobbying Firm Americans for Prosperity," ThinkProgress, August 7, 2009, at http://thinkprogress.org/2009/08/07/maddow-afp/.

19. Pew Research Center for the People and the Press, "Distrust, Discontent, Anger, and Partisan Rancor: The People and Their Government," April 18, 2010, at http://people-press.org/report/606/trust-in-government.

20. CBS/*New York Times*, "Polling the Tea Party."

21. Charles Tanner Jr., "Correlation Between Unemployment Levels and Tea Party Membership," NAACP Tea Party Nationalism, September 9, 2010, at http://teapartynationalism.com/index.php?option=com_k2&view=item&id=109:appendix-a-is-there-any-correlation-between-unemployment-levels-and-tea-party-membership?&Itemid=292.

22. "CNN Poll: Who Are the Tea Party Activists?" CNN Politics, February 17, 2010, at http://politicalticker.blogs.cnn.com/2010/02/17/cnn-poll-who-are-the-tea-party-activists/, full poll at http://i2.cdn.turner.com/cnn/2010/images/02/17/rel4b.pdf.

23. CBS/*New York Times*, "Polling the Tea Party."

24. John O'Hara, *The New American Tea Party: The Counterrevolution Against Bailouts, Handouts, Reckless Spending, and More Taxes* (New York: Wiley, 2010), 206.

25. Ibid., 1–2.

26. www.indeed.com/salary/q-Floor-Trader-l-Chicago,-IL.html. During his famous outburst, Santelli called the traders and the financial professionals surrounding him "a pretty good statistical cross-section of America."

27. McGrath, "The Movement."

28. Bessie, "Media Spreads."

29. Media Matters for America, "Beck Berates O'Donnell for Pointing Out Palin's Support of Bailout to Palin Supporter," Media Matters for America, November 19, 2009, at http://mediamatters.org/mmtv/200911190016.

30. Bessie, "Media Spreads."

31. Matt Taibbi, "Tea and Crackers: How Corporate Interests and Republican Insiders Created the Tea Party Monster," *Rolling Stone*, October 15, 2010.

32. Scott Rasmussen and Douglas Schoen, *Mad as Hell: How the Tea Party Movement Is Fundamentally Remaking Our Two-Party System* (New York: HarperCollins, 2010), 297.

33. CBS/*New York Times*, "Polling the Tea Party."

34. Rasmussen and Schoen, *Mad as Hell*, 275–280.

35. Benjamin I. Page and Lawrence R. Jacobs, *Class War? What Americans Really Think About Economic Inequality* (Chicago: University of Chicago Press, 2009). See also Martin Gilens, *Why Americans Hate Welfare: Race, Media, and the Politics of Antipoverty Policy* (Chicago: University of Chicago Press, 2000).

36. For sources and details, see Paul Street, *Barack Obama and the Future of American Politics* (Boulder, CO: Paradigm Publishers, 2008), Appendix A; and Katherine Adams and Charles Derber, *The New Feminized Majority* (Boulder, CO: Paradigm Publishers, 2008), 67–75. For additional opinion data, see Page and Jacobs, *Class War?* which demonstrates broad public support for policies aimed at narrowing the gap between rich and poor and creating genuine opportunity for all. Page and Jacobs find that most Americans support higher minimum wages, improved public education, wider access to universal health insurance coverage, and use of tax dollars to fund these programs.

37. Alex Castellanos quoted in David Paul Kuhn, "R.I.P. Political Establishment," RealClearPolitics, September 21, 2010, at www.realclearpolitics .com/articles/2010/09/21/rip_political_establishmen_and_tea_party _netroots_107238.html.

38. CBS/*New York Times*, "Polling the Tea Party."

39. Ibid.

40. Lisa Lerer, "Tea Party Economic Gloom Fuels Republican Momentum," Bloomberg News, October 13, 2010, at http://insurancenewsnet.com/ article.aspx?id=230316&type=newswires. Consistent with the right's alignment with the business class, a plurality of Tea Party backers told Selzer and Co. that they would not be less likely to support a candidate whose campaign ads were financed by anonymous business groups. For all likely voters, a plurality said that would affect their vote.

41. The classic study is Frank, *What's the Matter with Kansas?*

42. This notion is promoted by Rasmussen and Schoen in their widely circulated book on the Tea Party, *Mad as Hell*, 285.

43. By contrast, the overall CBS/*Times* sample included four Democrats among their top eight, ranked as follows: Barack Obama, Bill Clinton, Hillary Clinton, Newt Gingrich, Jimmy Carter, Sarah Palin, John McCain, and George W. Bush. CBS/*New York Times*, "Polling the Tea Party."

44. Ibid.

45. Ibid.

46. Ibid.; CBS/*New York Times*, "Polling the Tea Party."

47. Lerer, "Tea Party Economic Gloom."

48. "Tea Party Movement," *New York Times* Web site, September 7, 2010, at http://topics.nytimes.com/top/reference/timestopics/subjects/t/tea_party_movement/index.html.

49. Taibbi, "Tea and Crackers."

50. Dougherty, "Tea Party Crashers."

51. Taibbi, "Tea and Crackers."

52. Kate Zernike, "For Tea Party, Sway Beyond Mere Numbers," *New York Times*, October 15, 2010.

53. Kelley B. Vlahos, "Buzzkill at the Tea Party," Antiwar.com, March 23, 2010, at http://original.antiwar.com/vlahos/2010/03/22/liberty-forum/.

54. "Tea Party Closely Linked to Religious Right, Pol Finds" ABC News, October 5, 2010; Andy Sullivan, "Poll: Tea Partiers Back 'Christian Conservative Agenda,'" MSNBC, October 5, 2010, at www.msnbc.msn.com/id/39522464/ns/politics-more_politics/; Robert P. Jones and Daniel Cox, "Religion and the Tea Party in the 2010 Election," Public Religion Research Institute, October 2010, at www.publicreligion.org/objects/uploads/fck/file/AVS%202010%20Report%20FINAL.pdf.

55. "Tea Party Supporters," CBS News, April 14, 2010, at www.cbsnews.com/8301-503544_162-20002529-503544.html.

56. Alfredo Garcia, "Is the Tea Party Unbiblical?" Pew Forum on Religion and Public Life, July 22, 2010, at http://pewforum.org/Religion-News/Is-the-Tea-Party-unbiblical.aspx. See also the February 2010 Pew Research Center survey at http://people-press.org/dataarchive/.

57. Michelle Boorstein, "Tea Party, Religious Right Often Overlap," *Washington Post*, October 5, 2010, at www.washingtonpost.com/wp-dyn/content/article/2010/10/05/AR2010100501491.html.

58. Marc J. Hetherington and Jonathan D. Weiler, *Authoritarianism and Polarization in American Politics* (Cambridge, UK: Cambridge University Press, 2009), 57–60.

59. Amy Gardner, "Tea Party Picking Up Steam Nationwide," *Washington Post*, September 21, 2010.

60. Jane Mayer, "Covert Operations: The Billionaire Brothers Who Are Waging War Against Obama," *New Yorker*, August 30, 2010.

61. Ibid.

62. Lee Fang, "MEMO: Health Insurance, Banking, Oil Industries Met with Koch, Chamber, Glenn Beck to Plot 2010 Election," ThinkProgress, October 20, 2010, at http://thinkprogress.org/2010/10/20/beck-koch-chamber

-meeting/?utm_source=web&utm_medium=twitter. Thanks to Kelly Gerling for bringing this source to our attention.

63. Bessie, "Media Spreads."

64. Mayer, "Covert Operations."

65. Ibid.

66. McGrath, "The Movement."

67. Gardner, "Tea Party Picking Up Steam."

68. Fang, "MEMO."

69. William Greider, *Who Will Tell the People? The Betrayal of American Democracy* (New York: Simon and Schuster, 1992), 36–37.

Chapter Four

1. Kate Zernike, *Boiling Mad: Inside Tea Party America* (New York: Times Books, 2010), 5–6.

2. Kate Zernike, "Where Dr. King Stood, Tea Party Claims His Mantle," *New York Times*, August 27, 2010, at www.nytimes.com/2010/08/28/us/politics/28beck.html; Clay Waters, "Book Review: NY Times Reporter Kate Zernike Still Finding Tea Party Racism in 'Boiling Mad,'" Media Research Center, September 18, 2010, at www.newsbusters.org/blogs/clay-waters/2010/09/18/book-review-ny-times-reporter-kate-zernike-still-finding-tea-party-raci.

3. William Douglas, "Tea Party Protesters Scream 'Nigger' at Black Congressman," McClatchy Newspapers, March 20, 2010, at www.mcclatchydc.com/2010/03/20/90772/rep-john-lewis-charges-protesters.html.

4. Don Irvine, "Did the Media Muff Story on Racist Tea Party Protestors?" Accuracy in Media, March 21, 2010, at www.aim.org/don-irvine-blog/did-the-media-muff-story-on-racist-tea-party-protestors/.

5. Zernike, *Boiling Mad*, 5, 51, 139.

6. Benjamin Todd Jealous, "Tea Party Nationalism: Foreword," Tea Party Nationalism, 2010, at http://teapartynationalism.com/.

7. Fox News star Glenn Beck lamented "how easy" it is "to dupe people," in light of the obvious fact that the Tea Party "is not about race." Sean Hannity attacked the "all-out effort by the Democrats to create a caricature of the Tea Party movement as racist, as extreme," while Bill O'Reilly depicted media discussions of Tea Party racism in other media outlets as an example of how the liberal media were driven by "ideology" instead of serious concern over racism in American culture and politics. Glenn Beck, *The Glenn Beck Program*, March 24, 2010, 5 PM EST; Sean Hannity, *Hannity*, April 1, 2010, 9 PM EST; Bill O'Reilly, *The O'Reilly Factor*, April 5, 2010, 8 PM EST.

8. Ed Schultz, *The Ed Show*, July 23, 2010, 6 PM EST.

9. Keith Olbermann, *Countdown*, July 14, 2010, 8 PM EST; Rachel Maddow, *The Rachel Maddow Show*, July 21, 2010, 9 PM EST.

10. Chris Matthews, *The Chris Matthews Show*, July 13, 2010, 5 PM EST.

11. Michael Gerson, "Signs of Sanity from the Tea Party," *Washington Post*, July 21, 2010.

12. Michael Gerson, "A Primer on Political Reality," *Washington Post*, February 19, 2010.

13. Eugene Robinson, "The Tea Party Must Purge Racism from Its Ranks," *Washington Post*, July 20, 2010.

14. Charles Krauthammer, "The Buckley Rule," *Washington Post*, September 17, 2010; E. J. Dionne Jr., "The NAACP's Tea Party Challenge," *Washington Post*, July 15, 2010.

15. Colbert I. King, "The Tea Party Faithful Holler Back," *Washington Post*, April 10, 2010.

16. Charles M. Blow, "Dog Days of Obama," *New York Times*, July 17, 2010.

17. Charles M. Blow, "Trying to Outrun Race," *New York Times*, May 8, 2010.

18. National Association for the Advancement of Colored People, "Tea Party Nationalism," October 20, 2010, at http://teapartynationalism.com/. The authors of this report seemed unable to grasp the difference between racism understood at the level of explicit, old-fashioned public bigotry and outwardly "color-blind," post–civil rights era racism grasped at the deeper institutional and ideological levels discussed in this chapter.

19. Ann Gerhart and Phillip Rucker, "The Tea Party Is Still Taking Shape," *Washington Post*, February 6, 2010, at www.washingtonpost.com/wp-dyn/content/article/2010/02/05/AR2010020501694.html.

20. David Weigel, "Rand Paul, Telling the Truth," *Washington Post*, 2010, at http://voices.washingtonpost.com/right-now/2010/05/rand_paul_telling_the_truth.html.

21. Tim Wise, *Colorblind: The Rise of Post-Racial Politics and the Retreat from Racial Equity* (San Francisco: City Lights, 2010), 17–18.

22. For recent academic reflections and research on "color-blind racism," see Eduardo Bonilla-Silva, *Racism Without Racists: Color-Blind Racism and the Persistence of Racial Inequality in America* (Lanham, MD: Rowman and Littlefield, 2009); Michelle Alexander, *The New Jim Crow: Mass Incarceration in the Age of Colorblindness* (New York: New Press, 2010); Michael K. Brown, Martin Carnoy, Elliot Currie, Troy Duster, David E. Oppenheimer, Marjorie K. Schultz, and David Wellman, *Whitewashing Race: The Myth of a Color-Blind Society* (Berkeley and Los Angeles: University of California Press, 2005); and

Paul L. Street, *Racial Oppression and the Global Metropolis: A Living Black Chicago History* (Lanham, MD: Rowman and Littlefield, 2007). See also Paul Street, "Skipping Past Structural Racism: Center Trumps Left in Recent PBS Series on Race in America," *Black Commentator*, April 8, 2004, at www.black commentator.com/85/85_think_street.html; Paul Street, "A Lott Missing: Rituals of Purification and Deep Racism Denial," *Black Commentator*, December 22, 2002, at www.blackcommentator.com and www. nationinstitute.org/tomdispatch/index.mhtml?pid=258; Henry A. Giroux, *The Abandoned Generation: Democracy Beyond the Culture of Fear* (New York: Palgrave-MacMillan, 2003), 1–70; Henry A. Giroux, *The Terror of Neoliberalism: Authoritarianism and the Eclipse of Democracy* (Boulder, CO: Paradigm Publishers, 2004), 1–53; Adolph Reed Jr., "Undone by Neoliberalism: New Orleans Was Decimated by an Ideological Program, Not a Storm," *The Nation*, September 18, 2006, 26–30.

23. University of Washington Institute for the Study of Ethnicity, Race, and Sexuality, "2010 Multi-State Survey on Race and Politics," 2010, at http://depts.washington.edu/uwiser/racepolitics.html, detailed tables at http://depts.washington.edu/uwiser/mssrp_table.pdf and http://depts.washington.edu/uwiser/Stereotypes%20about%20Asians%20and%20whites%20by%20White%20tea%20Party%20Approval.pdf; "New Poll Finds Tea Partiers Have More Racist Attitudes," *Newsweek*, April 2, 2010, at www.newsweek.com/blogs/the-gaggle/2010/04/09/new-poll-finds-tea-partiers-have-more-racist-attitudes.html. The University of Washington surveyed 1,006 respondents across six "battleground states" (Georgia, Michigan, Missouri, Nevada, North Carolina, and Ohio) between February 8 and March 15, 2010. CBS/*New York Times*, "Tea Party Supporters: Who They Are and What They Believe," CBS News, April 14, 2010, at www.cbsnews.com/8301–503544_162–20002529–503544.html.

24. Martin Gilens, *Why Americans Hate Welfare: Race, Media, and the Politics of Antipoverty Policy* (Chicago: University of Chicago Press, 1999), 159.

25. Melvin L. Oliver and Thomas M. Shapiro, *Black Wealth/White Wealth: A New Perspective on Racial Inequality* (London: Routledge, 1997), 136–137.

26. David Leonhardt, "The Black-White Pay Gap," *New York Times*, September 16, 2010, at http://economix.blogs.nytimes.com/2010/09/16/the-black-white-pay-gap/

27. Gilens, *Why Americans Hate Welfare*, 159.

28. Estimates for educational segregation for the Chicago metropolitan area, as compiled by the authors of this book, are based upon our consultation of district-by-district high school racial demographic backgrounds in Cook County in 2008, provided through the Illinois State Board of Education's annual "Report Card." For more on national residential and educational segregation, see also

Charles Lamb, *Housing Segregation in Suburban America Since 1960: Presidential and Judicial Politics* (Cambridge, UK: Cambridge University Press, 2005); Oliver and Shapiro, *Black Wealth/White Wealth*, 139; Jonathan Kozol, "Still Separate, Still Unequal: America's Educational Apartheid," *Harper's*, September 2005, at www.harpers.org/archive/2005/09/0080727; and Jonathan Kozol, *The Shame of the Nation: The Restoration of Apartheid Schooling in America* (New York: Crown, 2005).

29. National Council of State and Housing Agencies, "NLIHC Finds Shortage of Affordable Housing Worsened for Low Income Households," National Council of State and Housing Agencies, January 7, 2010, at www.ncsha.org/resource/nlihc-finds-shortage-affordable-housing-worsened-lowest-income-households; Chicago Urban League, *Still Separate, Unequal: Race, Place, Policy, and the State of Black Chicago* (Chicago: Chicago Urban League, Department of Research and Planning, April 2005), 125–130.

30. Thomas J. Sugrue, *The Origins of the Urban Crisis: Race and Inequality in Postwar Detroit* (Princeton, NJ: Princeton University Press, 2005), 140–141; William Julius Wilson, *When Work Disappears: The World of the New Urban Poor* (New York: Vintage Books, 1996), 3–24; William Julius Wilson, *The Truly Disadvantaged: The Inner City, the Underclass, and Public Policy* (Chicago: University of Chicago Press, 1987), 44.

31. Sugrue, *The Origins of the Urban Crisis*, 92; Robert O. Self, *American Babylon: Race and the Struggle for Postwar Oakland* (Princeton, NJ: Princeton University Press, 2003), 256; Arnold R. Hirsch, *Making the Second Ghetto: Race and Housing in Chicago 1940–1960* (Cambridge, UK: Cambridge University Press, 1985), 15–16.

32. Chicago Urban League, *Still Separate, Unequal*, 140–145; Devah Pager, *Marked: Race, Crime, and Finding Work in an Era of Mass Incarceration* (Chicago: University of Chicago Press, 2007); Sugrue, *The Origins of the Urban Crisis:* 92; Self, *American Babylon*, 256; Arnold R. Hirsch, *Making the Second Ghetto: Race and Housing in Chicago 1940–1960* (Cambridge, UK: Cambridge University Press, 1985), 15–16.

33. Alexander, *The New Jim Crow*, 7, 59, 63–66, 73–77, 85–87, 95–136, 184, 191; Melissa Moore, "Covering Crime and Justice," *Justice Journalism*, 2010, at www.justicejournalism.org/crimeguide/chapter04/chapter04.html.

34. Alexander, *The New Jim Crow*, 49–50, 145–50, 206, 216–217; Paul Street, *The Vicious Circle: Race, Prison, Jobs, and Community in Chicago* (Chicago: Chicago Urban League, Department of Research and Planning, October 2002); Pager, *Marked*, 2007. Pager found that the discrimination experienced by black jobs applicants even without felony records was significantly more extreme than that experienced by whites with felony records.

35. Street, *The Vicious Circle*.

36. Andrew Grant Thomas and Gary Orfield, *Twenty-First Century Color Lines: Multiracial Change in Contemporary America* (Philadelphia: Temple University Press, 2009), 47–48; Steven D. Levitt and Stephen J. Dubner, *Freakonomics: A Rogue Economist Explores the Hidden Side of Everything* (New York: William Morrow, 2005), 64; Richard Rothstein, *Class and Schools: Using Social, Economic, and Educational Reform to Close the Black-White Achievement Gap* (Washington, DC: Economic Policy Institute, 2004); Harold Wenglinsky, "How Money Matters: The Effect of School District Spending on Academic Achievement," *Sociology of Education* 70 (July 1997): 221–237; John Mackenzie, "Public School Funding and Performance," University of Delaware Newark Working Paper, 2010, at www.udel.edu/johnmack/research/school_funding.pdf.

37. Kozol, "Still Separate, Still Unequal"; Kozol, *The Shame of the Nation*, 18–19, 20, 28, 60.

38. See, among many sources, Jonathan Kozol, "Educational Apartheid Fifty Years After *Brown*," *The Nation*, May 3, 2004; Alfie Kohn, "Standardized Testing and Its Victims," *Education Week* (September 17, 2004); Henry A. Giroux, *The Abandoned Generation: Democracy Beyond the Culture of Fear* (New York: Palgrave Macmillan, 2003), 75–76, 79, 82–90, 98; Asa Hillard III, comments in "Beyond Black, White, and Brown," *The Nation*, May 3, 2004; Paul Street, *Segregated Schools: Educational Apartheid in the Post–Civil Rights Era* (New York: Routledge, 2005), 78–80; and Street, *Racial Oppression*, 249–251.

39. Paul Kantor and Dennis R. Judd, *American Urban Politics in a Global Age* (New York: Pearson Longman, 2008); Kevin M. Kruse and Thomas J. Sugrue, eds., *The New Suburban History* (Chicago: University of Chicago Press, 2006); Kenneth T. Jackson, *Crabgrass Frontier: The Suburbanization of the United States* (Oxford, UK: Oxford University Press, 1985); Robert A. Beauregard, *When America Became Suburban* (Minneapolis: University of Minnesota Press, 2006); John R. Logan and Mark Schneider, "Racial Segregation and Racial Change in American Suburbs, 1970–1980," *American Journal of Sociology* 89, no. 4 (1984); Stephen Grant Meyer, *As Long as They Don't Move Next Door: Racial Segregation and Conflict in American Neighborhoods* (Lanham, MD.: Rowman and Littlefield, 2000); Lamb, *Housing*; Chicago Urban League, *Still Separate, Unequal*, 130; Environmental Justice Resource Center, "Suburban Sprawl and Transportation Racism," *Black Commentator*, September 23, 2004; Robert D. Bullard and Angelo Torres, eds., *Highway Robbery: Transportation Racism and New Highways to Equity* (Boston: South End Press, 2004).

40. Roy Brooks, *Integration or Separation: A Strategy for Racial Equality* (Cambridge, MA: Harvard University Press, 2002), ix.; Joel Feagin, *Racist America: Roots, Current Realities, and Future Reparations* (New York: Routledge, 2000),

261. For a discussion of the withdrawal of affluent, white taxes from social welfare spending for the poor, dating back to at least the 1970s, see Self, *American Babylon*.

41. Douglas S. Massey, "American Apartheid: Housing Segregation and Persistent Urban Poverty," Distinguished Lecture, Social Science Research Institute, Northern Illinois University, DeKalb, Illinois, 1994. In testimony supporting the University of Michigan's affirmative action program, historian Thomas Sugrue explained why it is a matter of no small significance for racial equality that "whites and minorities seldom live in the same neighborhoods." Expanding on the point, Sugrue observed, "The questions—where do you live? and who are your neighbors?—are not trivial. A person's perspectives on the world, his friends, her group of childhood peers, his networks and job opportunities, her wealth or lack of wealth, his quality of education—all of these are determined to no small extent by where he or she lives." Thomas Sugrue quoted in Chicago Urban League, *Still Separate, Unequal*, 23.

42. See, for example, Feagin, *Racist America*; and Brown et al., *Whitewashing Race*.

43. We are informed in part by Stokely Carmichael and Stanley Hamilton's perceptive response to the question "What is racism?" at the beginning of their book *Black Power*: "Racism is both overt and covert. It takes two, closely related forms: individual whites acting against individual blacks, and acts by the total white community against the black community. We call these individual racism and institutionalized racism. The first consists of overt acts by individuals, which cause death, injury or the violent destruction of property. This type can be recorded by television cameras; it can frequently be observed in the process of commission. The second type is less overt, far more subtle, less identifiable in terms of specific individuals committing the acts. But it is no less destructive of human life. The second type operates in the operation of established and respected forces in the society, and thus receives far less public condemnation than the first type."

Carmichael and Hamilton illustrate their distinction between overt "individual" racism and covert "institutionalized" racism with some compelling historical examples: "When white terrorists bomb a black church and kill five black children, that is an act of individual racism, widely deplored by most segments of the society. But when in that same city—Birmingham, Alabama— five hundred black babies die each year because of the lack of proper food, shelter and medical facilities, and thousands more are destroyed and maimed physically, emotionally and intellectually because of conditions of poverty and discrimination in the black community, that is a function of institutionalized racism. When a black family moves into a home in a white neighborhood and is stoned, burned or routed out, they are victims of an overt act of individual racism which many people will condemn—at least in words. But it is institutional racism that keeps black people locked in dilapidated slum tenements, subject to the daily prey of exploitative slumlords, merchants, loan sharks and discriminatory real estate agents. The society either pretends it does not know of this latter situation, or is in fact incapable of doing anything meaningful about it." Stokely Carmichael and Charles Hamilton, *Black Power: The Politics of Liberation in America* (New York: Vintage Books, 1967), 4, quoted in Stephen Steinberg, *Turning Back: The Retreat from Racial Justice in American Thought and Policy* (Boston: Beacon Press, 1995), 75–76.

44. Giroux, *The Abandoned Generation*, 1–70; Giroux, *The Terror of Neoliberalism*, 1–53.

45. Adolph Reed Jr., "Undone by Neoliberalism," *Nation* (September 18, 2005), 26–30.

46. Cathy Young, "Tea Partiers Racist? Not So Fast?" RealClearPolitics, April 25, 2010, at www.realclearpolitics.com/articles/2010/04/25/tea_partiers _racist_not_so_fast_105309.html.

47. See the various polls (CNN/Opinion Research, ABC News/*Washington Post*, CBS/*New York Times*, NBC News/*Wall Street Journal*, Princeton, *USA Today*, Gallup, and more) from 1999 to 2010 linked at Polling Report.com, "Race and Ethnicity," 2010, at www.pollingreport.com/race.htm.

48. Charles W. Mills, *From Class to Race: Essays in White Marxism and Black Radicalism* (Lanham, MD: Rowman and Littlefield, 2003), 216.

49. CNN, "CNN Opinion Research Poll," CNN/Opinion Research Corporation, February 17, 2010, at http://i2.cdn.turner.com/cnn/2010/images/ 02/17/rel4b.pdf. Although blacks and Latino/as have made significant inroads into the suburbs in recent decades, most suburbs in the inner and outer rings of metropolitan areas are still heavily segregated along class and color lines. See Haya L. Nasser, "Minorities Make Choice to Live with Their Own," *USA Today*, July 8, 2001, at www.usatoday.com/news/nation/census/2001–07–09 -minorities.htm; and Lamb, *Housing Segregation*.

50. Nicholas J. G. Winter, *Dangerous Frames: How Ideas About Race and Gender Shape Public Opinion* (Chicago: University of Chicago Press, 2008), 84, 144; Paul M. Kellstedt, *The Mass Media and the Dynamics of American Racial Attitudes* (Cambridge, UK: Cambridge University Press, 2003), 107–108; Gilens, *Why Americans Hate Welfare*, 98–99, 114, 106; Steve Macek, *Urban Nightmares: The Media, the Right, and the Moral Panic over the City* (Minneapolis: University of Minnesota Press, 2006); Robert M. Entman and Andrew Rojecki, *The Black Image in the White Mind* (Chicago: University of Chicago Press, 2000), 66, 81, 102; James Shanahan and Michael Morgan, *Television and Its Viewers: Cultivation Theory and Research* (Cambridge, UK: Cambridge University Press, 1999).

51. Macek, *Urban Nightmares*, 2.

52. University of Washington, "May 2010 Poll," at http://www.washingtonpoll.org/results/June1_teaparty.pdf.

53. Robert P. Jones and Daniel Cox, "Religion and the Tea Party in the 2010 Election," Public Religion Research Institute, October 2010, at www .publicreligion.org/objects/uploads/fck/file/AVS%202010%20Report%20 FINAL.pdf.

54. Editorial, "Dream Time," *New York Times*, September 19, 2010, at www.nytimes.com/2010/09/20/opinion/20mon2.html.

55. For some examples of local Tea Party groups attacking the Dream Act along these lines, see the Cleveland, Ohio, chapter, at http://clevelandteaparty patriots.blogspot.com/2010/08/lee-fisher-supports-dream-act-amnesty.html; the Gainesville, Florida, chapter, at http://gainesvilleteaparty.org/hot-topics/ immigration/dream-act-amnesty-plan/; and the New Hampshire Tea Party group, at www.nhteapartycoalition.org/tea/2010/09/23/push-for-dream-act -imminent/. For data challenging the notion that increased immigration threatens jobs, see Aviva Chomsky, *"They Take Our Jobs!" and 20 Other Myths About Immigration* (New York: Beacon Press, 2007).

56. Robert P. Jones and Daniel Cox, "Religion and the Tea Party in the 2010 Election," Public Religion Research Institute, October 2010, at www .publicreligion.org/objects/uploads/fck/file/AVS%202010%20Report%20 FINAL.pdf.

57. Gaiutra Bahadur, "Xenophobic Far-Right Militias Get a Tea Party Makeover," *Alternet*, November 4, 2010, at www.alternet.org/immigration/ 148664/null?page=entire; Deepa Kumar, "The Rise of Anti-Muslim Hate," *International Socialist Review*, November–December 2010, 18.

58. Cristina Silva, "Sharron Angle: Muslim Law Taking Hold in Parts of U.S.," Huffington Post, October 7, 2010, at www.huffingtonpost.com/2010/ 10/08/sharron-angle-muslim-law-_n_755346.html.

59. For more on the "Ground Zero Mosque" propaganda, see the following current events stories: Anthony DiMaggio, "Mediated Racism: Orientalism, Birtherism, and the Muslim Community Center," Truthout, September 9, 2010, at www.truth-out.org/mediated-racism-orientalism-birtherism-and-muslim -community-center63045; and Anthony DiMaggio, "The Rise of America's Idiot Culture," *Counterpunch*, August 12, 2010, at www.counterpunch.org/ dimaggio08122010.html.

60. The name referred to the Spanish city of Cordoba, a leading cultural center of the Muslim empire that ruled the Iberian peninsula during the medieval era. Cordoba represented both high intellectual accomplishment and peaceful coexistence among Muslims, Christians, and Jews.

61. Ralph Blumenthal and Sharaf Mowjood, "Muslim Prayers and Renewal Near Ground Zero," *New York Times*, December 9, 2009, A1; Adam Lisberg, "Mayor Bloomberg Stands Up for Mosque," Daily Politics Blog, August 23, 2010, at www.dailynews.com; Justin Elliot, "How the 'Ground Zero Mosque' Fear Mongering Began," Salon, August 16, 2010, at www.salon.com; Deepa

Kumar, "The Rise of Anti-Muslim Hate," *International Socialist Review* (November–December 2010), 14.

62. Rick Calder, "Brooklyn Tea Party Rallies Against Ground Zero Mosque, Multiculturalism," *New York Post*, September 27, 2010, at www.nypost.com/p/blogs/brooklyn/brooklyn_tea_party_rallies_against_PufOppdJalmYsPigd6z2AK.

63. Christine DeLargy, "NY Senate Tea Party Candidate: Ground Zero Mosque 'Hotbed for Trouble,'" CBS News, August 12, 2010, at www.cbsnews.com/8301–503544_162–20013501–503544.html.

64. Oliver Willis, "Mark Williams Calls Allah a 'monkey God'; Is He Still Welcome on CNN's Air?" Media Matters, May 18, 2010, at www.mediamatters.org; Bill Hutchinson, "Tea Party Leader Mark Williams Says Muslims Worship a 'Monkey God,' Blasts Ground Zero Mosque," *New York Daily News*, May 19, 2010, at www.nydailynews.com/ny_local/2010/05/19/2010–05–19_tea_party_leader_mark_williams_says_muslims_worship_a_monkey_god_blasts_ground_z.html. Williams has a history of appealing to racists on the right: In the summer of 2009, CNN's *Anderson Cooper 360* exposed him for warning that Obama was "an Indonesian Muslim turned welfare thug and a racist in chief." See Nicholas Graham, "Tea Party Leader Melts Down on CNN: Obama Is an 'Indonesian Muslim Turned Welfare Thug,'" Huffington Post, September 15, 2009, at www.huffingtonpost.com/2009/09/15/tea-party-leader-melts-do_n_286933.html.

65. Kumar, "The Rise of Anti-Muslim Hate," 14, 18.

66. NAACP, "Who Is an American? Tea Parties, Nativism, and Birthers," August 24, 2010, at www.teapartynationalism.com/index.php?option=com_k2&view=item&layout=item&id=100&Itemid=265.

67. Laurie Goodstein, " Across Nation, Mosque Projects Meet Opposition," *New York Times*, August 7, 2010, at www.nytimes.com/2010/08/08/us/08mosque.html; CNN, "Church Plans Quran Burning Event," CNN.com, July 30, 2010, http://articles.cnn.com/2010–07–29/us/florida.burn.quran.day_1_american-muslims-religion-cair-spokesman-ibrahim-hooper?_s=PM:US.

68. Goodstein, "Across Nation, Mosque Projects."

69. Kumar, "The Rise of Anti-Muslim Hate," 18.

70. Associated Press, "Tea Party's Next Wave Rising from Alaska to Colorado," Foxnews.com, July 3, 2010, at www.foxnews.com/politics/2010/07/03/tea-partys-wave-rising-alaska-colorado/.

71. Paul Steinhauser and Steve Brusk, "Haslam Is Projected Easy Winner in Tennessee Primary for Governor," CNN Politics, August 5, 2010, at www.cnn.com.

72. Media Matters for America, "Fox's Beck to First-Ever Muslim Congressman: 'What I Feel Like Saying Is: Sir Prove to Me That You Are Not Working with Our Enemies,'" Media Matters for America, November 15, 2006, at http://mediamatters.org/mmtv/200611150004.

73. Justin Elliot, "Tea Party Leader: Defeat Ellison Because He's Muslim," *Salon*, October 26, 2010, at www.salon.com/news/politics/war_room/2010/10/26/tea_party_nation_phillips_ellison_muslim. Phillips was incorrect: Representative Andre Carson (D-IN) was also a Muslim.

74. Resistnet, "#1 Most Dangerous Democrat Rep. Keith Ellison," Resistnet, January 30, 2010, at www.resistnet.com/group/mncd5/forum/topics/1-most-dangerous-democrat-rep-1?xg_source=activity.

75. Keith Ellison, "Press Release: Ellison Calls for End to Israel-Hamas Hostilities," Congressman Keith Ellison, December 31, 2008, at http://ellison.house.gov/index.php?option=com_content&task=view&id=200&Itemid=1. On a side note, CAIR has been attacked by right-wing racists for allegedly supporting terrorism by being affiliated with Hamas. These attacks coincided with the FBI's decision to end its cooperation with CAIR in its antiterrorist investigations. Worth pointing out, however, is the fact that no evidence was ever presented against CAIR and the group was never convicted of supporting terrorism. The FBI appears to understand that it has no tangible evidence demonstrating CAIR's support for terrorism, in line with CAIR's own long-standing rejection of terrorism. Contrary to the Tea Party narrative, CAIR originally threatened to end its cooperation with the FBI after reports surfaced that FBI agents were trying to "recruit terrorists" in a California mosque. CAIR demanded the FBI end its entrapment-style tactics, calling on the group to reassess "its use of agent provocateurs in Muslim communities." For more on this story, see Alexandra Marks, "FBI and American Muslims at Odds," *Christian Science Monitor*, March 25, 2009, at www.csmonitor.com/USA/Society/2009/0325/p02s01-ussc.html.

76. For more information on the thoroughly debunked claim that Obama is not a citizen, see the work of the nonpartisan group Fact Check: FactCheck.org, "Born in the U.S.A.," FactCheck.org, August 21, 2008. For more about the conservative–Tea Partiers' racist, paranoid, and propagandistic fear-mongering campaign that seeks to make this into a continued issue, see Rush Limbaugh, "What's the Difference Between God and Obama?" Rushlimbaugh.com, June 10, 2009, at www.rushlimbaugh.com/home/daily/site_061009/content/01125110.guest.html; Eric Kleefield, "Bachmann Joins Sing-Along with Birther Lyric," Talking Points Memo, February 16, 2010, at http://tpmdc.talkingpointsmemo.com/2010/02/bachmann-joins-sing-along-with-birther-lyric-video.php; Eric Kleefield, "Palin: The Public Is 'Rightfully' Making Obama's Birth Certificate an Issue," Talking Points Memo, December 4, 2009, at http://tpmdc.talkingpointsmeemo.com/2009/12/palin-the-public-is-rightfully-making-obamas-birth-certificate-an-issue.php; Media Matters for America, "Conservative Media Figures Allege Obama's Hawaii Trip Is About Discredited Birth Certificate Rumors," Media Matters for America, October 23, 2008, at http:mediamatters.org/research/200810230020; and Media Matters for America, "Dobbs Repeat-

edly Makes Obama Birth Certificate Claims His CNN Colleagues Call 'Total Bull,'" Media Matters for America, July 17, 2009, at http://mediamatters.org/research/200907170039.

77. CBS/*New York Times*, "Tea Party Supporters: Who They Are and What They Believe," CBS News, April 14, 2010, at www.cbsnews.com/8301 −503544_162−20002529−503544.html.

78. University of Washington, "2010 Multi-State Survey."

79. Jim Lobe, "Post-9/11 Immigration Roundup Backfired—Report," Common Dreams, June 27, 2003, at www.commondreams.org/headlines03/0627−03.htm.

80. Amanda Terkel, "Florida Tea Party to Host 'Radical Islamophobe' Who Said Muslims Shouldn't Hold Political Office," ThinkProgress, July 18, 2010, at http://thinkprogress.org/2010/07/18/tea-party-islamophobe/.

81. Pew Research Center, "Muslim Americans: Middle Class and Mostly Mainstream," Pew Research Center, May 22, 2007, at http://pewresearch .org/pubs/483/muslim-americans.

82. John L. Esposito, *Islam: The Straight Path* (Oxford, UK: Oxford University Press, 2004).

83. Lauren Vriens, "Islam: Governing Under Sharia," Council on Foreign Relations, October 5, 2001, at www.cfr.org/publication/8034/islam.html. Sharia is not viewed by those who share any understanding of the concept as the simple suppression of non-Christian Westerners to Islamic dictates, although this is the common misperception among Tea Partiers and others on the American right. Muslim scholars such as Abdullahi Ahmed An-Na'im argue that "enforcing Sharia through coercive power of the state negates its religious nature, because Muslims would be observing the law of the state and not freely performing their religious obligation as Muslims."

Other interpretations clearly allow for the fusion of government and religious law, as seen in the writings of Islamists such as religious theorists Sayyid Qutb and Hassan al-Banna, al Qaeda members such as Osama bin Laden and Ayman al-Zawahiri, and political leaders such as Ismail Haniyeh (of Hamas) and Hassan Nasrallah (of Hezbollah), among others. Even these figures, however, retain major disagreements about the "legitimate" teachings of Islam and what types of acts they allow Islamists to engage in (whether or not to engage in terrorist attacks against the United States, for example). None of this disagreement about precisely what Sharia is, or the nuances regarding whether it should be applied in relation to governance, however, is captured.

84. "Muslim Americans: Middle Class and Mostly Mainstream," Pew Research Center, May 22, 2007, at www.pewresearch.org.

85. "Tea Party Closely Linked to Religious Right," ABC News, October 5, 2010, at http://blogs.abcnews.com/thenote/2010/10/tea-party-closely-linked -to-religious-right-poll-finds.html.

86. For more, see the Beck-Ellison exchange discussed in endnote 74. See also the following works: Nacos and Torres-Reyna, *Fueling Our Fears*; Anthony DiMaggio, "Arabic as a Terrorist Language: The Right Wing's War on the Khalil Gibran Academy," *Counterpunch*, August 30, 2007, at www.counterpunch.org/dimaggio08302007.html; Anthony DiMaggio, "Fort Hood Fallout: Cultural Racism and Deteriorating Public Discourse on Islam," *Z Magazine*, December 3, 2009, at www.zcommunications.org/fort-hood-fall-out-cultural-racism-and-deteriorating-public-discourse-on-islam-by-anthony-dimaggio.

87. See Deepa Kumar, "Jihad Jane: Constructing the New Muslim Enemy," Fifth Estate, April 2010, at www.fifth-estate-online.co.uk/comment/Jihad_Jane_Deepa_Kumar.pdf; and Deepa Kumar, "Framing Islam: The Resurgence of Orientalism During the Bush II Era," *Journal of Communication Inquiry* 34, no. 3 (July 2010): 254–277.

88. Edward Said, *Orientalism* (New York: Vintage, 1994), 8, 27; Edward Said, *Covering Islam: How the Media and the Experts Determine How We See the Rest of the World* (New York: Vintage, 1997), xi, 13.

89. Matthew Alford, *Reel Power: Hollywood Cinema and American Supremacy* (London: Pluto Press, 2010), 173; Jack G. Shaheen, *Reel Bad Arabs: How Hollywood Vilifies a People* (Brooklyn, NY: Olive Branch Press, 2001), 1.

90. For more, see the first poll from endnote 84, which was used in our multivariate regression analyses. All variables discussed are significant at the 5 percent level or lower.

91. Matt Taibbi, "Matt Taibbi on the Tea Party," *Rolling Stone*, October 15, 2010, at www.rollingstone.com/politics/news/17390/210904?RS_show_page=1.

Chapter Five

1. John Broder, "Climate Change Doubt Is Tea Party Article of Faith," *New York Times,* October 21, 2010.

2. Richard Hofstadter, *The Paranoid Style in American Politics* (New York: Vintage Books, 2008), 3, 4–5.

3. Ibid., 7, 11, 30.

4. Ibid., 4.

5. David Niewert, *The Eliminationists: How Hate Talk Radicalized the American Right* (Sausalito, CA.: PoliPointPress, 2009), 84, 94, 121–131.

6. David Rovics, "Breaking Ranks," *Counterpunch*, April 15, 2010, at www.counterpunch.org/rovics04152010.html; Matthew Rothschild, "Chomsky Warns of Risk of Fascism in America," *The Progressive*, April 12, 2010, at www.progressive.orgwx041210.html.

7. For useful reflections, see Eric Hobsbawm, *The Age of Extremes: A History of the World, 1914–1991* (New York: Pantheon, 1994), 112–135; Leon Trotsky, *The Struggle Against Fascism in Germany* (New York: Pathfinder, 1971).

8. Glenn Beck, "The Progressive Takeover of America," Foxnews.com, January 8, 2010, at www.foxnews.com/story/0,2933,582638,00.html.

9. This belief is held by 24 percent of Tea Party supporters and 32 percent of Tea Party activists. CBS/*New York Times*, "Tea Party Supporters: Who They Are and What They Believe," CBS News, April 14, 2010, at www.cbs news.com/8301–503544_162–20002529–503544.html.

10. Bill O'Reilly and Glenn Beck regularly interrupt and "outshout" opponents on their programs before these individuals are allowed to make their cases. O'Reilly stops guests short, yelling, "I don't want to hear it" to those challenging his received wisdoms. He labels his critics "pinheads" and orders them to "shut up!" O'Reilly has physically threatened those on "the left" with whom he disagrees. Beck screams at callers-in, condemns his detractors as dangerous anti-Christian socialists, and calls for violent rebellion to "take the country back" from horrid leftist "progressives" and the "big government" they support. For more on Bill O'Reilly and Glenn Beck's latent fascism, see *Outfoxed: Rupert Murdoch's War on Journalism*, DVD, directed by Robert Greenwald (Disinformation Company, 2004); Media Matters for America, "Myths and Falsehoods About Health Care Reform Continued," Media Matters for America, November 13, 2009, at http://mediamatters.org/research/200911130002; Media Matters for America, "Beck 'Loses' His 'Mind': Screams at Caller: 'Get Off My Phone You Little Pinhead!'" Media Matters for America, July 15, 2009, at http://mediamatters.org/mmtv/200907150016; Reverend James Martin, "Glenn Beck vs. Christ the Liberator," Huffington Post, August 29, 2010, at www.huffingtonpost.com/rev-james -martin-sj/glenn-beck-vs-christ-the-_b_698359.html; and Mary C. Curtis, "Glenn Beck Tells NRA Members: Fight the 'Marxists' at the Polls," *Politics Daily*, May 16, 2010, at www.politicsdaily.com/2010/05/16/glenn-beck-tells -nra-members-fight-the-marxists-at-the-polls/.

11. This notion was regularly advanced at Tea Party gatherings meeting we attended and cited as a reason that local Tea Party chapters' agendas could not be made public. Such paranoia served as a roadblock to organizing, as local activists were unwilling to provide basic information about local chapter goals and events. The "infiltration" theory did contain a kernel of truth: Some national organizations have called on liberals and Tea Party critics to attend, disrupt, and ridicule Tea Partiers at their rallies. No evidence, however, has ever been presented demonstrating a systematic effort on the part of left-wing groups or the government to infiltrate and destroy local Tea Party chapters. We did in fact function as Tea Party infiltrators in order to conduct participant-observatory field research in 2009 and 2010, but we did not do so as parts or agents of any political organization, liberal or otherwise.

12. CBS/*New York Times*, "Tea Party Supporters."

13. For some important warnings, see Noam Chomsky, *Failed States: The Abuse of Power and the Assault on Democracy* (New York: Metropolitan, 2006); Sheldon Wolin, *Democracy Incorporated: Managed Democracy and the Specter of Inverted Totalitarianism* (Princeton, NJ: Princeton University Press, 2008); Henry A. Giroux, *The Terror of Neoliberalism: Authoritarianism and the Eclipse of Democracy* (Boulder, CO: Paradigm Publishers, 2004); and Paul Street, *Empire and Inequality: America and the World Since 9/11* (Boulder, CO: Paradigm Publishers, 2004).

14. See Paul Street, *The Empire's New Clothes: Barack Obama in the Real World of Power* (Boulder, CO: Paradigm Publishers, 2010), chap. 1; and Reed Abelson, "In Health Care Overhaul, Boons for Hospitals and Drug Makers," *New York Times*, March 21, 2010, at www.nytimes.com/2010/03/22/business/22bizhealth.html.

15. Laura Bassett, "James Carville Takes on Obama on Oil Spill: He's 'Risking Everything' with 'Go Along with BP Strategy,'" Huffington Post, May 21, 2010, at www.huffingtonpost.com/2010/05/21/obama-faces-new-wave-of-c_n_585620.html.

16. Jonathan Weisman, "GOP Doubts, Fears 'Post-Partisan' Obama," *Washington Post*, January 7, 2008, at www.washingtonpost.com/wp-dyn/content/article/2008/01/06/AR2008010602402.html.

17. Noam M. Levey, "Grants Awarded for State Health Insurance Exchanges," *Los Angeles Times*, September 30, 2010, at http://articles.latimes.com/2010/sep/30/nation/la-na-health-grants-20101001; Abelson, "In Health Care Overhaul."

18. Maggie Mertens, "Comparing Health Care Reform Bills: Democrats and Republicans 2009, Republicans 1993," *Kaiser Health News*, at www.kaiserhealthnews.org/Graphics/2010/022310-Bill-Comparison.aspx; Jeff Zeleny, "Obama Plans Bipartisan Summit on Health Care," *New York Times*, February 7, 2010, at www.nytimes.com/2010/02/08/us/politics/08webobama.html; Sam Stein, "Steele Calls Obama Health Care Socialism, Agrees This Is His Waterloo," Huffington Post, July 20, 2009, at www.huffingtonpost.com/2009/07/20/steele-calls-obama-health_n_240989.html.

19. "Still on the Table?" *Newsweek*, February 24, 2010, at www.newsweek.com/2010/02/24/still-on-the-table.html.

20. Ben Smith, "Health Reform Foes Plan Obama 'Waterloo,'" *Politico*, July 17, 2009, at www.politico.com/blogs/bensmith/0709/Health_reform_foes_plan_Obamas_Waterloo.html.

21. See Jon R. Bond and Richard Fleischer, eds., *Polarized Politics: Congress and the President in a Partisan Era* (Washington, DC: CQ Press, 2000); and Keith T. Poole and Howard Rosenthal, *Ideology and Congress: A Political-*

Economic History of Roll Call Voting (New Brunswick, NJ: Transaction, 2007). To see more of Keith Poole and Howard Rosenthal's empirical analysis of partisan polarization at a 130-year high, see http://voteview.com/polarized america.asp.

22. Jacob S. Hacker and Paul Pierson, *Off Center: The Republican Revolution and the Erosion of Democracy* (New Haven, CT: Yale University Press, 2005), 29. The limited "leftward" movement of the Democratic Party appears in large part to be the result of the disappearance of southern conservatives from the party in the wake of the onset of the civil rights era. See Hacker and Pierson, *Off Center*, 27.

23. For a comprehensive account and left critique of presidential candidate and U.S. senator Barack Obama as a "deeply conservative" corporate-neoliberal and militarist, see Paul Street, *Barack Obama and the Future of American Politics* (Boulder, CO: Paradigm Publishers, 2008). See also Paul Street, "Obama's Audacious Deference to Power: A Critical Review of Barack Obama's *The Audacity of Hope*," *ZNet Magazine*, January 24, 2007, at www.zmag.org/content/ showarticle.cfm?ItemID=11936.

24. Larissa MacFarquhar, "The Conciliator: Where Is Barack Obama Coming From?" *New Yorker*, May 7, 2007.

25. Steven DeLue, *Political Thinking, Political Theory, and Civil Society* (New York: Longman, 2002), 283; Robert C. Tucker, *The Marx-Engels Reader* (New York: Norton, 1978), 191–192, 219; Werner Blumenberg, *Karl Marx: An Illustrated History* (London: Verso, 1972), 76.

26. Karl Marx and Friedrich Engels, *The Communist Manifesto* (New York: Washington Square Press, 1964), 116, 94, 93.

27. Tucker, *The Marx-Engels Reader*, 70–72.

28. Mike Elk, "Abandoning EFCA Is Obama's Political Suicide," *Truthout*, January 6, 2010, at www.truth-out.org/0106091.

29. Alice Gomstyn, Matthew Jaffe, and Charles Herman, "GM Chief Wants Americans to See a 'Fantastic Return,'" ABC News, June 1, 2009, at http://abcnews.go.com/Business/Economy/story?id=7722655&page=1.

30. "Obama's Speech to the Business Roundtable," *Wall Street Journal*, February 24, 2010, at http://blogs.wsj.com/washwire/2010/02/24/obamas-speech -to-the-business-roundtable/. For a useful and concise summary of true socialist principles within and beyond the workplace, see Alan Maas, *The Case for Socialism* (Chicago: Haymarket, 2010), 73–87.

31. John Nichols, "The 'New GM': Layoffs, Factory Closings, and Offshoring," Common Dreams, June 2, 2009, at www.commondreams.org/ view/2009/06/02–0.

32. William Greider, "Obama's Weird Idea of Auto Industry Rescue: Use Our Money to Build Factories Abroad," AlterNet, May 11, 2009, at www

.alternet.org/workplace/139940/obama's_weird_idea_of_auto_industry_rescue:
_use_our_money_to_build_car_factories_abroad.

33. Noam Chomsky, "Coups, UNASUR, and the U.S.," *Z Magazine*, October 2009, 26.

34. Greg Palast, "Grand Theft Auto: How Stevie the Rat Bankrupted GM," GregPalast.com, June 1, 2009, at www.gregpalast.com/grand-theft-auto-how-stevie-the-rat-bankrupted-gm/.

35. Jim Puzzanghera, "U.S. Role at GM to Be Passive, Obama Vows," *Los Angeles Times*, June 2, 2009, at http://articles.latimes.com/2009/jun/02/business/fi-gm-reax2.

36. Bill Vlasic, "To Attract Shoppers, GM to Repay Debt to U.S.," *New York Times*, January 25, 2010, at www.nytimes.com/2010/01/26/business/26auto.html.

37. Palast, "Grand Theft Auto."

38. Floyd Norris, "U.S. Teaches Carmakers Capitalism," *New York Times*, November 20, 2009.

39. See Street, *The Empire's New Clothes.*

40. Charles E. Lindblom, *Politics and Markets: The World's Political-Economic Systems* (New York: Basic Books, 1977); David Lowery and Holly Brasher, *Organized Interests and American Government* (New York: McGraw-Hill, 2004); Frank Baumgartner, Jeffrey M. Berry, Marie Hojnacki, David C. Kimball, and Beth L. Leech, *Lobbying and Policy Change: Who Wins, Who Loses, and Why* (Chicago: University of Chicago Press, 2009); Thomas Ferguson, *Golden Rule: The Investment Theory of Party Competition and the Logic of Money-Driven Political Systems* (Chicago: University of Chicago Press, 1995); Anthony J. Nownes, *Pressure and Power: Organized Interests in American Politics* (New York: Houghton Mifflin, 2001); Darrell M. West and Burdett A. Loomis, *The Sound of Money: How Political Interests Get What They Want* (New York: Norton, 1998); G. William Domhoff, *The Power Elite and the State: How Policy Is Made in America* (Hawthorne, NY: Aldine de Gruyter, 1990); Floyd Hunter, *Community Power Structure: A Study of Decision Makers* (Chapel Hill: University of North Carolina Press, 1969); C. Wright Mills, *The Power Elite* (Oxford, UK: Oxford University Press, 2000); Charles C. Lindblom, "The Market as Prison," *Journal of Politics* 44, no. 2 (1982): 324–336.

41. Marc J. Hetherington and Jonathan D. Weiler, *Authoritarianism and Polarization in American Politics* (Cambridge, UK: Cambridge University Press, 2009), 158, 195.

42. Polling data in Figure 5.1 on media consumer habits related to Fox, CNN, and MSNBC from 2004 through 2009 are publicly available in the Pew Research Center database, at http://people-press.org/dataarchive/.

43. Kate Zernike, *Boiling Mad: Inside Tea Party America* (New York: Times Books, 2010), 107.

44. Scott Rasmussen and Douglas Schoen, *Mad as Hell: How the Tea Party Movement Is Fundamentally Remaking Our Two-Party System* (New York: HarperCollins, 2010), 155.

45. Sean Hannity, *Hannity*, September 3, 2010, 9 PM EST.

46. Glenn Beck, *The Glenn Beck Program*, March 5, 2010, 5 PM EST.

47. Wolin, *Democracy Incorporated*, 68, 166.

48. Sean Willentz, "Confounding Fathers: The Tea Party's Cold War Roots," *New Yorker*, October 18, 2010.

49. Ibid.

50. Ibid.

51. Ibid.

52. Andrew Romano, "America's Holy Writ," *Newsweek*, October 17, 2010, at www.newsweek.com/2010/10/17/how-tea-partiers-get-the-constitution -wrong.html.

53. To read the Illinois Tea Party's mission statement, see www.illinoistea .org/missionstatement.html.

54. Jill Lepore, *The Whites of Their Eyes: The Tea Party's Revolution and the Battle over American History* (Princeton, NJ: Princeton University Press, 2010), 96, 123–124.

55. Romano, "America's Holy Writ."

56. Wilentz, "Confounding Fathers."

57. Joseph Story, *Commentaries on the Constitution* (Durham, NC: Carolina Academic Press, 1995).

58. Cornell University, "United States v. Butler," Cornell University Law School, 2010, at www.law.cornell.edu/anncon/html/art1frag29_user.html; Cornell University, "Helvering v. Davis," Cornell University Law School, 2010, at www.law.cornell.edu/socsec/course/readings/301us619.htm.

59. Zernike, *Boiling Mad*, 128.

60. Karl Polanyi, *The Great Transformation: The Political and Economic Origins of Our Time* (Boston: Beacon Press, 1944).

61. For more sources and elaboration, see Paul Street, "By All Means, Study the Founders: Notes from the Democratic Left," *Review of Education, Pedagogy, and Cultural Studies* 24, no. 4 (October–December 2003): 281–303.

62. Thomas Jefferson quoted in Adam Cohen, "A Century-Old Principle: Keep Corporate Money Out of Elections," *New York Times*, August 10, 2009, at www.nytimes.com/2009/08/11/opinion/11tue4.html.

63. Noam Chomsky quoted in Street, "By All Means."

64. James Madison quoted in Thom Hartmann, *Unequal Protection: How Corporations Became People—and How You Can Fight Back* (San Francisco: Berrett-Koehler, 2010), 82.

65. James Madison, *The Writings of James Madison: 1819–1836* (New York: Putnam's Sons, 1910), 281.

66. Barry C. Lynn, *Cornered: The New Monopoly Capitalism and the Economics of Destruction* (Hoboken, NJ: Wiley, 2010).

67. David Sirota, "What a Second Stimulus Should—and Shouldn't—Look Like," Common Dreams, September 7, 2010, at www.commondreams.org/view/2010/09/07–1.

68. CBS/*New York Times*, "Tea Party Supporters"; Lisa Lerer, "Poll: Tea Party Economic Gloom Fuels Republican Momentum," Bloomberg News, October 13, 2010, at www.bloomberg.com/news/print/2010–10–14/tea-party-s-economic-gloom-fuels-republican-election-momentum-poll-says.html. The repeal of the Glass-Steagall Act, which set up a barrier between traditional commercial and investment banks, was bipartisan, for example.

69. CBS/*New York Times*, "Tea Party Supporters." For information on the tremendous budget deficits and debt under the George W. Bush and Ronald Reagan administrations, see Congressional Budget Office, "Budget and Economic Outlook: Historical Budget Data," Congressional Budget Office, January 2010, at www.cbo.gov/ftpdocs/108xx/doc10871/HistoricalTables.pdf.

70. For a discussion of the lack of a one-to-one relationship between debt and economic vitality, and for a discussion of conservative dishonesty in claims that the debt is at its highest levels in history (referring only to the national debt in hard dollars, rather than as a percentage of gross domestic product), see Dean Baker, *False Profits: Recovering from the Bubble Economy* (Sausalito, CA: PoliPointPress, 2010).

71. Sam Stein, "Tax Day Fact Check: Most Americans Got a Tax Cut This Year," Huffington Post, April 15, 2010, at www.huffingtonpost.com/2010/04/15/tax-day-2010-protesters-i_n_538556.html.

72. Jeanne Sahadi, "Health Reform: The $$$ Story," CNN.com, March 25, 2010, at http://money.cnn.com/2010/03/20/news/economy/cbo_reconciliation/index.htm.

73. For a comprehensive discussion of the literature covering the failure of tax cuts (especially those for the rich to promote meaningful, sustained economic growth), see Anthony DiMaggio, "Taking on Trickle Down Economics: The Public Rejects Conservative Tax Cuts as a Means of Economic Stimulus," Firedoglake, September 16, 2010, at http://seminal.firedoglake.com/diary/71683; and Anthony DiMaggio, "The Coming Tax War: How Letting the Bush Tax Cuts Expire Could End the Economic Crisis," Truthout, August 13, 2010, at www.truth-out.org/the-coming-tax-war-how-letting-bush-tax-cuts-expire-could-end-economic-crisis62154.

74. See Bill McKibben, *Earth: Making Life on a Tough New Planet* (New York: Times Books, 2010), 1–101.

75. CNN.com, "Surveyed Scientists Agree Global Warming Is Real," CNN.com, January 19, 2009, at http://articles.cnn.com/2009–01–19/world/

eco.globalwarmingsurvey_1_global-warming-climate-science-human
-activity?_s=PM:WORLD; Naomi Oreskes, "Beyond the Ivory Tower: The
Scientific Consensus on Climate Change," *Science*, December 3, 2004, at www
.sciencemag.org/cgi/content/full/306/5702/1686; Peter T. Doran and Maggie
Kendall Zimmermann, "Examining the Scientific Consensus on Climate
Change," University of Illinois, Chicago, 2009, at http://tigger.uic.edu/~pdoran/
012009_Doran_final.pdf; Scott Barker, "Scientists Agree on Climate Change,
Differ on Severity," *Knoxville News Sentinel*, October 25, 2003, at www.knox
news.com/kns/local_news/article/0,1406,KNS_347_2377424,00.html.

76. John M. Broder, "Skepticism on Climate Change an Article of Faith
for Tea Party," *New York Times*, October 20, 2010, at www.nytimes.com/
2010/10/21/us/politics/21climate.html.

77. Willentz, "Confounding Fathers."

Chapter Six

1. See, for one example among many, Naftali Bendavid, "Tea Party Activists Complicate Republican Comeback Strategy," *Wall Street Journal*, October 16, 2009, at http://online.wsj.com/article/SB125564976279388879.html.

2. Adam Bessie, "Media Spreads Tea Party Leaders as 'Anti-establishment' Myth," *Media-Ocracy*, September 20, 2010, at www.media-ocracy.org.

3. Lisa Lerer, "Poll: Tea Party Economic Gloom Fuels Republican Momentum," Bloomberg News, October 14, 2010, at www.bloomberg.com/news/
print/2010–10–14/tea-party-s-economic-gloom-fuels-republican-election
-momentum-poll-says.html.

4. Nedra Pickler, "Voters Embrace Several Tea Party Candidates," Associated Press, November 3, 2010, at www.forbes.com/feeds/ap/2010/11/03/
politics-us-tea-party_8070103.html,

5. BBC, "Millions Join Global Anti-war Protest," BBC News, February
17, 2003, at http://news.bbc.co.uk/2/hi/europe/2765215.stm.

6. Howard Zinn, *A People's History of the United States* (New York: Harper
Perennial, 1999), 629.

7. Edward S. Herman and David Peterson, *The Politics of Genocide* (New
York: Monthly Review Press, 2010); Edward S. Herman and Noam Chomsky,
Manufacturing Consent: The Political Economy of the Mass Media (New York:
Pantheon, 1988); Noam Chomsky and Edward S. Herman, *The Washington
Connection and Third World Fascism: The Political Economy of Human Rights*, vol.
1 (Boston: South End Press, 1979); Noam Chomsky and Edward S. Herman,
*After the Cataclysm: Postwar Indochina and the Reconstruction of Imperial Ideology:
The Political Economy of Human Rights*, vol. 2 (Boston: South End Press, 1979).

8. Julie Hollar, "Tea Party v. U.S. Social Forum," Fairness and Accuracy in Reporting, September 2010, at www.fair.org/index.php?page=4143.

9. As Republican House majority leader, Dick Armey supported legislation that would subsidize energy corporations with taxpayer money by funding the transport of more than 77 million tons of nuclear waste to the Yucca Mountain repository and pay to store it there indefinitely. Armey authorized massive military appropriations that greatly benefited corporate military contractors, enthusiastically supported agribusiness subsidies, voted against a bipartisan campaign finance reform bill that would have imposed limits on the amount of money corporations could contribute to political campaigns, and sided with health insurance providers over consumers by attacking a Senate bill attempting to establish a "patient's bill of rights."

As a House Republican from Minnesota and a prominent speaker for the Tea Party, Michele Bachmann has amassed a significant record colluding with corporate America. Her top campaign contributors in 2008 included the securities and investment industry, insurance corporations, pharmaceutical interests, and real estate firms. Nearly three-quarters of Bachmann's campaign contributions from political action committees are from business interests, a significant violation (in and of itself) of her alleged support for "free-market" approaches such as the separation of business and state.

Sarah Palin may have failed in her vice-presidential run in 2008, but she was embraced as one of the leading proponents of the Tea Party, speaking regularly at the group's rallies and receiving favorable ratings from most Tea Partiers in opinion surveys. She has also built a career on corporate welfare. She ran under a ticket in 2008 that received millions from oil and gas contributions, with these industries combined ranking the eleventh largest contributor to the McCain campaign. Most perversely with regard to the Tea Party and its alleged "free-market" approach is her vocal support for the bailout, as expressed during her 2008 vice-presidential run within the McCain campaign. Such support, expressed immediately prior to her rise to fame as an "antibailout" Tea Partier, suggests the extreme extent to which Tea Party rank-and-filers are being manipulated by the Washington Republican political establishment. See http://projects.washingtonpost.com/congress/members/a000217/; Opensecrets.org, "Michele Bachmann," Center for Responsive Politics, 2010, at www.opensecrets.org/politicians/pacs.php?cycle=2010&cid=N00027493&type; Opensecrets.org, "John McCain: Top Industries," Center for Responsive Politics, 2010, at www.opensecrets.org/pres08/indus.php?cycle=2008&cid=N00006424; and David Weigel, "Yes, Palin Backed the Bailouts," *Washington Independent*, November 20, 2009, at http://washingtonindependent.com/68578/yes-palin-backed-the-bailouts. For more information on Armey's voting record, see http://projects.washingtonpost.com/congress/members/a000217/.

10. "Polling the Tea Party," *New York Times*, April 14, 2010, at www .nytimes.com/interactive/2010/04/14/us/politics/20100414-tea-party-poll -graphic.html.

11. Tea Party turnouts for Joliet and Chicago are listed at http://en.wikipedia .org/wiki/List_of_Tea_Party_protests,_2010.

12. Comprehensive information on national Tea Party protests is notoriously difficult to find. The only comprehensive list we were able to discover is available at http://en.wikipedia.org/wiki/List_of_Tea_Party_protests,_2010.

13. Kate Zernike, "Tea Party Convention Is Canceled," *New York Times*, September 24, 2010, at http://thecaucus.blogs.nytimes.com/2010/09/24/tea -party-convention-is-canceled/.

14. Stephanie Mencimer, "Tea Party 'Liberty XPO' Fail," *Mother Jones*, September 10, 2010, at http://motherjones.com/mojo/2010/09/tea-party -liberty-xpo-fail.

15. Evan McMorris Santoro, "Tea Party's 9/12 Rally Looking Much, Much Smaller Than Last Year's," Talking Points Memo, September 12, 2010, at http://tpmdc.talkingpointsmemo.com/2010/09/tea-partys-912-rally -looking-much-much-smaller-than-last-years.php.

16. Alexander Cockburn, "Whatever Happened to the Anti-war Movement?" *New Left Review*, July–August 2007, at http://newleftreview.org/ ?view=2677.

17. For estimates of turnout at Iraq war protests, see http://en.wikipedia .org/wiki/Protests_against_the_Iraq_War; and Tim Perone, "Beck and Call: Tea Party Stars Lead 300,000 in DC Rally," *New York Post*, August 29, 2010, at www.nypost.com/p/news/national/beck_and_call_Bys1VIlPrpRVMz5o HEyR6K.

18. New York Times, "Polling the Tea Party"; The Note, "Tea Party Closely Linked to the Religious Right," ABC News, October 5, 2010, at http://blogs.abcnews.com/thenote/2010/10/tea-party-closely-linked-to -religious-right-poll-finds.html.

19. Kathleen Hall Jamieson and James Cappella, *Echo Chamber: Rush Limbaugh and the Conservative Media Establishment* (Oxford, UK: Oxford University Press, 2010).

20. Sean Hannity, *Hannity*, March 22, 2010, 9 PM EST

21. Glenn Beck, *The Glenn Beck Program*, August 3, 2009, 5 PM EST.

22. "Miller: Rising Federal Debt Is Unconstitutional," Foxnews.com, September 19, 2010, at www.foxnews.com/politics/2010/09/19/miller-rising -federal-debt-unconstitutional/.

23. Sean Hannity, *Hannity*, March 22, 2010, 9 PM EST.

24. Glenn Beck, *The Glenn Beck Program*, October 29, 2009, 5 PM EST.

25. Sean Hannity, *Hannity*, April 29, 2010, 9 PM EST.

26. Bill O'Reilly, *The O'Reilly Factor*, January 29, 2010, 8 PM EST.

27. Glenn Beck, *The Glenn Beck Program*, June 22, 2010, 5 PM EST.

28. Glenn Beck, *The Glenn Beck Program*, October 5, 2010, 5 PM EST.

29. Glenn Beck, *The Glenn Beck Program*, July 6, 2010, 5 PM EST.

30. Media Matters for America, "Limbaugh, Hannity, and the GOP: An Iron Triangle of Stimulus Misinformation," Media Matters for America, February 7, 2009, at http://mediamatters.org/research/200902070003; Sean Hannity, *Hannity*, October 5, 2010, 9 PM EST; Sean Hannity, *Hannity*, September 23, 2010, 9 PM EST; Sean Hannity, *Hannity*, August 25, 2010, 9 PM EST.

31. "CBO: Health Care Bill Will Cost $115 Billion More Than Previously Assessed," ABC News, May 12, 2010, at http://blogs.abcnews.com/political punch/2010/05/cbo-health-care-bill-will-cost-115-billion-more-than-previously -assessed.html.

32. Bill O'Reilly, *The O'Reilly Factor*, March 18, 2010, 8 PM EST.

33. Sean Hannity, *Hannity*, March 18, 2010, 9 PM EST.

34. Glenn Beck, *The Glenn Beck Program*, April 12, 2010, 5 PM EST. In fact, the CBO report concluded that the Democrats' health reform would not contribute to the national debt.

35. Lydia Saad, "Tea Partiers Are Fairly Mainstream in Their Demographics," Gallup, April 5, 2010, at www.gallup.com/poll/127181/tea-partiers-fairly -mainstream-demographics.aspx.

36. Jeremy Scahill, "Media Matters with Robert McChesney," AM 580, April 18, 2010, at http://will.illinois.edu/mediamatters/show/april-18th -2010/.

37. Scott Keyes, "Tea Party Leader Dick Armey: Social Security Is a Corrupt 'Ponzi Scheme,'" ThinkProgress, September 20, 2010, at http://think progress.org/2010/09/20/armey-social-security/; "Dick Armey Calls Medicare 'Tyranny,'" *Politico*, August 16, 2009, at www.politico.com/blogs/politicol-ive/0809/Dick_Armey_calls_Medicare_tyranny.html.

38. Jonathan Mermin, *Debating War and Peace: Media Coverage of U.S. Intervention in the Post-Vietnam Era* (Princeton, NJ: Princeton University Press, 1999); Daniel C. Hallin, *The "Uncensored War": The Media and Vietnam* (Oxford, UK: Oxford University Press, 1986); W. Lance Bennett, Regina G. Lawrence, and Steven Livingston, *When the Press Fails: Political Power and the News Media from Iraq to Katrina* (Chicago: University of Chicago Press, 2007); Anthony R. DiMaggio, *When Media Goes to War: Hegemonic Discourse, Public Opinion, and the Limits of Dissent* (New York: Monthly Review Press, 2010).

Chapter Seven

1. Lance Selfa, "Preparing for a Republican Comeback?" *International Socialist Review*, September–October 2010, 1–2.

2. Al Fram, "Ailing Economy, Tea Party Fuel GOP," Associated Press, November 3, 2010, at http://news.yahoo.com/s/ap/us_exit_polls. This is a report on an Edison Research exit poll conducted for the Associated Press and television networks with 18,132 voters nationwide.

3. Michael O'Brien, "Biden: 'The Republican Tea Party Is the Alternative,'" *The Hill*, September 20, 2010, at www.thehill.com/ . . . /119811-biden -the-republican-tea-party-is-the-alternative.

4. Jeff Zeleny and David M. Herszenhorn, "G.O.P. Captures House, but Not Senate," *New York Times*, November 3, 2010; Maureen Dowd, "Republican Party Time," *New York Times*, November 3, 2010.

5. Krissah Thompson and Dan Balz, "Rand Paul Comments About Civil Rights Stir Controversy," *Washington Post*, May 21, 2010, at www.washington post.com/wp-dyn/content/article/2010/05/20/AR2010052003500.html; "Rand Paul: 'We've Come to Take Our Government Back," CNN, November 2, 2010, at http://politicalticker.blogs.cnn.com/2010/11/02/rand-paul-weve -come-to-take-our-government-back.

6. Selfa, "Preparing for a Republican Comeback."

7. Lisa Lerer and Catherine Dodge, "Republicans to Control House, Gain in Senate," Bloomberg Business Week, November 3, 2010, at www.businessweek .com/news/2010–11–03/republicans-to-control-u-s-house-gain-in-senate.html.

8. Nelson D. Schwartz, "Power Shift Is Expected by C.E.O.s," *New York Times*, November 2, 2010.

9. Ibid.

10. Jack Rasmus, *Epic Recession: Prelude to Global Depression* (Ann Arbor, MI: Pluto Press, 2010); Mary Engel, "The Real Unemployment Rate? 16.6%," MSN Money, June 4, 2010, at http://articles.moneycentral.msn.com/ learn-how-to-invest/The-real-unemployment-rate.aspx; Ron Scherer, "U.S. Adds 3.8 Million to Ranks of Poor as Poverty Rate Jumps," *Christian Science Monitor*, September 16, 2010; Palash R. Gosh, "U.S. Poverty Rate Spikes," *International Business Times*, September 16, 2010, at http://www.ibtimes.com/ articles/63050/20100916/poverty.htm

11. Selfa, "Preparing for a Republican Comeback."

12. Benjamin I. Page and Robert Y. Shapiro, *The Rational Public: Fifty Years of Trends in American Policy Preferences* (Chicago: University of Chicago Press, 1992

13. Anthony DiMaggio, "Obama and the Housing Crisis: Forecasting the 2010 Midterm Elections," *Counterpunch*, April 24–26 2009, at www.counter punch.org/dimaggio04242009.html.

14. Gary C. Jacobson and Samuel Kernell, *Strategy and Choice in Congressional Elections* (New Haven, CT: Yale University Press, 1983); Edward R. Tufte, "Determinants of the Outcomes of Midterm Congressional Elections," *American Political Science Review* 69, no. 3 (1975): 812–826.

15. Gary Langer, "Exit Polls: Economy, Voter Anger Drive Republican Victory," ABC News, November 2, 2010, at http://abcnews.go.com/Politics/vote-2010-elections-results-midterm-exit-poll-analysis/story?id=12003775.

16. Fram, "Ailing Economy."

17. Ibid.

18. The percent decline in personal income from 2008 to 2010 averaged-1.9 percent for states where Republicans picked up Senate seats, as compared to an average decline of-1.6 percent in those states where Democrats claimed victories. Similarly, the limited personal financial growth that did take place (as reflected in states that saw weak growth during 2010) appears to have aided Republicans as well. Personal financial gains from 2009 to 2010 averaged .87 percent in states where Republicans claimed Senate victories, compared to a growth rate average of .91 percent for those states where Democrats won seats.

19. Fram, "Ailing Economy."

20. Our statistical analysis of the 2010 midterm elections employs multivariate bivariate logistic regression, analyzing the relationship between various independent variables and electoral victories and defeats for individual candidates running for Congress. The regression includes six independent variables for individual candidates: (1) incumbent/nonincumbent, (2) level of campaign contributions, (3) Republican/non-Republican, (4) Democrat/non-Democrat, (5) Tea Partier/Non–Tea Partier, and (6) third party/non–third party. Our analysis shows that of the six independent variables, just two—campaign contributions and incumbency—are statistically significant, incumbency at the .01 percent level and campaign contributions at the 1 percent level. Being a Tea Party candidate is not a significant predictor of victory or loss in the midterm elections.

21. Opensecrets.org, "Incumbent Advantage," Center for Responsive Politics, 2010, at http://www.opensecrets.org/overview/incumbs.php.

22. Alexandra Moe, "Just 32 Percent of Tea Party Candidates Win," MSNBC, November 3, 2010, at http://firstread.msnbc.msn.com/_news/2010/11/03/5403120-just-32-of-tea-party-candidates-win.

23. To see the various local-polling-based predictions of which Tea Party candidates would win and lose, see "Where Tea Party Candidates Are Running," *New York Times*, October 14, 2010, at www.nytimes.com/interactive/2010/10/15/us/politics/tea-party-graphic.html.

24. For information on Tea Partiers' campaign contributions, see the data from Opensecrets.org, at www.opensecrets.org/races/index.php.

25. For more on this pattern, see endnote 18.

26. Leo Leopold, "Obama Is No FDR, We're No Mass Movement," Huffington Post, February 10, 2010, at www.huffingtonpost.com/les-leopold/obama-is-no-fdr-were-no-m_b_457452.html.

27. For an egregious, over-the-top example of the liberal and progressive hope in Obama to which Leo Leopold refers, see Robert Kuttner, *Obama's Challenge: America's Economic Crisis and the Power of a Transformative Presidency* (White River Junction, VT: Chelsea Green, 2008). For Kuttner disappointed, chastened, and a little depressed, see his recent book *A Presidency in Peril: The Inside Story of Obama's Promise, Wall Street's Power, and the Struggle to Control Our Economic Future* (White River Junction, VT: Chelsea Green, 2010).

28. Paul Street, *Barack Obama and the Future of American Politics* (Boulder, CO: Paradigm Publishers, 2008); Selfa, "Preparing for a Republican Comeback.

29. Selfa, "Preparing for a Republican Comeback?" For evidence that Obama has governed in ways that are deeply continuous in many core aspects with the George W. Bush administration, see Paul Street, *The Empire's New Clothes: Barack Obama in the Real World of Power* (Boulder, CO: Paradigm Publishers, 2010.

30. Kevin Phillips, *The Politics of Rich and Poor: Wealth and the American Electorate in the Reagan Aftermath* (New York: Harper, 1989), 32

31. Selfa, "Preparing for a Republican Comeback."

32. Bob Herbert, "They Still Don't Get It," *New York Times*, January 23, 2010.

33. Sheldon Wolin *Democracy Incorporated: Managed Democracy and the Specter of Inverted Totalitarianism*: (Princeton, NJ: Princeton University Press, 2008), 206. Other authors also had little difficulty predicting the limited progressive outcomes of a Democratic victory in the polls in 2008. See Street, *Barack Obama and the Future*; Lance Selfa, *The Democrats: A Critical History* (Chicago: Haymarket, 2008); and John R. MacArthur, *You Can't Be President: The Outrageous Barriers to Democracy in America* (New York: Melville House, 2008.

34. "Robin Hahnel, "Election Redux: Learning from the 2010 Midterm Elections, Part 1: Lessons for Others," *ZNet*, November 4, 2010, at www.zcommunications.org/election-redux-learning-from-the-2010-midterm-elections-part-1-lessons-for-others-by-robin-hahnel.

35. Pew Research Center, "Democrats Stirring But Fail to Match GOP Support, Engagement," Pew Research Center, October 21, 2010, at http://pewresearch.org/pubs/1773/poll-2010-midterm-gop-lead-early-voting-campaign-outreach-engagement-reactions-victory-defeat.

36. Dan Balz, "Tea Party Fuels GOP Midterm Enthusiasm, Action," *Washington Post*, October 9, 2010, at www.washingtonpost.com/wp-dyn/content/article/2010/10/09/AR2010100902749.html.

37. "Democrats See Lowest Primary Turnout Ever, Study Says," Politerati Blog, *Washington Post*, September 17, 2010, at www.whorunsgov.com/politerati/uncategorized/democrats-see-lowest-midterm-primary-turnout-ever-study-says.

38. Karlyn Bowman, "What the Voters Actually Said on Election Day," *The American*, November 16, 2010, citing CBS exit polls, at www.american .com/archive/2010/november/what-the-voters-actually-said-on-election-day.

39. David Von Drehle "Where the Rout Leave the Democrats," *Time*, November 3, 2010, at www.time.com/time/politics/article/0,8599,2029174 ,00.html.

40. Gary Langer, "2010 Elections Exit Poll Analysis: The Political Price of Economic Pain," ABC News, November 3, 2010, at http://abcnews.go.com/ Politics/2010-midterms-political-price-economic-pain/story?id=12041739.

41. Pew Research Center, "Republicans Faring Better with Men, Whites, Independents, and Seniors," Pew Research Center, August 10, 2010, at http://people-press.org/report/643.

42. John Judis, "End the Honeymoon," *New Republic*, February 13, 2009, at http://www.tnr.com/politics/story.html?id=5bff5e94–6fa6–4a69–9ff2–8f 08cb437ccc

43. See the chilling account in Christopher Hayes, "Tuesdays with Rahm," *The Nation*, October 26, 2009.

44. David Sirota, "Will Obama Get a Primary Challenge in 2012?" Huffington Post, August 13, 2010. For critical reflections on the performance of the American "progressive movement" in the first yea of Obama's presidency, see the Afterword to Street's *The Empire's New Clothes*.

45. Matthew Rothschild, "Rampant Xenophobia," *The Progressive*, October 16, 2010, 8.

46. On the October 2 rally, see Jared Ball, "One Nation Under a Grip, Not a Groove," *Black Agenda Report*, October 6, 2010; and Glen Ford, "Ignominious Surrender on the Mall," *Black Agenda Report*, October 6, 2010, both at www.blackagendareport.com/?q=node&page=1. On the remarkable European protests and the telling contrast with the comparatively demobilized and left-bereft United States, see Richard D. Wolff, "European Workers Distance from U.S. Through Action," *ZNet*, October 6, 2010, at www.zcommunications.org/ european-workers-distance-from-us-through-action-by-richard-d-wolff; and Richard D. Wolff, "French Labor Activism, U.S. Labor Passivism," *ZNet*, October 16, 2010, at www.zcommunications.org/french-labor-activism-us-labor -passivism-by-richard-d-wolff.

47. Moe, "Just 32 Percent of Tea Party Candidates Win."

48. Michele Bachmann, "Members of the Tea Party Caucus," Congresswoman Michele Bachmann, 2010, http://bachmann.house.gov/News/DocumentSingle .aspx?DocumentID=199440.

49. Catherine E. Shoichet and Shannon Travis, "Election Projections Fuel Tea Party Fervor," CNN, November 3, 2010, at www.cnn.com/2010/ POLITICS/11/03/tea.party/index.html.

50. Sean J. Miller, "Poll: Tea Party Fires Up the Democrats More Than It Influences Republicans," *The Hill*, November 9, 2010, at http://thehill.com/house-polls/thehill-anga-poll-week1/123097-tea-party-is-firing-up-the-democrats.

51. Dalia Sussman, "Poll Finds Mixed Views, or None at All, on Tea Party," *New York Times*, September 15, 2010, at http://thecaucus.blogs.nytimes.com/2010/09/15/tea-party-has-time-to-shape-perceptions.

52. Pew Research Center, "Distrust, Discontent, Anger, and Partisan Rancor," Pew Research Center, April 18, 2010, at http://people-press.org/report/?pageid=1703; Frank Newport, "Tea Party Supporters Overlap Republican Base," Gallup, July 2, 2010, at www.gallup.com/poll/141098/tea-party-supporters-overlap-republican-base.aspx.

53. Fram, "Ailing Economy."

54. Newport, "Tea Party Supporters."

55. Ibid; www.bloomberg.com/news/2010–10–14/tea-party-s-economic-gloom-fuels-republican-election-momentum-poll-says.html.

56. Kate Zernike, "Tea Party Comes to Power on an Unclear Mandate," *New York Times*, November 3, 2010; Fram, "Ailing Economy."

57. William Galston quoted in Michael Scherer, "Tea Party Time: The Making of a Political Uprising," *Time*, September 16, 2010, at www.time.com/time/politics/article/0,8599,2019504,00.html.

58. See the interesting commentary by Timothy Egan, "How Obama Saved Capitalism and Lost the Midterms," *New York Times*, November 2, 2010, at http://opinionator.blogs.nytimes.com/2010/11/02/how-obama-saved-capitalism-and-lost-the-midterms/?src=me&ref=opinion.

59. Edward S. Herman, "Big Government, Deficits, Entitlements, and 'Centrists,'" *Z Magazine* (April 2010).

60. Zernike, "Tea Party Comes to Power."

61. On Obama and the Obama phenomenon as a heavily mass-mediated, expertly marketed, clean-slate, "man-for-all-seasons" development and on Obama's remarkable and vaguely defined open-brand "novelty dividend," see Street, *Barack Obama and the Future*, xvii–xxxvi, 59–72; and Street, *The Empire's New Clothes*, 1–5.

62. Pollingreport, "USA Today/Gallup Poll," Pollingreport.com, August 27–30, 2010, at www.pollingreport.com/budget.htm; "Bloomberg Poll," Polling report.com, March 19–22, 2010, at www.pollingreport.com/budget.htm; CNN, "CNN/Opinion Research Corporation Poll," Pollingreport.com, September 21–23, 2010, at www.pollingreport.com/budget.htm; "Bloomberg Poll," Polling report.com, December 3–7, 2009, at www.pollingreport.com/budget2.

63. Rob Walton, "Campaign Finance and the United States' Corruption Perception Problem," Huffington Post, October 31, 2010, at www.huffingtonpost

.com/rob-walton/campaign-finance-and-the_b_776740.html; "U.S. Mid-Term Election to Be Costliest Ever," *Agence France Presse*, October 11, 2010, at www.newsmax.com/InsideCover/USMid-TermElectionsCostliest/2010/ 10/11/id/373235.

64. Hahnel, "Election Redux."

65. As Hahnel notes, "From 2008–2010 the Democrats had larger majorities than the Republican Party enjoyed at any point over the past 80 years in the House of Representatives and the US Senate. . . . If a progressive agenda could not move forward in the last two years, if effective responses to the highest unemployment rates in 80 years were 'off the table,' if the White House refused to get behind any climate bill, and the Senate would not even bring a single piece of climate legislation up for a vote, then only a fool would expect any better results in a Washington awash with triumphant Republicans and cowed Democrats." Ibid.

66. "The Legacy of Howard Zinn," *Socialist Worker*, November 2, 2010, at http://socialistworker.org/blog/critical-reading/2010/11/02/legacy-howard-zinn.

67. E. J. Dionne Jr., "The Tea Party Movement Is a Scam," RealClear Politics, September 23, 2010 at www.realclearpolitics.com/articles/2010/09/ 23/the_tea_party_movement_is_a_scam.html.

Chapter 8

1. Monica Davey, "For Wisconsin Governor, Battle Was Long Coming," *New York Times,* February 19, 2011.

2. Media Matters, "Right Wing Media Push Misleading Stat That Wisconsin Public Workers Make More Than Private Employees," *Media Matters for America* (February 22, 2011) at http://mediamatters.org/research/201102 220021; Paul Krugman, "Wisconsin Power Play," *New York Times*, February 20, 2011 at http://www.nytimes.com/2011/02/21/opinion/21krugman.html ?partner=rssnyt&emc=rss.

3. Editors, "Spreading Anti-Union Agenda," *New York Times*, February 22, 2011, read at http://www.nytimes.com/2011/02/23/opinion/23wed1.html ?ref=todayspaper; Davey, "For Wisconsin Governor."

4. See DeWayne Wickham, "In Wisconsin, Union-Busting as GOP Strategy,'" *Tucson Citizen*, February 21, 2011, at http://tucsoncitizen.com/usa -today-news/2011/02/21/in-wisconsin-union-busting-as-gop-strategy/. As Wickham explained, "Walker's bill is a shoot-the-wounded assault on the Democratic Party's base, which when combined with a voter ID law that's also being pushed through Wisconsin's Republican-controlled legislature, could put the Badger State firmly in GOP hands for decades. . . . The proposed ID law would restrict the right to vote to people with military IDs, driver's li-

censes, and a state-issued ID card. Passports and photo ID cards issued to college students (even those from state universities) would not be acceptable. College students and public unions are pillars of the Democratic base. Wisconsin's ID law would suppress voter participation among students. . . . " GOP-controlled legislatures in Missouri, Ohio, and Texas were advancing similar voter identification bills, Wickham added—all part of the GOP's "quest for political hegemony."

5. Elizabeth McNichol, Phil Oliff, and Nicholas Johnson, "States Continue to Feel Recession's Impact," *Center on Budget and Policy Priorities*, February 10, 2011, http://www.cbpp.org/cms/?fa=view&id=711; Joanne Huist Smith, "Revenue Shortfalls, Not Bargaining, Drive States' Deficits," *Dayton Daily News*, February 28, 2011, at http://www.daytondailynews.com/news/dayton-news/revenue-shortfalls-not-bargaining-drive-states-deficits-109 2931.html?cxtype=rss_local-news; "Right Wing Media Push 'Bogus' Argument That Collective Bargaining Correlates With State Budget Deficits," Media Matters (March 1, 2011) at http://mediamatters.org/iphone/research/201103010016.

6. David A. Patten and Kathleen Waller, "Gov. Walker: Obama Should Fix His Own Budget Crisis," Newsmax.com, March 4, 2011, at http://www.newsmax.com/Headline/scott-walker-obama-wisconsin/2011/03/04/id/388424.

7. Monica Davey and Steve Greenhouse, "Wisconsin May Take Axe to State Workers' Benefits and Their Unions," *New York Times*, February 11, 2011, read at http://www.nytimes.com/2011/02/12/us/12unions.html.

8. Eric Lipton, "Billionaire Brothers' Money Plays Role in Wisconsin Dispute," *New York Times*, February 21, 2011, at http://www.nytimes.com/2011/02/22/us/22koch.html.

9. Ryan J. Foley, "On Prank Call, Governor Discusses Strategy," Associated Press, February 22, 2011; Lipton, "Billionaire Brothers' Money."

10. Lipton, "Billionaire Brothers' Money"; Foley, "On Prank Call."

11. Foley, "On Prank Call." See also Paul Krugman. "Shock Doctrine USA," *New York Times*, February 24, 2011, at http://www.nytimes.com/2011/02/25/opinion/25krugman.html.

12. Kate Zernike, "Wisconsin's Legacy of Labor Battles," *New York Times*, March 6, 2011, at http://www.nytimes.com/2011/03/06/weekinreview/06midwest.html.

13. Foley, "On Prank Call."

14. Ryan J. Foley, "Wisconsin Governor Says State Could Lead Nation in Weakening Unions as Protests Enter Day 6," Associated Press, February 20, 2011, at http://www.chicagotribune.com/news/local/breaking/sns-ap-us-wisconsin-budget-unions,0,3070407.story; Davey, "For Wisconsin Governor, Battle Was Long Coming."

15. *New York Times* editors, "Spreading Anti-Union Agenda."

16. Ibid.

17. Davey and Greenhouse, "Wisconsin May Take Axe to State Workers' Benefits and Their Unions."

18. Dan Hinkel, "Wisconsin Budget Battle Rallies Continue," *Chicago Tribune*, February 19, 2011, http://www.chicagotribune.com/news/local/breaking/chibrknews-wisconsin-budget-battle-rallies-continue-20110219,0,1990710.story.

19. Doug Henwood, "Wisconsin Erupts," *Left Business Observer*, February 16, 2011, at http://lbo-news.com/2011/02/16/wisconsin-erupts/.

20. Steve Verburg, "Labor Group Calls for General Strike if Budget Bill Is Approved," *Wisconsin State Journal*, February 23, 2011, at http://host.madison.com/wsj/news/local/govt-and-politics/article_64c8d7a8-3e8c-11e0-9911-001cc4c002e0.htm.

21. Kate Zernike, "Standoffs, Protests, and a Prank Call," *New York Times*, February 23 2011.

22. Ann Sanner, "Union Bill Whizzing Through Ohio Legislature," Associated Press, March 3, 2011, at http://news.yahoo.com/s/ap/20110223/ap_on_re_us/us_wisconsin_budget_unions.

23. Zernike, "Standoffs."

24. Jonathan Weisman, "Obama Sits Out State Fights," *Wall Street Journal*, February 24, 2011, A4.

25. Jackie Calmes, "Less Drama in White House After Staff Changes," *New York Times,* March 3, 2011, at http://www.nytimes.com/2011/03/04/us/politics/04staff.html?_r=3.

26. For details and sources, see Paul Street, "Cold-Blooded Calibration: Reflections on Egypt, Honduras, and the Art of Imperial Re-branding," *ZNet*, February 11, 2011, at http://www.zcommunications.org/cold-blooded-calibration-by-paul-street.

27. Weisman, "Obama Sits Out."

28. Robert Reich, "Obama's Republican Narrative of Our Economic Woes," The Berkeley Blog, December 2, 2010, at http://blogs.berkeley.edu/2010/12/02/two-competing-stories-of-whats-wrong-with-the-economy/.

29. Miller quoted in Weisman, "Obama Sits Out."

30. Dennis Cauchon, "Poll: Americans Favor Union Bargaining Rights," *USA Today*, February 22, 2011, at http://www.usatoday.com/news/nation/2011-02-22-poll-public-unions-wisconsin_N.htm.

31. Anthony DiMaggio, "The Great Budget Repair Swindle,'" *ZNet*, March 4, 2011, at http://www.zcommunications.org/the-great-budget-repair-swindle-by-anthony-dimaggio

32. Henwood, "Wisconsin Erupts."

33. Johann Hari, "How to Build a Progressive Tea Party," *Nation*, February 3, 2011, at http://www.thenation.com/article/158282/how-build-progressive -tea-party?page=full.

34. Alissa Bohlig, "U.S. Uncut's Anti-Austerity Protest Hits Bank of America," *Truthout*, February 28, 2011, at http://www.truth-out.org/us-uncuts-anti -austerity-protests-start-small-strong-against-bank-america68108; Art Levine. "U.S. Uncut Spreads Spirit of Madison," *In These Times*, February 24, 2011, at http://www.inthesetimes.com/working/entry/6998/us_uncut_spreads_the_spirit _of_madison_protests_saturday_over_budget_c/.

35. Hari, "How to Build a Progressive Tea Party."

Acknowledgments

Paul Street
I am deeply indebted to my wife, Janet Razbadouski, who saw me through a difficult period as this book neared completion in the fall and winter of 2010–2011. Special thanks also to my good friend, Kathleen Shankman, for going beyond the call of duty to undertake a remarkably thorough and helpful content and copyedit of this manuscript.

Anthony DiMaggio
I'd like to thank my wife, Mary, for tolerating my long hours and nights working on this project. I'd also like to thank the rest of my family for supporting my research, and my son, Frankie, for his inspiration. Finally, I'd like to thank Paul Street for his tireless and impressive work on this project, in addition to Noam Chomsky and Henry Giroux for their supportive words with regard to reviewing the manuscript.

Index

About the Authors

Paul Street is an independent journalist, policy adviser, and historian. He has published widely in popular and scholarly media and is author of numerous books including, most recently, *The Empire's New Clothes: Barack Obama in the Real World of Power* (Paradigm, 2010). **Anthony DiMaggio** is the author of the newly released *When Media Goes to War* (Monthly Review, 2010) and *Mass Media, Mass Propaganda* (Lexington Books, 2008). He has taught U.S. and Global Politics at Illinois State University and North Central College.